Special Tribute Reviews

Never before have I read a book that impacted me in a myriad of ways. I was complimented, embarrassed, encouraged, insulted, challenged, and changed. I had to read the foreword and the first two chapters over and over again just to try to understand what Dr. Saheli was trying to communicate to me. I got it. It's my silence that's eerie.

Dr. Saheli took me through a scholarly journey to a practical osmosis but did not stop there. Confronted with my religious dogma, this preacher opened my mind to God's eternal purpose. He closed the book by going back to the scholarly journal that left me shaking with guilt but gave me hope, knowing that it's not too late to repent. – **Dr. Billy Curl, Bishop, Crenshaw Church of Christ, Los Angeles**

Eerie Silence exposes racism in America; racism thrives through covert and blatant actions. Covert racism is by far the most devastating and *Eerie Silence* no longer allows us to sweep it under the rug. Warning! When you read *Eerie Silence,* your closet racism character will scream out in public. – **John Jeffrey, Father of the Author**

This book is full of heart. To ask these questions, to make these connections, to seek this level of accountability, requires caring strongly and feeling deeply. *Eerie Silence* will require the reader to decide how much he or she cares. Prepare to be challenged. – **Marcus Thompson II, Journalist/Columnist and best-selling author of *Golden: The Miraculous Rise of Steph Curry***

Eerie Silence exposes how American institutions related to Christianity, education and criminal justice intersect to maintain a Eurocentric, racist culture that misrepresents, constrains and exploits people of color, especially those of the African diaspora. It is a strongly recommended read. – **Robert S. Adams, Ph.D., Retired Deputy Probation Officer**

EERIE SILENCE

RACE/RACISM EXPLORED ACROSS EDUCATIONAL, THEOLOGICAL,
AND JUSTICE CONTINUUMS AMIDST AMERICA AND BEYOND

AMMAR SAHELI

WESTBOW
PRESS®
A DIVISION OF THOMAS NELSON
& ZONDERVAN

Scripture quotations marked KJV are taken from the King James Version of the Bible.

Scripture quotations marked NIV are taken from the Holy Bible, New
International Version®, NIV® Copyright © 1973, 1978, 1984, 2011 by
Biblica, Inc.® Used by permission. All rights reserved worldwide.

Scripture quotations marked NLT are taken from the Holy Bible, New Living Translation,
Copyright © 1996, 2004, 2015 by Tyndale House Foundation. Used by permission of
Tyndale House Publishers, Inc., Carol Stream, Illinois 60188. All rights reserved.

Scripture quotations marked ASV are taken from the Holy Bible, American Standard
Version (The Revised Version, American Standard Edition of the Bible). Public domain.

WestBow Press books may be ordered through booksellers or by contacting:

WestBow Press
A Division of Thomas Nelson & Zondervan
1663 Liberty Drive
Bloomington, IN 47403
www.westbowpress.com
1 (866) 928-1240

Because of the dynamic nature of the Internet, any web addresses or links contained
in this book may have changed since publication and may no longer be valid. The views
expressed in this work are solely those of the author and do not necessarily reflect the
views of the publisher, and the publisher hereby disclaims any responsibility for them.

Any people depicted in stock imagery provided by Getty Images are models,
and such images are being used for illustrative purposes only.
Certain stock imagery © Getty Images.

ISBN: 978-1-9736-4384-5 (sc)
ISBN: 978-1-9736-4385-2 (hc)
ISBN: 978-1-9736-4383-8 (e)

Library of Congress Control Number: 2018912904

Print information available on the last page.

WestBow Press rev. date: 06/11/2020

CONTENTS

CONTENTS

DEDICATION

This book and contribution to the struggle of love, equity, and justice for the marginalized and underserved is dedicated to my mother and her radical spirit of advocacy, literacy, and scholarship.

Mrs. Andrea Jeffrey
January 27, 1945 - April 5, 2015

ACKNOWLEDGMENTS AND APPRECIATIONS

Glory to God for His divine providence and using me as a vessel of service for my family, community, and the human condition. To my beautiful and blessed wife Tonya, thanks for loving me deeply and motivating me through this project. You inspire and energize me daily. Thanks for allowing our home to be overrun with books for a season and granting me the sacrificial space and time to read incessantly, research, write, and complete this project.

To my beloved father John, your continued example, love, and mentoring are unmatched. Thanks for loving, guiding, and teaching me what it means to be a man, husband, father, advocate, and follower of Christ. I so wish my mother was still physically with us. I know we would have unbelievable conversations around this book and the current climate of our nation and world.

To my four living children, Sadé, Najja, Zion, and Shiloh, thanks for the encouragement you provide every day and the thirst you have for life and innovation. To our deceased son, Seven Enoch, daily you evoke the celestial inspiration for me to be an advocate for life and to do all I can to prevent any form of death, whether physical, educational, psychological, or spiritual.

West Oakland Church of Christ, your willing spirit to operate outside the box of religious traditionalism, allowing the infusion of love and justice to be incorporated in our missional, evangelistic, and educational efforts are genuinely appreciated and valued. Your prayers and supplications through this project are cherished. Your willingness to break through silence is refreshing. Thanks to Marcus Thompson II for the book cover design.

To my educational family in the Bay Area, California, across America and the globe, thanks for your love and support. And thanks to all *Saheli7 Educational Consulting* partners, workshop, and professional development participants. Keep pushing for critical consciousness and interracial justice.

Lastly, to my Western Addition *(Fillmoe)* and San Francisco family, this project is just another testimony of our community resilience and resolve. We always overcome the odds. London Breed, a true born and raised San Franciscan, congratulations on becoming the first African American woman Mayor of the City! The neighborhood, city, state, and nation are proud.

FOREWORD

Have you ever had an experience where you felt like you were the victim of a racist undertone, action or innuendo, but the experience was accompanied by such a lack of acknowledgment by the other people who were present in the room that it left you questioning what just occurred? I vividly recall this very thing happening to me in 2008 when I was a second-year law student on the first day of my *Property* class. Excited about my first day of the class, I sat down and anxiously anticipated seeing how my *Property* professor, who was also a property lawyer, would begin what I believed to be one of the most important law school courses in my program. He set up the LCD for a movie to introduce the concept of *Property*, and all I can remember seeing on the screen were several Black people with chains around their necks; the film he chose to introduce the concept of *Property* was *Amistad*, and the subject was African slaves. When I realized what was occurring, my stomach dropped. At that moment it felt like the 97% white class locked their eyes on me and the two other Black students in the room. I needed someone to validate what I felt because the silence that followed was deafening. At that time I could have used a book like Saheli's *Eerie Silence*.

Twenty-two years ago when I was a sophomore at the University of San Francisco, I visited a nearby church on a Sunday in September and witnessed the most powerful oration of a prayer. At that time, I had no idea that the person administering the prayer would become my husband. This person was Dr. Ammar Saheli. Ammar has always had a way of captivating me and many others through his verbose and deep thoughts, especially those surrounding race and racism in America. Many underestimate the value of having access to this type of powerful epistemic. This thought is encapsulated in the total embodiment of *Eerie Silence: Race/Racism Explored Across Educational, Theological, and Justice Continuums Amidst America and Beyond*. This book does a masterful job of acknowledging the silence that occurs whenever a racist innuendo or blatant racist action occurs, all while capturing the professional and personal experiences of Ammar Saheli, which make him most qualified to pen this exquisite work. *Eerie Silence* takes you on a journey into how to approach and manage the numerous problems which plague the Black community and the underserved in the form of racism, injustice, and racial identity development.

A champion for racial, educational, and theological justice, Ammar Saheli has dedicated his life to asking the hard questions and devising solutions for equity and interracial-justice healing. This book will transform the lives of those who have not entirely been able to name the devastating effects of race and racism on multiple levels.

Although Ammar began writing this project in January 2018, after completing his essay, "Finding Your Position on the Racialized Battlefield: A Brief Examination of Racism, Silence, Fragility, Resistance, & Justice," his research and stimulus began in 1995 when he met and was mentored by Dr. Laura Head at San Francisco State University, enrolling in her *Introduction to Black Psychology* course. Through that profound and life-changing class and experience, racial shackles of self-hate and dehumanization were shattered—replaced by deep racial liberation, transformation, pride, empowerment, and commitment to racial advocacy and justice. It was there that Ammar was exposed to the scholarship of Frances Cress Welsing, Claude Steele, and many other African American experts committed to antiracist practices, the development of Black positive racial identity attitudes, Black Nationalism, and Pan-Africanism, as solutions to colorism, pigmentocracy, and African dehumanization. His research and exposure continued through transformative literature revealed through his University of San Francisco doctoral program, heavily connected to the influential work of Paulo Freire and bell hooks. During that time, Ammar was introduced to the deep writings of Du Bois and Cornell West by his father. From that point forward the foundation was set from which to launch into comprehensive intellectual waters, coupled with twenty years of working in the trenches of public education and pastorally serving a church in West Oakland for almost eighteen years. Through this, the birth of *Eerie Silence* was conceived.

The eerie silence tolerated around the African Diaspora has been remarkable. Some Black people in America are delayed in making the connection and realization that the reason there are so many people who share their phenotype and genotype, living all across the world, is directly related to the African slave-trade. This realization is amplified and exacerbated when government agencies and institutions have an agenda to silence this fact. After France won the 2018 World Cup, Trevor Noah, host of the *Daily Show*, congratulated both France and Africa on the win since the majority of the team is comprised of men of African descent. Clearly, Noah made too much noise around this topic on his show because he received a letter from French government officials correcting him that the men he labeled African were, in fact, French. Trevor replied, intimating that they are only French because France colonized Africa.

Those same government officials also took the indignant stance in the letter to highlight that—unlike America—their citizens do not need to hyphenate their French citizenship with anything else because they are *only* French. One could argue that this is merely another attempt to keep silent about the manner in which many Africans arrived in France. This is not to negate the fact that some Africans voluntarily immigrated to France just as some volitionally arrived in America and other countries, however, to remain silent around the entire story that connects numerous countries to the African slave-trade is not only eerie but criminal.

The centuries of chattel slavery in America often overshadow years of African servitude in other countries, yet, like America, these same countries continue to prosper financially from the contributions resulting from enslaved Africans, while embracing a "hush-hush" mentality. This has caused some within the African Diaspora, outside America, who are ignorant or in denial about their lineage and connection to the Middle-Passage, to think they are superior to involuntary Africans in America. The fact that students can go through an entire schooling system in many countries, blind to the fact that African slavery was a global undertaking is unfathomable. Imagine the power, empowerment, and unity that could potentially come from sparking this conversation.

Eerie Silence was birthed out of racialized pain and the visible injustice that surrounds American inaction and sets the platform for this dialogue. Historically, dialectic encounters have always included within their nexus, theological and educational formations of epistemology. Especially within Eastern contexts, religion, theology, and intellectualism did not operate on binary levels, they were inseparable and discussed holistically. J. Deotis Roberts (2005), said in *Liberation and Reconciliation: A Black Theology*, "So closely are God and humans tied together in theological reflection that it is almost a matter of indifference whether one begins reflection upon humans and moves to God, or whether one begins with God and moves to humanity" (p. 37).

Not as an evangelistic plea of conversion, but *Eerie Silence* integrates theological concepts with the discussion of racial responsiveness, responsibility, and accountability because religion has always existed at the epicenter of humanity, peace, conflict, and interpersonal engagement. It is only through our modern era and epoch that we seek to silence and alienate religious and theological influences from paideia and an assessment of historical, human, cultural, tribal, and racial developments and contributions.

Despite *Eerie Silence* being focused on breaking inaction toward glaring episodes of injustice and their dehumanizing outgrowths, it may first appear as an uneven theologically dense text, but when contextually navigated through a critical worldview, religious epistemologies are sometimes used as a framework to explain and clarify how inflicted practices, in the name of religion, were feigned to enslave, dehumanize, oppress, and marginalize people. *Eerie Silence* is a complex introductory tool designed for religious centers, churches, schools, universities, and social justice organizations, fighting disparate racial outcomes. It can be used by both silent and vocal churches as a scaffold to enter and sustain racial conversations with embedded theological concepts, detailing the social justice footprint in the Scriptures. Religion and public education are complicated twenty-first century domains, but if schools, school districts, and educators wrestle through the way the author boldly juxtaposes race, racism, silence, and injustice—with the intersection of religious institutionalism, it is a powerful tool that will benefit and assist them and their students with understanding issues of justice, race, equity, and critical pedagogy—while simultaneously disrupting and dismantling toxic racist systems within education and society.

While I am the person in this relationship professionally trained as a lawyer, this author is the better racial justice advocate and champion and it is masterfully illustrated in this book. He should be confident that there will be many grateful readers that will gain a broader perspective of what it means to experience eerie silence as it relates to race and racism across many continuums in America and beyond.

Tonya DJ Saheli, JD, MS
Saheli Legal Mediation, Owner
Professor of Business Law & Ethics
Saheli7 Educational Consulting, CFO
Author: *The Memoirs of a Young Millennium Preacher's Wife: A Story of Life, Love and the Testing of Faith*

A VERITABLE CALL TO ARMS

This work is simply a force of thought and evidence of an important mind and thinker. Its bridging of theology, law, education policy, popular culture, intellectual discourse, ministry, media and race, personal experience and biography, is short of brilliant. That it was written in a breath of time brings to mind Martin Delaney's opus, "The Condition, Elevation, Emigration, and Destiny of the Colored People of the United States, Politically Considered," written in 30 days calling for widespread spiritual and social change. Concerning this study's sweeping coverage, it is a striking work that made reading it to its end, an urgent matter.

It is a veritable call to arms, a manifesto to the Church and world to first take stock of the debilitating role that racial division has played across the noted categories in U.S. society and culture, and how it diminishes the spiritual and institutional potential of the Church among the most socially and civically isolated segments of society. This is followed by a call to engagement in the real world of affected communities and individuals, touched by violence, institutional biases, and religious division and polarization.

The Pact of Silence on the idolatry of the Church's embrace, tolerance, and reflection of society's overarching racial inequities is challenged throughout the study. Decades of forums, lectureships, joint worship efforts, pulpit exchanges, retreats, and sermons have had negligible impact in distinguishing the Church from secular and social institutions that perpetuate inequities and marginalization of subordinate social groups. Social institutions pledged to foster the spiritual and educational development of all people, instead routinely mirror and emulate society's injustices. The Pact of Silence permeates the fellowship of Believers as readily as it does education policy and approaches, and popular culture.

Breaking the silences across church, education curricula, and popular culture is a necessary foundation for the kind of transformational ministry engagement that Ammar Saheli calls for in this work, and has eluded many well intended outreach efforts among the most vulnerable individuals in society. The Believer is asked to understand the vital importance of society's soul crushing racial injustices as a prerequisite to meaningful engagement with communities, just as the department colleague, school principal, or college Dean is asked to understand the ministry of education as a call to transform the life chances of individuals out of conditions that too often lead to dead end options, crushed hopes, and dreams.

This is a work that readers will want to consult again and again to measure their growth in awareness and consciousness toward the book's call to comprehensive care for others, which is the root word for education (*educare*), and the sacred ministry of the Church that changes lives and saves them in a heartsick world, that is poised to accept ministry that accepts people in all of their complexities, spiritual, intellectual, and social. This is a wine that will not last long in the wineskins of traditionalism, conservatism, anti-ism, self-righteousness, and isolated fellowship with link minded others, it is a call to ministry to break down the middle wall of racial partition in the church and society in order that generations of women, men, and young people might go unencumbered in their full potential and development.

James L. Taylor, Ph.D
Professor of Politics
San Francisco, California

CHAPTER 1
THE PERVASIVE TOXICITY OF EERIE SILENCE

Race and racism are inescapable in America and sweep generationally. Two brief contextual encounters connected to a couple of men from my congregation continually traverse my mind and blend well as a foretaste to this project. The men are Sam Holmes and Alex Rowe. Brother Holmes is the eldest man at the West Oakland Church of Christ, and his late mother was a pioneer member, beginning in 1960. I cannot remember what, but I said something in a sermon or Bible study lecture years ago that prompted Sam Holmes to share a noose with me that has been in his possession for almost forty years; there was a disturbing story connected. He began his career in 1964 with a company that ultimately merged decades later. In 1980 Sam Holmes was hired as the first African American machinist at the Brockway Glass Company in Oakland, California. He eventually retired from the company after fifty successful years of service. However, during his very first day on the job in 1980, his white coworker walked him around the facility pointed and said, "There is your locker." Mr. Holmes opened it and hung inside was a noose. No investigation, intervention, or discipline followed the incident; silence remained, and Sam Holmes still has the evidentiary noose.

Alex Rowe served in the US Navy before successfully retiring after thirty-three years; he enlisted in 1971 and retired in 2009. Alex returned home from service in the Vietnam War, Desert Shield/ Desert Storm, and Operation Iraqi Freedom. Race and racism were always an issue, but things shifted on more insidious levels in 2007 when Barack Obama began his presidential campaign. Suddenly Mr. Rowe started receiving disparaging hate-filled anonymous emails on his US government computer about Barack Obama. As the only African American man in his immediate group, he also received hateful emails that were not anonymous. Nothing was explicitly done to address the hate. The continuance of the hateful emails amplified the false sense of community that existed, and trust was broken. Alex retired ten days after President Barack Obama was inaugurated on January 20, 2009. Mr. Rowe intimated the hypocrisy of what it would mean to serve in battle with teammates who defamed the president of the United States and commander in chief. How could those who sent hateful messages about a Black president be expected to protect a Black sailor in battle? Nothing was addressed; silence remained, and Mr. Alex Rowe retired.

Eerie Silence Introduced

Why is America so silent toward the pervasiveness of race, racism, and unjust encounters? Problematically, eerie silence prowls through the psychic, spiritual, and cosmic walls of postmodern educational, religious, theological, and cultural systems across America and the globe. The subject of this silence is unconsciously elusive, defended, tucked-away, and closeted as a prized possession of power and privilege. The protective force surrounding this conception is breathtaking; even passively unassuming people vigorously arise with grand display, shielding this sacredly forbidden topic and stance. The subject is race and its companion racism in all their covert and overt formations. This literary work serves as a brief exploration of the intersections between silence, race, racism, religion, theology, education, racial identity development, the American assimilation project, and the influence of Eurocentric hegemony and *coloniality*.

The purpose is to examine the role and pervasive toxicity of inaction and avoidance in the face of injustice.

Operating through an explicit lens of equity, Neely Fuller Jr. (2016) explains the difficulty in discussing racism and white supremacy in *The United-Independent Compensatory Code/System/ Concept: A Compensatory* Counter-Racist *Code*. He said, "There is no way to talk about race and tell the truth, and make logical suggestions based on the truth, without White people being offended, and without Non-White people being embarrassed" (p. 403). Part of this manifested impetus is looming eerie silence—and in the witness of injustice, silence is a transgression and painful omission. Ta-Nehisi Coates, in *We Were Eight Years in Power: An American Tragedy,* captures the emotive and overpowering force behind mainstream US silence toward injustice. Especially for a Black or non-white person navigating and existing in America Coates said, "It is to understand what it means to live in a country that will never apologize for slavery, but will not stop apologizing for the Civil War" (2017, p. 80).

The eerie silence of America is indicative of national inter-personal and interracial relationship underdevelopment. Although it is a global phenomenon, the hegemon (regardless of type) is rarely analyzed or challenged in America. The sophistication of the in-concert silence is astounding. Healthy relationships allow for honest, challenging, and vulnerable critique; but in America, distinct and apparent gender, racial, educational, and economic discriminations and predictable negative trends are expected to be ignored and silenced. Based on the principles and qualities of mature relationships, the arrogant, racist, and eerie silence of America, renders it immature. National immaturity affects every aspect of American institutionalism, including religion, politics, education, and race. It transmits compliance and complicity in future generations. The American dominant power structure strangely determines what it will be outraged over and what it is willing to ignore or defend. Although this level of silence influences everyone, the ability of whiteness to witness injustice and remain silent is agonizingly scandalous. I have observed this collective behavior in schools, universities, churches, police-settings, political arenas, families, communities, and assuredly mainstream media.

Through the conceptions of sixteenth-century Eurocentric dominance, Will Durant reported in *The Reformation: The Story of Civilization, Part VI,* "The Spanish who in this time period conquered Mexico, California, Central America, and Peru were first of all adventurers, tired of poverty and routine at home, and facing with pleasure the perils of distant alien lands." He went on to say, "Amid the hardships of their reckless enterprise they forgot civilized restraints, frankly adopted the morality of superior guns, and accomplished an act of continual robbery, treachery, and murder" (1957, p. 864). In *Savage Anxieties: The Invention of Western Civilization,* Robert A. Williams Jr. discusses how the people and lands affected by robbery, treachery, murder, Manifest Destiny, and the Doctrine of Discovery have not been healed; the hegemon has not repented. Racialized diversity is America's most celebrated asset, while simultaneously acting in parallel—it is America's most significant paradox because of the creation of race and the byproduct of European hegemonic treatment toward those vilified and marginalized. As stated by Moraña, Dussel, and Jáuregui in *Coloniality At Large: Latin America and the Postcolonial Debate,* "The political and philosophical thought emerging from colonialism 'invented' *race* as the pivotal notion that supported the process of world classification" (2008, p. 8). They went on to say, "Situated as one of the axes of modernity, the issue of race became the 'rationale' used to support, justify, and perpetuate the practice of imperial domination" (2008, pp. 8-9). The roots of American and global eerie silence were established in coloniality and domination.

As an example that will serve as a repetitive theme throughout this project, Walter D. Mignolo said in his essay, "Preamble: The Historical Foundation of Modernity/Coloniality and the Emergence of Decolonial Thinking," that "higher education can be controlled through theology and egology; that is the epistemic authority of God and secular reason" (2008, p. 25). The goal is to explore how these conceptions influence thinking, customs, and institutions in the twenty-first century, whether implicitly or explicitly. Mignolo also explained the effect of coloniality on indigenous frames and customs:

> The undeniable presence of indigenous ways of life, of thinking, of doing, of acting, are repressed beneath the rhetoric of modernity. Modernity/coloniality is a coin with two faces, the same in the center as the periphery. In other words, center and periphery are so because modernity/coloniality became the rhetoric of salvation and the logic of oppression that managed the world order in the past 500 years. (2008, p. 25)

Of course, because of this invisible repressive pressure, many but not all in Christendom are afraid, seduced, and outwitted when it comes to the concept of race and racism. This is also true across educational and cultural systems. The consequence of this silence has left the church and educational institutions, especially in America, with an undiagnosed condition with incalculable effects. This reality affects all marginalized groups, especially people of the African diaspora in America, but we also cannot underestimate its cloaked devastation on white intellect and racial identity development. While Black folk and people of color seek to work through inflicted psychological and racial identity formations of inferiority, white people must come to terms with and overcome their destructive unconscious/conscious feelings of superiority. As the Black-White binary contemplates, non-white, non-Black, and bi-racial people and groups must determine their racial identity and position, safeguarding it from the seduction and proclivity toward white superiority. The protective covering of religion and the church does not shield people from racial and societal ills, and in America, it is subliminally reinforced through what I call, *colonized Christianity*, the result of sanitized approaches to religion and education.

Resistant religious and educational reactions to people who

evoke conversations about race and racism are categorized as divisive. Because the ecclesia is a cosmic and salvific habitation for the sanctified, a mantra is touted that there is no need to discuss race, its history, or its current effects. The evasive and defensive message presents an assertion that salvation shields a person from global trends, events, harm, and oppression; this paradigm is deeply dangerous and negligent. It limits the spiritual and psychological power of those within Christendom, and it is imperative that lingering conditions of silence be assessed and remedied.

In *The Wretched of the Earth*, Frantz Fanon said, "People must know where they are going and why. The politician should be aware that the future will remain bleak as long as the people's consciousness remains rudimentary, primary, and opaque. We, African politicians, must have very clear ideas about our peoples' situation" (1963, p. 135). Also, and in response to dynamics of politics, education, religion, and culture, religious leaders and adherents therein must also be keenly aware and critically conscious. When Christians ignorantly and irresponsibly use biblical passages to stifle conversations about race or other difficult topics, it asphyxiates the authenticity of relationship and ignores apparent realities of our world. This is especially true when examining the American condition for Africans in America, some of which who subscribed to the Christian ethos and liberating expression while enslaved in chains. Cornel West said in *Prophesy Deliverance: An Afro-American Revolutionary Christianity* (2002): "Black people became Christians for intellectual, existential, and political reasons. Christianity is, as Friedrich Nietzsche has taught us and liberation theologians remind us, a religion especially fit for the oppressed" (p. 35).

Through *Prophetic Fragments: Illuminations of the Crisis in American Religion & Culture* (1988) Cornel West explosively analyzes, confronts, and exposes the theology and behavior of postmodern American Christianity. West said "American religious life— despite its weekly rituals and everyday practices—is shot through with existential emptiness. This emptiness—or lack of spiritual depth—results from the excessive preoccupation with isolated personal interests and atomistic individual concerns in American religious life" (p. ix). What West described of American formations of Christianity is the opposite of an authentic Christological ethos. Examining the transfigured ministry of Jesus pushes us to understand that He was concerned about the salvation of humanity, inclusive of justice and judgment. He endured the highest form of social injustice as a guiltless man. The Christian pathos is powerful, yet some attempt to diminish its force by elucidating a contrived, stale, and safe biblical narrative. A passage that is often launched to block racial dialogue in the church is shared below:

> And all who have been united with Christ in baptism have put on Christ, like putting on new clothes. [28]There is no longer Jew or Gentile, slave or free, male and female. For you are all one in Christ Jesus. [29]And now that you belong to Christ, you are the true children of Abraham. You are his heirs, and God's promise to Abraham belongs to you. (Galatians 3:27-29 NLT)

Confrontational Love Over Silence

Thinking critically, Galatians 3:27-29 is not a passage that precludes discussions of race, oppression, or white supremacy; it serves as a pivotal thesis that necessitates such dialogue. The written message the Apostle Paul shared with the Galatian church speaks to the perfected goal of interrelated Christian ontology. However, until we arrive at a place where biased and discriminatory practices are eradicated in the church, we must continue to navigate through bold and uncomfortable conversations. The Bible is written as an ideal; it is a blueprint of equity and equality that people must vigorously strive to apprehend. Until that moment of biblical virtue for radical love is reached, the struggle must continue. In the same epistle to the

Galatians, the Apostle Paul shared with them how he confronted the Apostle Peter, because of his biased actions. He said:

> But when Peter came to Antioch, I had to oppose him to his face, for what he did was very wrong. [12]When he first arrived, he ate with the Gentile believers, who were not circumcised. But afterward, when some friends of James came, Peter wouldn't eat with the Gentiles anymore. He was afraid of criticism from these people who insisted on the necessity of circumcision. [13]As a result, other Jewish believers followed Peter's hypocrisy, and even Barnabas was led astray by their hypocrisy. (Galatians 2:11-13 NLT)

Love is not evidenced by a lack of confrontation. Because Paul loved God and his apostolic colleague, he confronted Peter under difficult and emotional circumstances. If silence was the mature and preferred spiritual panacea for keeping the peace, this could have been a prime opportunity for Paul to refrain from the radical confrontation. Because of love, confrontation is not comfortable, but it is necessary. Through the investigation of Galatians 3:27-29, the goal is to strive toward the ideal of perfected and vulnerable relationships. The day is sought where race, ethnicity, socio-economic status, culture, gender, and political affiliation will not be factors that determine how people are treated or prejudicially perceived. However, reality and experience inform us that patterns of discrimination and racism still exist; even in the church. Since this is real, why should the earthly church act like it is exempt from discussing difficult social issues, including race and racism? Like churches and religious institutions, educational and political domains cannot escape and also are not exempt from active engagement.

Exposing race is not designed to fetishize a racial dialectic or treat it neurotically, it is about normalizing the dialogue, so when racial discussions are necessary, they are not atypically viewed. Discussing truth is not divisive—especially in the church. Pursuit of truth is the epistemological, axiological, and ontological thrust of the church, humanity, and intellectualism. If done with the right spirit, purpose, and tone, it is an act of love. Much of the 1 *Corinthians* epistle to the Corinthian church is a radical project of *confrontational love.* The blueprint and model can be used across all forms of Socratic and dialectical processes, and theologian Kenneth E. Bailey (2011) said in his classic work, *Paul Through Mediterranean Eyes: Cultural Studies in 1 Corinthians:*

> But a surgeon does not offend a patient by cutting out a deadly tumor. The operation may be painful and the recovery slow, but for the health of the body, such a procedure is necessary. In the case of the Corinthian church Paul's surgery offered the only hope for healing. (p. 289)

For some people, the irresponsible use and placation of Galatians 3:27-29, engenders the premise that Christians escape the everyday problems of hate, discrimination, racism, marginalization, and oppression because the assaults of such vices are rendered powerless toward church members. If that was the case, why is divorce, substance abuse, premarital pregnancies, alcoholism, jealousy, and more found in the church? A brief survey of first-century church behaviors identifies that type of biblical intellectualism or theology as baseless. Shortly after the first-century church was established in Jerusalem, they were summarily forced to develop a ministry to address and further prevent discrimination. Luke recorded, "But as the believers rapidly multiplied, there were rumblings of discontent. The Greek-speaking believers complained about the Hebrew-speaking believers, saying that their widows were being discriminated against in the daily distribution of food" (Acts 6:1 NLT). There you have it;

discrimination in the church. The apostles did not ignore or tolerate the ignorance, they developed an internal system to address it.

In response to the problematic condition, rooted in ethnic and linguistic discrimination, "...The Twelve called a meeting of all the believers. They said, "We apostles should spend our time teaching the word of God, not running a food program" (Acts 6:2 NLT). They boldly, spiritually, and strategically addressed the situation. Through their actions, no one claimed the Apostles were divisive for explicitly naming and addressing ethnic and cultural discrimination? They said, "...So, brothers, select seven men who are well respected and are full of the Spirit and wisdom. We will give them this responsibility" (Acts 6:3 NLT). After the men were selected to remedy the ministry dilemma, acting in love, justice, and equity the Jerusalem church grew: "So God's message continued to spread. The number of believers greatly increased in Jerusalem, and many of the Jewish priests were converted, too" (Acts 6:7 NLT). The blueprint in God's church is not to ignore issues, but address them with love, wisdom, and mature spirituality. Whether in churches, schools, or other social settings, silence toward oppression is not to be admired, embraced, or praised.

Advocacy and Liberation

It is important to highlight and extract from the biblical text, points of injustice that were addressed and remedied during the first century. Such biblical encounters should be used to help persuade and inform individuals that assume a posture of silence or an ill-contrived theology that confrontation is unbiblical, divisive, and the absence of love in action. Some of the episodes of justice can be missed, but in First Corinthians chapter nine, the Apostle Paul addressed the Corinthians regarding the treatment of some Apostles and preachers. Paul pointed out the discrepancy with the church being willing to sponsor the travel and accommodations for some preachers and their wives, but refused to pay for the wife of Barnabas. This encounter provides a profound principle of advocacy. Paul addressed them in the passage below:

> This is my answer to those who question my authority. [4]Don't we have the right to live in your homes and share your meals? [5]Don't we have the right to bring a believing wife with us as the other apostles and the Lord's brothers do, and as Peter does? [6]Or is it only Barnabas and I who have to work to support ourselves? (1 Corinthians 9:3-6 NLT)

Paul demonstrated voice and advocacy, refusing to be silent. With the example above, it is important to address the obvious and subtle nuances. First, through advocacy of voice, Paul addressed the apparent partiality of the church. The church was willing to host the apostles and their spouses, but in the case of Barnabas, the church declined to offer hospitality. Secondarily, why would the Apostle Paul care? Paul was not married, so why would he take on an issue that did not impact him directly? Regardless of religion or spirituality, this is a lesson everyone must learn, especially when a spirit of subliminal supremacy prevails. Authentic advocacy, inside and outside religious connotation, cannot just manifest concern with matters of personal interest; it must be comprehensive or at least travel beyond individual affairs. Paul consistently practiced the art of advocacy and confrontation, even when it did not relate to his direct lifestyle. If religious and secular institutions are only concerned about issues of justice that impact them directly, they miss the thrust of humanity, theology, and trajectory of Christ. As recorded in the *Gospel of Freedom* (2013), attempting to repair his relationship with Black resistant ministers that disagreed with his approach, Dr. King said, "I'm tired of preachers riding around in big cars, living in fine homes, but not willing to take their part in the fight... If you can't stand up with your own people, you are not fit to be a leader" (Reider, 2013, p. 32).

In addition to Paul advocating for Barnabas and his wife, he responded to the selfish element in Corinth through their defilement of the Eucharist. Through investigating the dynamics of the second half of First Corinthians chapter eleven and the communion process, a pivotal piece is often missed. Often the most expressed element of the narrative is that the Corinthians were intoxicated during the Eucharistic experience. Although that is true, there was a more sinister problem that concerned Paul. The people of the church consisted of two groups: the poor and the wealthy. To explicitly address the concern the Apostle Paul said:

> When you meet together, you are not really interested in the Lord's Supper. [21]For some of you hurry to eat your own meal without sharing with others. As a result, some go hungry while others get drunk. [22]What? Don't you have your own homes for eating and drinking? Or do you really want to disgrace God's church and shame the poor? What am I supposed to say? Do you want me to praise you? Well, I certainly will not praise you for this! (1 Corinthians 11:20-22 NLT)

Discovered within the text is another issue of injustice addressed. The wealthy Christians consumed the common meal that flowed into the Eucharist, but when the hungry, poor, and working-class Christians arrived, expecting and needing the fellowship meal, it had already been eaten. Paul was not silent, he addressed the issue. The first-century church has a documented history of addressing issues of injustice, discrimination, and oppression. About this issue Bailey (2011) wrote, "The problems are deeper and more threatening. By their actions they are 'despising the church of God' and 'humiliating those who have nothing'" (p. 318).

Paul was not willing for this kind of behavior to be representational of church fellowship and love. Bailey also captured the words of

Murphy-O'Connor who wrote, "The unity of the church is something more than physical juxtaposition in a determined space....Their behavior, in addition to humiliating the 'have-nots,' shows that they hold true community in contempt" (p. 318). Bailey also said, "Paul exposes the fact that they have broken up into the satisfied rich and the hungry poor, with no awareness of what it means to be the church of God" (p. 318). Strong confrontational words were expressed through the spirit and pen of Paul, but they were rooted in genuine love for the Corinthian church. Does this level of advocacy mesh with your holistic disposition, religiously and secularly, or have you contorted silent passivity into pseudo-humility?

The Education and Theology Nexus

There has always been a scholarly link between education, theology, and faith. Paulo Freire is often discussed, read, and researched because of his contributions to educational epistemology, but he also addressed theology, the Christian faith, and church. Thus, in addition to the pedagogy of the oppressed, there is also a theology of the oppressed. Even Ivan Van Sertima (2003) said, "Diplomacy was diplomacy, trade was trade, but culture and religion were inseparable strands of a native and sacred tradition" (p. 43). The work of Freire continues to challenge the advocacy of educators and the church. "For Freire, to know the word of God is to both hear the word and put it into practice. Consequently, one cannot know God's word unless one is first dedicated to human liberation through concrete actions" (Elias, 1994, p. 142). Similarly, Deotis Roberts (2005) said in *Liberation and Reconciliation: A Black Theology*, "No one can fully understand the revelation of God if he or she does not know the meaning of the cross, not merely as unmerited suffering but also as a healing balm" (2005, p. 76). Through critical examination and consciousness, advocacy pushes through the barriers of race, class, gender, and power paradigms—seeking equality and justice. Freire said in *Pedagogy of the Oppressed*, "Those who authentically commit themselves to the people must re-examine themselves constantly.... Conversion to the people requires a profound rebirth. Those who undergo it must take on a new form of existence..." (p. 60).

Churches, schools, and communities that lack examination, silent in the realm of advocacy, unknowingly uphold the system of structural hegemony. They claim the proclamation of biblically religious work and educational paideia in schools and universities, but according to Elias, "Under the guise of defending the faith they defend class interests" (p. 143). According to the theology of Freire, prophetic churches are uniquely identified and distinguished from others because they are found "denouncing injustices in the world and announcing a more just world to be brought about through historical-social praxis of the oppressed" (Elias, p. 143). Freire categorizes churches under three types: Traditionalist, Modernizing, and Prophetic. The prophetic church addresses the eerie silence in America and across the world. This eerie silence is highly sophisticated, collectively engaged by the white power structure, and religiously "Freire praises prophetic churches, places where leaders and people have achieved critical consciousness. These churches engage in a critical analysis of society and commit themselves to radical social change on behalf of the oppressed" (Elias, p. 144). Using the Freirean premise and without religionizing people, we also need more prophetic schools, governments, politicians, leaders, and communities.

The Illusionary Prize of Whiteness

Especially in the US, the hegemonic system of acceptance is couched in American assimilation. The goal in America is for people to join the *melting-pot* phenomenon. For America and across many parts of the globe, the destination of assimilation is whiteness. As stated by Paul Kivel in *Uprooting Racism: How White People Can Work for Racial Justice*, "Racism is based on the concept of whiteness—a powerful fiction enforced by power and violence. Whiteness is a constantly shifting boundary separating those who are entitled to have certain privileges from those whose exploitation and vulnerability to violence is justified by their not being white" (1996, p. 17). Du Bois said in *Darkwater: Voices from Within the Veil*, "But what on earth is whiteness that one should desire it? Then always somehow, some way, silently but clearly, I am given to understand that whiteness is the ownership of the earth forever and ever, Amen!" (p. 17). As a result and along with educational institutions, Christians and religious leaders must be cautious of allowing the essence of white cultural assimilation to enter the ranks of churches, mosques, and synagogues as a seductive imperialist package. White assimilation already rules the current ethos of American and Eurocentric Christianity and epistemology, but eerie silence prevents it from being acknowledged and confronted. In 2005 during my first mission trip to Ghana, as I walked into the home of the hosting preacher, the only picture on his living-room wall was that of a phenotypically European Jesus. "If we pay attention to the images around us we can literally see the pervasive influence that racism has on our everyday lives" (Kivel, p. 27).

The essence of white supremacy is overpowering to the extent where even in Africa the coloniality of imagery is dominated. Despite formations of human silence, the Bible speaks against this form of privilege and bias. The grip of white supremacy is strong to the point that even in the February 2018 Movie *Black Panther*, despite its deeply African foundation, it could not completely break free from the classic white supremacy depiction of whiteness as the hero and savior. The white savior was not as prominent as in most Hollywood movies, but it was apparent. With some regard, it was the white CIA spy that saved the day, miraculously flying the technologically advanced spaceship of *Wakanda*. Black Panther was the ultimate hero or victor, but the grip of Hollywood could not rest without the traditional white savior, even in a *Marvel* film dedicated to the depths of a non-colonized African nation. In addition to the white savior element, Christopher Lebron said in his February 17, 2018 Boston Review article:

Black Panther presents itself as the most radical black experience of the year. We are meant to feel emboldened by the images of T'Challa, a black man clad in a powerful combat suit tearing up the bad guys that threaten good people. But the lessons I learned were these: the bad guy is the black American who has rightly identified white supremacy as the reigning threat to black well-being; the bad guy is the one who thinks Wakanda is being selfish in its secret liberation; the bad guy is the one who will no longer stand for patience and moderation—he thinks liberation is many, many decades overdue. And the black hero snuffs him out.

Despite the pride that swept through segments of Black America because of the fame and financial record success of the film, just months later, along with many others, the Black Panther character evaporated into dust in *Avengers: Infinity War*. Through the box office *Black Panther* has earned more than 1.344 billion dollars in America. The movie opened on February 16, 2018 and by April 27, 2018, the character was dead by the powers of *Thanos*. What is the big deal? This is just comic book history through the gigantic cinema screen. However, when viewed through the structural systems of American supremacy, the Black racial nexus of *Black Panther* and *Avengers: Infinity War* is deeply symbolic of Black racial progress, followed by European destruction. Not only did T'Challa die in *Avengers: Infinity War*, the land of Wakanda was the location of the epic battle and was desecrated during the war. Many Black moviegoers, especially those unfamiliar with the *Marvel* Comic series, left the theater dejected. No one expected to see the Black superhero that had been built up for the previous two months all across the world, dead by the end of the movie. The allegorical and metaphorical implications are shocking.

In film and beyond it is critical that the intersections of race and white supremacy undergo consistent analysis. This is true in religious, educational, cinematic, musical, and media settings because race is always in motion. Kenneth E. Bailey, in *Paul Through Mediterranean Eyes*, addresses the concept of ethnicity and division in the early church. The Bible does not treat issues of ethnicity and culture as static, stale, or immaterial. God created ethnicity and difference, which means it is a visible and viable part of Christian and kingdom existence. Many Christians present themselves as if race, culture, and ethnicity are insignificant elements in the church and lives of believers; this attitude also surfaces through the multiple domains of education. About Paul seeking to bring unity to the Corinthian church, Bailey said, "No one was expected to cast aside any ethnic identity when he/she came to faith in Christ, but rather to purify and enrich it" (2011, p. 331). Bailey said as positioned by Paul, "He tells his readers that regardless of their ethnic origins (Jewish or Greek) there is an 'assignment,' a 'calling' from the Lord tailored to who they are that does not require becoming someone else" (p. 217). Bailey further paraphrases Paul by saying "God has a calling for you that will be shaped by your own unique cultural identity—be it Jewish or Gentile, slave or free" (p. 218). To the Corinthian church the message of Paul was "We do not have to break up into ethnic enclaves. There is space for all of us to bring the best of our cultural heritages into the body of Christ" (p. 101).

Race is a sociological construct more than it is a biological reality (Price, 1999). Although formations of race were not developed as is the case today, the first-century church began as a deeply diverse institution. The view of the church and Christianity is through a prism of whiteness because of racial conditioning, consequently perceived as a European institution. Based on Acts 2:9-11, the ethnic groups present on the day of *Pentecost* were, "Parthians, Medes, Elamites, people from Mesopotamia, Judea, Cappadocia, Pontus, the province of Asia, [10]Phrygia, Pamphylia, Egypt, and the areas of Libya around Cyrene, visitors from Rome [11](both Jews and converts to Judaism), Cretans, and Arabs." After the deeply *Christological* sermon of the Apostle Peter in Jerusalem, 3000 people were baptized (Acts 2:41).

Along with the twelve Apostles, this was the beginning fabric of the church. It must be assumed that people from all the ethnic groups were represented in the baptismal number, inclusive of those from Africa. The first-century church did not ignore issues of diversity, they embraced and addressed them.

Weaponized Silence

Inclusive of educational strands, silence is used as a weapon, preventing the full manifestation of the radical biblical edict that transcends a forced generosity or cooperation. Given the construction of the early church in Jerusalem (and as it spread), an ethnically and racially diverse group of people assembled, operating in voluntary love and cooperation. Jesus could not be a socialist, because socialism attempts to create forms of resource equality, regardless of intentional generosity and sharing from the heart. Radical love is displayed in Acts 2:44-46 KJV, "And all that believed were together, and had all things common; [45]And sold their possessions and goods, and parted them to all men [and women], as every man [and woman] had need. [46]And they, continuing daily with one accord in the temple, and breaking bread from house to house, did eat their meat with gladness and singleness of heart." Although greed and capitalism can cripple the mind, "For the love of money is the root of all kinds of evil" (1 Timothy 6:10 NLT), I do not believe Jesus would have an issue with capitalism on its face. Malcom X may disagree, he said, "you can't have capitalism without racism. And if you find [anti-racists] usually they're socialists or their political philosophy is socialism" (Marble, 2007, p. 88).

For me, the premise would be for those who have benefitted the most from a capitalist system to cooperatively share their resources and wealth with the poor and oppressed, without being forced. As soon as money and resources are offered because of force and not through a willing spirit of the one who beholds the resource, it is no longer Christian. Christianity can never be confused with socialism.

Socialism can be beneficial in a system where greed usurps morality and humanity, but it is never to be contorted into a form of spirituality or a Christian ethos. Related to multiculturalism, race, and justice, what story does the church in America, over the last three-hundred years, portray? Is it one of vocal advocacy toward love, equality, comprehensive spiritual liberation, and justice, or is it that of eerie silence? Educational institutions must answer the same question. An example of radical voluntary love and sharing is described in the fourth chapter of Acts:

> All the believers were united in heart and mind. And they felt that what they owned was not their own, so they shared everything they had. [33]The apostles testified powerfully to the resurrection of the Lord Jesus, and God's great blessing was upon them all. [34]There were no needy people among them, because those who owned land or houses would sell them [35]and bring the money to the apostles to give to those in need. (Acts 4:32-35 NLT)

When it comes to racial confrontations and injustice, eerie silence is the pervasive norm in America and across the globe. This is true in every pocket of society and includes educators, law enforcement, lawyers, judges, clergy, preachers/pastors, physicians, and people from every sector of blue-collar and white-collar professions. Ibram Kendi (2016) captures a pivotal concept in *Stamped from the Beginning: The Definitive History of Racist Ideas in America,* referencing the actions and disposition of the antislavery Puritan pastor of Rhode Island, Samuel Hopkins. Kendi compares the paradoxical and contradictory rhetoric of Thomas Jefferson with the powerful and direct anti-racist pursuit of Pastor Hopkins. Kendi said, "Hopkins became the first major Christian leader outside of the Society of Friends to forcefully oppose slavery, but he sat lonely on the pew of antislavery in 1776" (p. 107). Critically Dr. Kendi went on to say, "Other preachers stayed away from the pew, and so did the delegates declaring independence" (p. 107). The preachers who stayed away from the pew were those who acted in silence in the eighteenth century and many educators, clergy, and Christians continue the practice in the twenty-first century.

Absurdity of a Post-racial America

Why is it so easy for white people to call police on Black people? Resmaa Menakem (2017) said in *My Grandmother's Hands: Racialized Trauma and the Pathway to Mending Our Hearts and Bodies*:

> The white body sees itself as fragile and vulnerable, and it looks to police bodies for its protection and safety. Its view of the Black body is more complex and deeply paradoxical. It sees Black bodies as dangerously impervious to pain and needing to be controlled. Yet it also sees them as potential sources of service and comfort. (pp. 27-28)

America is not in post-racial colorblind space and reminders emerge daily about US racist toxicity. Through 2018 alone, countless episodes exploded through social media platforms of African American citizens being harassed and surveilled, with white people calling 911 out of the erroneous perception of Black suspicion. One of many incidents that garnered national attention in May 2018, unraveled into an absolute debacle when a white woman called the Oakland Police Department on Black people grilling barbeque at Lake Merritt, claiming their charcoal use was illegal. Similar to the multiple racial Waffle House incidents, the Oakland encounter was captured on video and streamed across social media outlets. The racial and racist episodes are not new; it is just with greater frequency that they are being captured on video because of Smartphone technology, quick social media access, and publishing. Following the Oakland Lake Merritt fiasco was an incident where a white woman labeled "Permit Patty" called authorities on a mother and her eight-year-old

African American daughter, for selling water near San Francisco Giants AT&T Park.

May 23, 2018, marked the day National Football League Commissioner, Roger Goodell, announced that every player on the field for the National Anthem must stand or face a fine. This decision, supported by most NFL owners, is backlash for the silent and peaceful protest of then-San Francisco 49ers quarterback, Colin Kaepernick. Since his protest, Kaepernick has not secured a job as an NFL quarterback, despite multiple players of lesser talent and experience landing QB roster spots on teams across the league. Kaepernick's peaceful protest was a statement against police brutality and mass incarceration. President Trump supports the position of the NFL, causing many to ponder the missed purpose of the protest. Kneeling for the National Anthem is not a protest against the flag, America, or the military; it highlights the need to address police brutality and racism. Demanding all NFL players to stand for the National Anthem is how eerie silence works. Categorically white advocacy was loud in opposition to the Kaepernick peaceful protest, but silent toward the cause that prompted him to sit and then kneel during the opening NFL ceremony.

Soon after the NFL anthem policy announcement, cancelation of the highly popular *Roseanne* show was announced on May 29, 2018 because of her racist tweet-tirade toward Valerie Jarrett, an African American woman that served as senior adviser to Barack Obama. Roseanne Barr made racist comments in the past, but the structure of whiteness deemed it appropriate to bring back the show in 2018. Apparently, America did not have much of an issue with her past racist behavior because before it was canceled, it was one of the most popular shows on television. Clearly, we are not living in a post-racial American society. We exist in a time where Jeff Sessions, US Attorney General, recklessly quoted Romans 13:1, attempting to biblically justify the separation of children from parents crossing the American border. Continual racially hegemonic incidents like that displayed by Sessions, is fact enough that America is far from a post-racial society.

To claim America exists in post-racial space is absurd. In June 2018, a change in immigration practices, resulting in zero-tolerance enforcement was highlighted across American mainstream media. The elevated attention compelled Sessions to address the nation, but he may have presumed his comments would squelch concerns, as opposed to sharpening them. The fact that children were separated from parents or guardians as families attempted to cross the US-Mexico border illegally was exposed. April 2018 marked the phase where the White House declared all immigrants attempting illegal entry into the US would be prosecuted, regardless of the reason, including first-time offenders. The new zero-tolerance enforcement was stated to be a US *deterrent* to immigrant illegal entry, but attempts increased. Pictures of young children in cages pushed some American citizens into an outrage. Many Republicans were also mortified and called for change. Former US first lady Laura Bush spoke in protest of the zero-tolerance enforcement. During the six weeks between April 19, 2018 and May 31, 2018, the Department of Homeland Security sent almost 2000 children to detention stations or foster placements. After White House denial of the separations and then exclaiming the condition could not be reversed without Congress, on June 20, 2018, President Trump signed an Executive Order, partially ending the practice. Racist encounters that appear ripe for the seventeenth-century or Jim Crow era are publically happening today.

Pockets of Black American reaction to the mainstream media coverage of the zero-tolerance outcome on Brown children and families were complex. Because of the history of Black people being kidnapped and brought to America through the Trans-Atlantic Enslavement Trade, the brutal American practice of child and family separation serves as a stark reminder and traumatic trigger. Some Black people were alarmed at the sustained rage of African American citizens, postulating that some seemed more concerned about immigrant conditions than the current plight of Black America. In essence, "How could Black people be so upset, considering our historical and current position in America?" What some may have overlooked is the actual source of Black community outrage for the treatment of migrant children. In addition to being outraged for immigrant Black and Brown family suffrage, although not identical, it painfully spotlights and resurfaces Black family trauma and separation at the hands of American sanctioned Government actions. About the tragedy and trauma of slavery, Derrick Bell said "But it is not comparative slavery policies that concern me. Slavery is, as an example of what white America has done, a constant reminder of what white America might do" (pp. 11-12). It was Dr. King who said in his Birmingham Jail Letter, "…An injustice anywhere is a threat to justice everywhere?" Moreover, that sentiment is the source of Black outcry, rage, and advocacy toward multiple forms of injustice, shattering the eerie silence.

The Colorblind Motif and Community Devastation

Scholar and theologian, James Cone, expressed that there is a tendency to view America as innocent and no one is expected to speak honestly about race. Despite there being no directive to that end, people have learned how to act in cognitive dissonance and denial when it comes to racial and racist dynamics. Cornel West adds that America is often spoken about in sanitized terms and anthologies. To dismiss the toxic blow of race and racism, especially in America, some have attempted to advance a racially colorblind motif. Michelle Alexander, in her epic work, *The New Jim Crow: Mass Incarceration in the Age of Colorblindness*, declares the conception of racial color blindness as destructive. She said, "…Colorblindness has proved catastrophic for African Americans" (p. 240). A racially colorblind scheme was introduced in America as a way to resolve and mask racist and discriminatory treatment toward Black people and other colorized groups. Glenn Singleton said in *Courageous Conversations About Race: A Field Guide for Achieving Equity in Schools* (2015), "… Many White Americans have been raised to believe that it is racist to notice race—that it is virtuous to be colorblind, so to speak….White educators view talking about race as inappropriate, particularly while in mixed racial company" (p. 129).

When color is dismissed, educational disparities can be veiled and explained away, labeling those who disaggregate data and context as divisive, racially neurotic, or simply *playing the race card.* Alexander also said, "Since the days of slavery, black men have been depicted and understood as criminals, and their criminal 'nature' has been among the justifications for every caste system to date" (p. 240). If race is removed from the equation, punishment, castigation, and vilification can be framed in individualized victim-blame language, *masquerading* the assault on a single racial group. This type of subtle and passive approach seeks to conceal the assertive and aggressive essence behind the racist outcomes of marginalized treatment. Speaking through an American lens, this has been the pattern across all systems, inclusive of those religious, economic, and educational. Nothing is immune from the ethereal influence of race and racism. Silence does not make it disappear.

It was racism and a racially colorblind ethos that paved the way for twentieth and twenty-first century mass incarceration. Racially speaking, eerie silence is a seductive trap that operates with such melodic effectiveness its results are only realized years after the strike of destruction. It reminds me of the phrase used in Ephesians 2:22, describing the unseen hand of evil as the "prince of the power of the air." As an example, we can briefly explore a political era that swept through churches, schools, and communities with limited critique. But more than thirty years later the bewildered dialogue is rich. Just five days before my twenty-second birthday, Bill Jefferson Clinton was inaugurated as the forty-second President of the United States of America. Native to Arkansas he had a certain swag and Black America embraced him; he had some roots in Little Rock, the birthplace of my father, and years before the forty-forth president, Barack Obama, Clinton was declared the first Black president of the United States. In 2002 he was inducted into the Arkansas Hall of Fame as an honorary member. He had an appreciation for blues, jazz, and played the saxophone—so aside from a few other stereotypes—I guess this gave him enough credit to jokingly and with some solemnity, be declared the first Black American president. He blew his saxophone in multiple settings with crowds in a beloved frenzy. What could not truly be detected behind his American swag and love for the blues was the racialized destruction and devastation he would leave behind. He did not start the criminal carnage of mass incarceration, but when he had his opportunity to equalize mandatory minimums for crack and powder cocaine, he declined.

Naomi Murakawa discusses in *The First Civil Right: How Liberals Built Prison America*, the destruction of Bill Clinton's presidential policies on Black and even Brown America. She critically reveals the juxtaposed responses to crime and drugs toward an early-to-mid 1900s America, versus the mid-1980s onward. "Congress passed harsh drug-related mandatory minimums in 1951 and 1956, repealed them in 1970 even as public punitiveness hit new highs, and then passed them again in biennial fashion, beginning in 1884" (Murakawa, 2014, p. 119). It is interesting how during the aforementioned epoch, Congress was willing to step away from harsh sentences. The only way to find any significance in the repeal is to look at the targets of the punishment during that time. When the impacted subjects were mostly white, it was easier to pass less punitive laws, but when the subjects were Black or Brown, punishment and sentencing was ratcheted upward. At the start of 1933, Franklin D. Roosevelt was the President and by 1950 Harry Truman was in office. Murakawa said, "Narcotics arrests were 11 percent black and 67 percent white in 1933. By 1950, however, a year before Congress passed the Boggs Act, narcotics arrests were 50 percent black and 46 percent white" (p. 119). Dwight D. Eisenhower was in office from 1953-1961 and Murakawa went on to say in *The First Civil Right*, "A year before Congress fortified narcotics penalties with the 1956 Narcotic Control Act, narcotics arrests were 63 percent black and 36 percent white. Concern about the racial composition of drug addicts infused congressional debates around the 1951 Boggs Act and the 1956 Narcotic Control Acts. Despite the rampant racism and the growth of crime being fixed to segments of Black America, there appeared to be some concern about labeling people for minor offenses. Murakawa continued regarding the fact that "... Congress repealed mandatory penalties for all drug violations in the Comprehensive Drug Abuse Prevention and Control Acts of 1970," while Richard Nixon was president:

> Members of Congress justified repeals with sweeping critiques of mandatory minimums, arguing that they hamper the process of rehabilitation, infringe on proper judicial roles, and exacerbate problems of youth alienation by enforcing a rigid and excessively punitive system. In particular, they rejected the inflexibility of mandatory minimums, suggesting that severe penalties wrongly punished casual violators as if they were hardened criminals. (p. 120)

This position soon changed and the devastation on the Black family was more than noticeable. The impact was present within religious and educational settings. The stage for mass incarceration was in motion, the church was relatively silent, and compounding the problem, school districts adopted zero-tolerance policies adversely impacting Black and Brown children. While Black fathers were incarcerated, Black boys were being kicked out of class, suspended from school, and expelled from school districts. During the inner-city crack cocaine influx of America, the position of sensitivity toward *youth alienation* and *casual violators* was ended and Bill Clinton played a significant role. By 1984:

> Congress' stance on mandatory drug penalties reversed once again, and Congress passed mandatory drug penalties in 1984, 1986, and 1988.... Consequences of the 1986 and 1988 Anti-Drug Abuse Act were apparent almost immediately. By

1993, African Americans accounted for 88.3 percent
of all federal crack cocaine distribution convictions,
Latinos 7.1 percent, whites 4.1 percent, and Asians
and Native Americans 0.5 percent. (Murakawa,
2014, pp. 121-122)

Although then-President Clinton did not start the policy process,
when he had an opportunity to equalize mandatory minimums for
crack and powder cocaine, he refused. With an opportunity to fall in
line with the 1995 US Sentencing Commission's recommendation "to
reduce crack-related penalties, President Clinton opposed 'equalizing'
penalties; his obligation to protect devastated communities trumped
his heart-felt 'concern with the number of young African-Americans
who enter the criminal justice system'" (Murakawa, 2014, p. 123).
This happened in relative silence. Thus, educational formations and
Black theology, a true depiction of biblical theology, must consistently
challenge repressive institutions and policies. Manning Marble said in
Beyond Black and White: From Civil Rights to Barack Obama, "When
millions of people are absolutely convinced that they are being
systematically destroyed, whether by an onslaught of drugs, criminal
violence, or medical mayhem, any nascent racial polemicist can gather
a constituency around himself and acquire a degree of legitimacy"
(pp. 13-14). Regarding this latter twenty-first century systemic Black
inquiry, he went on to say:

> Why is it so much easier to obtain crack cocaine
> and heroin in our neighborhoods than it is to buy
> fresh milk, eggs, and bread? Why are so many
> white educators so hostile toward the introduction
> of African-American Studies and multicultural
> requirements within the core curricula of public
> schools and colleges? (p. 14)

A Model Toward a Church Shattering Silence

In light of such historical and current trends, severely impacting the Black community and a radical push through denial and a racially colorblind disposition, propelling church participants forward with efforts of breaking silence and addressing deeper emotional and painful issues, on July 23-26, 2017, the West Oakland Church of Christ hosted the 9th annual Ministry Summit with the theme, "The Therapeutic Healing Blood of Jesus." Dr. Jesse Trice was the keynote speaker at the four-day event. I also facilitated a presentation regarding church statistics, trends, and strategies for being responsive to *Millennials*. Based on feedback, the presentation set the stage for deeper dialogue regarding race, racism, justice, and the role of the church. Shortly after the late-July Ministry Summit, protests and riots erupted in Charlottesville, Virginia on August 11-12, 2017. Because of the Charlottesville episode, homicide, and blatant acts of racial and racist division, I began receiving phone calls, text-messages, and Facebook inbox communications from Christians about frustrations, outrage, and their role. There was a basic level of confusion and an unconscious challenge of church silence. This further resulted in an all-out night of dramatic and radical dialogue on September 15, 2017.

For traditional church encounters, what we engaged in was atypical. All churches are not silent in the face of race, racism, and injustice, but for those who are vocal and activated, they are the exception. Raphael G. Warnock said in *The Divided Mind of the Black Church: Theology, Piety & Witness,* that we need "to *create together* within the black church and black community spaces for serious, sustained, and regular scheduled dialogue about the nature of black liberationist praxis in this postmodern moment" (p. 175). The Friday evening dialectic was described as "A Night of Dialogue and Reflection from Biblical/Spiritual Perspectives About Church, Outrage, Racism, Activism, God, and Equity." The title of the evening was "Love, the Church, & Social Justice: Breaking Silence through

Critical Dialogue, Reflection, & Application." The descriptive frame and program-booklet welcome message for the event is listed below:

> The leadership and membership of the West Oakland Church of Christ are pleased that you decided to join us tonight for this critical evening of fellowship, dialogue, love, learning, and prayer. Clearly, we are here to address difficult issues concerning our nation and world, such topics as are typically silenced or deemed taboo in our modern church era. In one discussion a fellow Christian said to me, "I believe that such a meeting can be beneficial but let us all remember that we are all children of the Most High God. Much is being said of a small and insignificant group as the KKK whose total membership is less than 8,000 souls across the USA." In my opinion, the statement above makes the purpose of the convening sound as if it is disconnected, unnecessary, ancillary, or separate-and-apart from a true Christian ethos or something that should be of concern to the church. However, this convening is in place because we are unapologetically Christian, the church, and have a righteous duty to be a shining light toward struggle, manifested love, and justice. In addition, despite the stated membership number of Ku Klux Klan membership, the subtle spirit of Eurocentric supremacy, dominance, and impact cannot be ignored in the world or church. Satan operates as the invisible prince and power of the air, thus the Klan and Alt-right agitators are not the issue; it's about addressing the subtle and covert spirits of hegemony and superiority that permeates America and the globe.

In terms of who we are called and chosen to be as a global church, through a prophetic Word Jesus said, *"Ye are the salt of the earth: but if the salt have lost his savour, wherewith shall it be salted? it is thenceforth good for nothing, but to be cast out, and to be trodden under foot of men. [14]Ye are the light of the world. A city that is set on an hill cannot be hid"* (Matthew 5:13-14 KJV). Issues of the world and America impact the church; therefore the body of Christ is not commissioned to be silent and hidden in matters that hurt, harm, oppress, and kill. In the mind of God, the church is a strategically powerful unit, sanctified to fulfill His purpose. To describe this assertive and conspicuous force Christ also said, *"...Upon this rock I will build my church, and all the powers of hell will not conquer it"* (Matthew 16:18 NLT).

It is imperative that the church operates out of its biblical mandate of love and advocacy. Through my keynote, I will share more about this premise, but as an example, the recent White House decision to terminate or revise immigration policy concerning Deferred Action for Childhood Arrivals (DACA), is cause for church advocacy and intervention. If you have members in your church and church community impacted by immigration policy termination/ reform and the potential loss of employment and/ or deportation, how could the church be silent or act as if those members in the church matter less? The church is comprised of people and salvation in Christ does not excuse members of the church from suffering through the tragedies, oppressions, and layers of violence that surface in our world. Thus, if the church is silent on issues that impact the church, we are guilty just as Jesus charged in *Matthew 25:45 KJV*, *"Verily I say unto you, Inasmuch as ye did it not to one of the least of these, ye did it not to me."* Silence, denial, and passivity is not just inaction toward humanity, it is inaction toward God.

It was prophet Amos who exclaimed, *"But let justice roll down as waters, and righteousness as a mighty stream" (Amos 5:24 ASV).* As a challenge and critique of the church, Dr. Martin Luther King Jr. said in Letter from Birmingham Jail, "Their witness has been the spiritual salt that has preserved the true meaning of the gospel in these troubled times. They have carved a tunnel of hope through the dark mountain of disappointment. I hope the church as a whole will meet the challenge of this decisive hour. But even if the church does not come to the aid of justice, I have no despair about the future."

It was in 1963 when Dr. King penned those prolific, relevant, and timeless words. Thus church, in your quest for love, truth, justice, and advocacy where do you stand? It is our hope and prayer that you enjoy this starting point and evening of dialogue, reflection, planning, and action.

Shalom,
Dr. Ammar Saheli, Ministering Evangelist
West Oakland Church of Christ

The church building was full, and each participant was there to gain validation and understanding, integrating the Word of God with their plea and need for justice. Does God have a word for the oppressed and persecuted? Is the church a passive organism? Does the word of

God address personal and social despair and grief? We will come back to this, but we must also ask: Does the God of the Bible resemble the biblical God preached about in America? The evening MC was my wife Tonya Saheli and the night included spoken-word, small-group dialogue, breakout sessions, a panel discussion, prayers for *Hurricane Harvey* and *Irma* victims and recovery, and an opening and closing keynote. I presented the opening keynote entitled, "The Visible Motif of Social Justice, Advocacy, & Love in the Scriptures." The evening moderator was Dr. James L. Taylor, professor of African American Studies and Political Science at the University of San Francisco, and author of the powerful book, *Black Nationalism in the United States: From Malcolm X to Barack Obama*. Dr. Margaret Norris, co-founder of the Omega Boys Club and Alive & Free was present and facilitated a powerful breakout session. Dr. Joseph Marshall, co-founder of Omega Boys Club, Alive & Free, and radio host of Street Soldiers also shared words. The small group conversations focused on three questions:

1. What has been difficult for you emotionally and/or spiritually in watching and processing the racialized events in America, such as Charlottesville and the Bay Area?
2. How do you feel about the intersection between social injustice and the impact on and role of the church?
3. What feelings, frustrations, or solutions are you left with and what questions remain for you?

Illustrating the energy in the building, it was after 11:00 PM when Dr. Taylor delivered his closing keynote. It was one of the most powerful speeches anyone could ever hear and truly revolutionary. Profoundly this transpired within the walls of a church building. After midnight we were still engaged in dialogue; the buzz in the building was electric from 6:00 PM through 12:30 AM. Based on the call and needs of the people, this night of dialectic engagement was necessary and the response and spiritual movement of God in the place validated and affirmed the effort. In a nation and world where racial justice is often denied and ignored, the issue and presence of race had to be placed on the table that night. It was not the first time my congregation had this conversation, but it was our first time inviting the Greater San Francisco Bay Area to participate in this collective and collaborative effort. There comes a time where a choice must be made to engage in spiritual activism and justice, or the result is a retreat into unconscious assimilation, producing American imperial *mores*. Mignolo (2009) explains the radical choice of action this way:

> The border between black skin and white mask is the border on the colonial difference at all levels, but also at the epistemic level: knowledge and epistemology are located in the white-skinned body, not in the black. And that is why the black-skinned body has two kinds of options: to become white or, like Fanon, to unveil the colonial racial matrix and its epistemic consequences. (p. 29)

As and through the gospel message of Christ, this call is urgent. The September 15, 2017 event sparked a three-month Bible study investigation that I presented to my congregation during the 2017 months of October-December. The title of this lecture series was, "In Search of Colorized Identity in the Sacred Scriptures: An Investigation of Biblical Truth Before Eurocentric/American Hegemony." It was this study that led to the creation of the deeper portions of this book, to which we now turn.

CHAPTER 2

THE PROBLEM OF SILENCE IN THE FACE OF VIOLENCE, JUSTICE, AND THEOLOGY IN AMERICA

> Even an accurate body count of black lynching
> victims could not possibly reveal how hate and
> fear transformed ordinary white men and women
> into mindless murderers and sadistic torturers,
> or the savagery that, with increasing regularity,
> characterized assaults on black men and women in
> the name of restraining their savagery and depravity.
> (Litwack, 2000, p. 12)

For the majority of my teenage and adult life I have contemplated
the unspoken and taboo elements of race and culture in the church.
However, it was the traumatic evening of November 8, 2010, where
my wife's unarmed brother, Derrick DD Jones, was murdered in a
dark alley on Trask and Seminary by two Oakland Police Department
officers, that shifted *justice* elements within my psyche and spirituality.
In 2009 Oscar Grant was killed and after the Derrick Jones murder,
Trayvon Martin, Tamir Rice, Michael Brown, Eric Garner, Alton
Sterling, Sandra Bland, Philando Castile, Laquan McDonald, John
Crawford III, Walter Scott, Freddie Gray, Mario Woods, Terence
Crutcher, Botham Shem Jean, and more were killed.

On June 19, 2018, seventeen-year-old Antwon Rose, of East Pittsburgh, was shot in the back and killed after fleeing a car. The officer was sworn in hours earlier. A few months earlier, the backyard police killing of Stephon Clark in Sacramento, California on March 18, 2018, was eerily reminiscent of the Derrick Jones murder. Around 9:25 PM and after police yelled "Gun, gun, gun" Stephon Clark was shot at twenty times in his backyard and fatally struck by eight of the bullets. Six of the shots entered his back. Only a cell phone was discovered at the scene. Although it is not the intent of this project, police and community engagement, through a lens of critical consciousness is needed, as explained by Brandon Lee in *Best Practices in Community Consciousness Policing: A Reflection on Law Enforcement Community Building Workshops;* and as demonstrated by the model and efforts of Captain Michael Carroll of the Alameda County Sheriff's Department, in the California Bay Area.

Through the lens of structural dominance, the church in America is tucked away behind the veil of white superiority. American whiteness has maintained a proclivity toward repetitively ignoring and spinning issues of righteousness and injustice. In the face of blatant injustice, Christendom still has the tendency to embrace a disposition of silence toward hegemonic abuses of power. The bigger ill is that a form of insidious *racist socialization* continues to find space in the church. Vocally breaking the intellectual and spiritual shackle of cognitive dissonance is problematic and met with resistance when the Eurocentric commandeered story is accurately reconstructed. What would the white power structure say to a Christian archaeologist or anthropologist who makes a racial, cultural, or ethnic discovery that challenges current notions of white supremacy? Would they be labeled divisive?

During Jim Crow South and a racist North, Black children were forced to live with the traumatic aftermath of lynching and today they suffer through the devastation of police murders of unarmed citizens. As chillingly chronicled by Timothy B. Tyson in *The Blood of Emmett Till,* young Emmett did not have to travel to Money, Mississippi to see racism; it already existed in his Chicago hometown. Tyson exposes the deadly Jim Crow white mob violence that ruled the city of Chicago as early as 1910 and through the civil rights era. The deadly American pattern of disproportionate slayings of unarmed Black men, women, male, and female teenagers are venomously seething. That cold night Derrick Jones was killed painfully awakened my challenge to the theological role of silence in the church, especially toward issues of injustice. Before the tragic night of Derrick being shot at close range, seven times in the chest and legs, I preached on issues of race, racism, and injustice, but not with the level of conviction, passion, and love I possess today. It was like Job who said about his life-changing encounter with God, "I had only heard about you before, but now I have seen you with my own eyes" (Job 42:5 NLT). Whether spiritually, educationally, or psychologically, there are episodes we experience that move us from theory to praxis. Job acknowledged that, though faithful, at one point in his life he only knew about God auditorily, but after God allowed distressing affliction to his body, the death of his children, and economic ruin, he boldly proclaimed that he came to know God experientially.

Eight years after being the preacher of the West Oakland church of Christ DD was killed. My father-in-law served as one of the congregational elders, and he and my mother-in-law were faithful members of the congregation for over forty years before my arrival. The city of Oakland was still whirling from the emotions related to the early morning New Year's day Fruitvale Bart station murder of Oscar Grant, by Bay Area Rapid Transit Police Officer Johannes Mehserle. On November 5, 2010, three days before the murder of Derrick Jones, Mehserle was sentenced to two years, minus time served. Coupled with the Mehserle verdict and Derrick Jones murder, the city of Oakland was on edge. My wife and family connected with the family of Oscar Grant and continued efforts of social justice organizing.

Sparked by the unarmed shooting of Derrick Jones, we spoke with Oakland City Hall Officials, advocated at meetings and rallies, met with then-Oakland Chief of Police, Anthony W. Batts, and Alameda

County Supervisor Nate Miley arranged a private meeting for the family to meet with Nancy O'Malley, Alameda County District Attorney. The family secured John Burris as an attorney, there was an investigation by the Citizens Review Board, Oakland Police Department Internal Affairs, Office of Civil Rights, and the Federal Bureau of Investigations. Along with disturbed citizens, many church members from Oakland, San Francisco, and the Bay Area marched and peacefully protested the unwarranted shooting of Derrick Jones. My epiphany surfaced as I observed an awkward disposition and confused silence within a segment of my congregation.

This was no longer a situation that was external; in real time this police killing struck the tentacles and sinews of my wife, children, family, and congregation. Early morning on November 9, 2010 when our home phone rang, upon answering my wife screamed and fell to the floor, notified that her brother was murdered the previous night. It was around 7:00 AM and our children were getting dressed for school and I was leaving out the door for work. Through the midst of the chaotic scene, while my wife was on the floor screaming and in tears, our oldest son Zion (almost eight at the time) was yelling, "where is my little brother, where is my brother." My wife was on the floor screaming and I was trying to decipher exactly what was happening. Zion's confused teary-eyed inquiry was initially ignored because it took time for his psychological reaction to his mother screaming to register in my mind. On April 12, 2006 Seven Enoch Saheli was born and he died in the arms of my wife and me, three days later, on April 15, 2006. The last time Zion heard his mother scream with such grief was when his baby brother died. Thus, during her November 2010 screams, Zion assumed his eight-month old baby brother, Shiloh, had also passed away. He was not aware that Shiloh was in his crib sleep upstairs. It was clear how the death of my wife's brother was vociferously impacting my family, but the church reaction required more analysis.

King, the Black Church, and a Social Justice Ethos

Growing up in a predominantly Black church experience, a blurred line and delicate nuance always existed between church activity, politics, and social justice issues. Although race was a discussion in my home, I do not recall any substantive discussions about racism or racial socialization in the church. I often wondered why every biblical figure was portrayed as white, but I was never privy to a conversation about the development and monopoly of white biblical imagery. People were exposed to horrible incidents reported on television, read about in newspapers and magazines, and experienced in their personal lives, but in my daily life, the church remained relatively silent on collective levels of injustice. About Dr. Martin Luther King Jr. in *Black Prophetic Fire*, Cornell West said, "At the time he was shot dead, 72 percent of Americans disapprove of him and 55 percent of Black Americans disapprove of him. He is isolated. He is alienated. He is down and out. He was wrestling with despair" (p. 70). According to Manning Marble in *Race, Reform, and Rebellion: The Second Reconstruction and Beyond in Black America,* the same sentiment was evident at and after the death of Malcolm X. "A prominent journalist and black appointee in the Johnson Administration, Carl Rowan, described him as 'an ex-convict, ex-dope peddler who became a racial fanatic... a Negro who preached segregation and race hatred'" (Marble, 2007, p. 89).

Today many people view Malcolm X as an American freedom fighter for racial and economic justice, but during the civil rights epoch, like King, he was loathed by many. Today Dr. King is revered as an iconic international peacekeeper, but during his lifetime significant portions of Christendom, and America in general, disagreed with his activism and non-violent methods. In general, Dr. King was accused of being too progressive, urged by the white power structure to operate as a *gradualist*. This kind of double consciousness and late-arrival love for historic figures who fought for civil rights compelled me to write a January 1, 2018 paper for my Sahealing.org blog and fellow educators entitled, "Finding Your Position on the Racialized Battlefield: A Brief

Examination of Racism, Silence, Fragility, Resistance, & Justice." As was the case with the paper, even this project is designed to help us all establish our position.

Dr. Martin Luther King Jr. was not confused about the perfectly wedded nexus of the gospel of Jesus Christ and issues of racial and social justice. He refused to be silent about racial oppression and marginalization. His Christian and biblical intellect was not an existential element of his push for freedom, equity, and equality—it was the core of his rationale. During the last years of his life, the King message became more radical, revolutionary, and direct. His love for God, people, and America fueled the risk and sacrifice of his life and ministry. His pursuit of justice was not a misguided emotional mission, it was *agape* love that both inspired and propelled him. Today, how can people laud Dr. King, but remain silent in the face of current persecution and injustice? He was deeply concerned about America and the powerful depths of white resistance toward his efforts for Black liberation. Raphael G. Warnock, Senior Pastor of the historic Ebenezer Baptist Church challenges the theology of all that Christendom elucidates by saying, "The only way to test whether our spiritual piety is authentic, and our theological speech and proclamation is indeed good news is to see whether the poor will hear it and receive it as such (Luke 4:18)" (2014, p. 175). Does the poor of today embrace the gospel or are they reluctant and skeptical of the message and those who share it?

Dr. King had a conversation with Harry Belafonte in his home five days before he was executed on the balcony outside his Lorraine Motel room. The chilling exchange was after a successful strategy meeting about the *Poor People's Campaign*. Mr. Belafonte felt the gathering was a success, but he noticed that Dr. King was frustrated. King acknowledged his annoyance and spoke about his desegregation pessimism; he knew integration would take root in America, but a new thought vexed his soul and psyche. With anguish and worry he told Mr. Belafonte, "I've come to the realization that I think we may be integrating into a burning house." King was troubled by this thought on March 31, 1968, and we can ask, "is America still a burning house today?" If it is still ablaze, what justification do we have for an eerie silence?

Reider reported in the *Gospel of Freedom* about King meeting with white men in Birmingham to discuss desegregation, "From the start, the very idea of blacks and whites sitting down together to negotiate the end of racial separation was a dicey and even absurd affair" (p. 50). The thought of Black America entering a burning house intensely stirred in the heart of Dr. King. It was now time for one of his most prolific sermons to his Ebenezer Baptist Church members. It would also be a message to the world. On the early afternoon of April 4, 1968, the day King was assassinated, Tavis Smiley reported in his 2014 book, *Death of a King: The Real Story of Dr. Martin Luther King Jr.'s Final Year:*

> Doc is feeling refreshed. While his aides are in court arguing for the legalization of Mondays march, he calls Dora McDonald, his secretary in Atlanta, to share his sermon topic for next Sunday's service at Ebenezer so that she can get it into the church bulletin. His theme is one that has been resonating in his head and heart for the past twelve months: *Why America may go to hell.* (p. 244)

Dr. King consistently broke his terrestrial silence in hope of a celestial day of American and racially global, economic, and political emancipation. Preaching is a therapeutic act that helps the minister or pastor redeem equilibrium, peace, and regeneration. From his home-base and on deepened levels, positioned atop his Ebenezer Baptist Church pulpit, Dr. King was again ready to challenge American racism and injustice with one of his most rousing sermons. He never made it back to Atlanta to proclaim the most powerful message America has never heard: *Why America May go to Hell.* Smiley said about the last moments of King's life, as he stood on his Lorraine Motel balcony speaking to Jesse Jackson at the ground level:

> "Doc, you remember Been Branch? He's our saxophonist. Memphis musician." "Oh, yes," Doc calls down, he's my man. How are you, Ben?...Make sure you play 'Precious Lord, Take My Hand' in the meeting tonight. "Play it real pretty." Then a shot rings out. The bullet finds its mark. Doc falls. At age thirty-nine, his life on earth ends. (p. 246)

Unlike some Christians today, Dr. King refused to allow white supremacy to silence and cripple his spiritual activism and biblical worldview. About the resilience of King and him metaphorically putting on his cemetery clothes, going to battle for racial and economic justice, Cornell West said in *Black Prophetic Fire*, "...You just have to be coffin-ready for this bearing of witness and struggle in the midst of a very sick country run by greedy oligarchs and avaricious plutocrats whose interest is very entrenching, whose power is mighty" (p. 68). The murder of my brother-in-law thrust our congregation out of theory and into *praxis* and gave me the uniform of resilient cemetery clothes. No longer were the police killings of unarmed Black men, women, and teenage girls and boys externally traumatic episodes replayed on CNN and Fox News, they were at the front door and inside the house. Although everyone in my congregation respected Dr. King as a trusted freedom-fighter for justice, with injustice, trauma, grief, and death looking us intensely in the face, there was an awkward and clumsy church reaction. There was a limited framework for connecting spirituality and theology with social justice and activism.

Despite honoring and watching Dr. King brilliantly connect his embrace of the cross and blood of Christ with a pursuit of civil rights, it was apparent that in the case of this unarmed shooting that left my wife and her siblings without their brother and parents without their son, social justice and religion was viewed as an *either-or* disposition, as opposed to a *both-and* stance. Through unspoken actions it was clear that Christianity operated on a binary; either a person was a Christian or an activist, but there was no biblical room or schematic for both. Old Testament prophets and New Testament Apostles were deeply spiritual, theological, radical, and strategically political. However, observing modern-day church inaction and uneasiness was both troubling and redemptive for me. It instantly crystalized my quest and embrace of authentic Christianity and a prophetic faith. The death of my son Seven Enoch spiritually liberated me from the manacles of biblical legalism, the death of Derrick Jones left me spiritually revolutionized with a social justice theology, and the Easter-Sunday (2015) death of my mother caused a deeper ministerial consciousness of the "burning fire shut up in my bones" (Jeremiah 20:9).

After the death of Derrick, one Sunday after church my father-in-law invited the organization, *By Any Means Necessary* (BAMN), to speak to the church. I had never heard of the organization. I knew that *BAMN* presenting to the church about civil rights organizing and peaceful protests would be a strained encounter, but since it was my father-in-law that invited them, he would be forced to deal with any backlash. I was going to sit back and observe the process. Church ended, and everyone was asked to remain to hear from *BAMN*. As I made my way to the back for a moment, my father-in-law stopped me and said he needed me to introduce *BAMN*.

My first internal response was a type of anger, for I felt set up or left holding the bag. If anything was to go wrong with the presentation, already knowing it was atypical for such groups to present to some churches, the blame and need for cleanup and damage control would be on my shoulders. My anger quickly turned to radical liberation and I approached the pulpit from which I had just finished preaching and introduced *BAMN*. It was in that moment and through that encounter that my spirituality and biblical worldview supremely and radically interlocked, with the gospel message, the cross, love, and justice at the root. Like King, the pressure and weight of institutional racism, white supremacy, and pockets of Black-church apprehensiveness could not keep me silent. Churches are often ill-equipped to respond to community and racial injustice from deeply biblical places, and the silence that is masked in fear, racial repression, and dehumanization— is masqueraded as unity and humility.

Prophetically the behavior of Jesus at the cross of Calvary is professed in Isaiah 53:7. Prophet Isaiah said, "He was oppressed, and he was afflicted, yet he opened not his mouth: he is brought as a lamb to the slaughter, and as a sheep before her shearers is dumb, so he openeth not his mouth" (Isaiah 53:7 KJV). The silence of Jesus during His persecution and execution is mistaken for a modern-day form of piety and humility. Some refuse to speak because advocacy for the marginalized does not comport with their interests. James Cone said in *God of the Oppressed*, "It is not that the problem of faith and history is unimportant. Rather, its importance, as defined by white theologians, is limited to their social interests" (p. 42).

Jesus was silent in His own persecution, but He spoke boldly for the marginalized, oppressed, and impoverished. As recorded by Luke the physician, Jesus said, "The Spirit of the Lord is upon me, because he hath anointed me to preach the gospel to the poor; he hath sent me to heal the brokenhearted, to preach deliverance to the captives, and recovering of sight to the blind, to set at liberty them that are bruised, [19]To preach the acceptable year of the Lord" (Luke 4:18-19 KJV). The ministry of Jesus was always about *the least of these,* which renders a silent disposition in the church today, related to injustice, as un-Christian. Jesus was not silent toward injustice, oppression, dehumanization, or humiliation.

At the age of seventeen on the evening of February 26, 2012, Trayvon Martin was fatally shot by George Zimmerman. Mr. Zimmerman was the neighborhood watch coordinator and Trayvon was returning from the store, walking back through the housing community of his relatives. Zimmerman was told by police dispatch to not follow Trayvon, but he did, and it resulted in the death of the seventeen-year-old high school student. After his death, the division of America peeled back its veil and people scrutinized the character of

Trayvon. Although there was nothing there to smear his humanity, his academic and school discipline records were publicized.

Trayvon was a typical teenager, but some looked for youthful mistakes to discredit him, seeking to justify his death. On July 23, 2018 a white man randomly and savagely slit the throat of eighteen-year-old Nia Williams and her twenty-year-old sister La'Tifah Williams as they exited the BART train at the MacArthur station in Oakland, California. Nia died from the attack at the BART station and her sister was transported to the hospital. In less than twenty-four hours after her death, Fox KTVU News aired an unrelated social-media photo of Nia holding what appeared to be a gun, but was actually a cell phone case. Regardless, of all the photos selected, why was the contextually offensive and insensitive photo included? Six years have passed since the Trayvon Martin murder, but smear tactics that amount to Black disregard and marginalization continue. The same smearing formula was attempted on the day of the funeral of Botham Shem Jean, which compelled me to write an open letter to Dallas city officials on September 15, 2018.

The reaction to the death of Derrick Jones was unnerving because I heard some people in the church community question the character of my brother-in-law after he was unjustly killed. Some were silent toward justice but vocal in their private corners about his character. This is the prevalent blueprint toward the marginalized and maligned in America. It is a racialized malignancy that obscures an equitable treatment of humanity. Instead of seeking justice, the pattern for the African American male and female image is to castigate and demonize the victims, seeking to spark an erroneous method of homicidal justification. The church is not immune from this form of predictable thinking. Some in the church stand guilty and we must ask why. This is not a shaming of church inaction and silence, it is designed to be a challenge and framework to help church members and beyond, find their necessary voice and position.

As evidenced by King and others, historically the church in America has not been completely silent toward injustice and antiracism, but the outspoken advocates have always been in the minority. Since the death of my brother-in-law, I have been advocating for a deeper need and level of urgency for racialized discussions. On August 1, 2016 I began a fourteen-part sermon series entitled "The Church on Center Stage with a Nation in Crisis: We Must Get this Right." Part fourteen ended on December 18, 2016 and the complete series focused on the blueprint and model of the first-century church in response to issues of race, racism, oppression, and injustice as a call from the cross of Christ. It was also a plea for churches to come together and have discussions about racial division and injustice as a model. How could the church not be proactive in establishing a blueprint for deeply spiritual social justice ministry and consistent forms of dialogue and action? It was during this sermon series, September 16, 2016, that Betty Jo Shelby, Tulsa Police Department officer and Church of Christ member, shot and killed Terence Tafford Crutcher, Sr. Now an officer-involved killing of an unarmed Black man was at the doorsteps of the church of Christ.

Churches of Christ no longer could process such killings through an external prism, it was now internal. It would have been great if we had already been engaged in intentional and deep forms of interracial dialogue, but that was not the case. Betty Jo Shelby was arrested and tried for the shooting. She was found not guilty on May 17, 2017. The killing of Mr. Crutcher Sr. is a grave tragedy and the fact that America refuses to address its racial fears, implicit bias, and institutional racism remains disastrous. Because of the shooting on September 6, 2018, his family and churches of Christ on national and international levels are forced to process the death of Botham Shem Jean, killed by Dallas police officer, Amber Guyger, in his apartment. He was beloved and a graduate of Harding University and a praise and worship leader at the Dallas West Church of Christ.

Despite the silence found in some churches and after the ousting of Bernie Sanders from the presidential race, there was an emboldened voice regarding the 2016 presidential election process between Hilary Rodham Clinton and Donald J. Trump. Under the guise of Christianity and the church, divisive postures were present, superimposing political affiliation and partisanship over Christian spiritual positioning in Christ. For some it seemed there was more allegiance to political party and the flag than the *cross*. One voice I heard circling throughout segments of Christendom was Lance Wallnau. His book categorized candidate Trump as a type of King Cyrus of the Bible. Before exploring that premise, notice the words of Dyson (2017), regarding the Obama/Trump nexus:

> We have, in the span of a few years, elected the nation's first black president and placed in the Oval Office the scariest racial demagogue in a generation. The two may not be related. The remarkable progress we seemed to make with the former has brought out the peril of the latter. (p. 3)

Make America Great Again Hypocrisy

Before president Trump was elected, Dr. Lance Wallnau branded him as a type of irreligious messiah and savior. In his 2016 book, *God's Chaos Candidate: Donald J. Trump and the American Unraveling*, Wallnau depicted Trump as the modern-day biblical King Cyrus. At first glance, the classification and labeling may seem harmless, but when compared to the *Make America Great Again* slogan of President Trump, it is worthy of deeper analysis. Why were so many in the Christian community willing to be vocal about Trump, but retreat to silence when issues of social and racial justice surface? Since Trump was viewed as a modern-day Cyrus, it is to that explanation we explore. What did King Cyrus do and represent and how does that archetype fit and aid the American project?

King Cyrus reigned after the destruction of Solomon's Temple and provided the decree for the Hebrew people to be freed from Babylonian captivity. Although not a believer in the God of the Hebrew people, Cyrus was used by God to rebuild the second temple, establishing a climate that made it possible for the people of Israel to return to Jerusalem. J. Daniel Hays said in his exciting work, *The Temple and the Tabernacle: A Study of God's Dwelling Places from Genesis to Revelation*, "In 539 BC King Cyrus of Persia conquers the Babylonians and consolidates his power in the region. One year later Cyrus issues a decree that allows the Israelites who have been exiled by the Babylonians to return home to Judah and Jerusalem and to rebuild their city and their temple" (p. 128). As recorded by Ezra the scribe in Scripture, the Bible declares:

> Now in the first year of Cyrus king of Persia, that the word of the LORD by the mouth of Jeremiah might be fulfilled, the LORD stirred up the spirit of Cyrus king of Persia, that he made a proclamation throughout all his kingdom, and put it also in writing, saying, ²Thus saith Cyrus king of Persia, The LORD God of heaven hath given me all the kingdoms of the earth; and he hath charged me to build him an house at Jerusalem, which is in Judah. (Ezra 1:1-2 KJV)

Just a few verses later Ezra reports the jubilance of the people as they were able to return to Jerusalem to rebuild the temple:

> Then rose up the chief of the fathers of Judah and Benjamin, and the priests, and the Levites, with all them whose spirit God had raised, to go up to build the house of the LORD which is in Jerusalem. ⁶And all they that were about them strengthened their hands with vessels of silver, with gold, with goods, and with beasts, and with precious things, beside all that was willingly offered. (Ezra 1:5-6 KJV)

Under the context of *Make America Great Again*, the Wallnau *Trump/Cyrus* connection is ghostly. Through the analogy of Trump likened to King Cyrus, who are the American people allegorically restored to a time of rebuilding? I cannot help but see it through a lens of white supremacy and superiority. Trump can be viewed as Cyrus because Christian theology is often promulgated from a schematic of Eurocentric hegemony and not a pedagogy or andragogy of the oppressed. This kind of ethereal God is existential and disconnected from the conditions of humanity. It is the development of that kind of venomous thinking that concocts a God that divinely commands chattel slavery and the *Maafa* in America, *Manifest Destiny, Doctrine of Discovery,* and Hitler's Holocaust of the Jews in Germany.

In *God of the Oppressed* James Cone said, "God's revelation is inseparable from the social and political affairs of Israel" (p. 57). Cone said of the God of the Bible and not that of an entity framed out of white supremacy, "God is a political God, the Protector of the poor and the Establisher of the right for those who are oppressed" (p. 57). Additionally, for the people of America and "For theologians to speak of this God, they too must become interested in politics and economics, recognizing that there is no truth about Yahweh unless it is the truth of freedom as that is revealed in the oppressed people's struggle for justice in this world" (p. 57). Does this premise match with the Trump comparison of liberation and deliverance?

Trump exclaims, *"Make America Great Again,"* but what time-frame is he referencing? During what epoch was America great? The president depicted as King Cyrus is a metaphor for *King Trump,* setting the stage for the spirit of bolstered white supremacy to return, rebuilding and growing its empire. It is unfortunate that someone would abuse the biblical text to such an extent. With reference to biblical analysis, Orpheus Heyward discusses in *Baptism: Dead, Dipped Delivered,* "It is vitally important to any word study to realize that context plays a significant part in defining any term. Therefore, the surrounding information of a passage sheds light on the meaning of a word" (p. 13). To that end, the Trump comparison is wholly out of context and he is not connected to the work of God as a regenerated King of Persia. If this book was strictly about theological interpretation, time would be taken to explain the biblically correct hermeneutical implications of King Cyrus, but that would be another project. In short, the role of King Cyrus speaks to the political and theological reestablishment of the temple and people of God, ultimately pointing to the salvific work of Christ on the cross (John 2:15-21).

The racism and racist ideas fostered by President Trump were clearly displayed as he defaced immigrants and the lineage of Africa, Haiti, and El Salvador, by using a loathsome term I will not repeat, but praised and hoped for immigrants from Norway. Though controversial and perhaps opportunistic, Omarosa Manigault Newman captures White House Trump sentiments in *Unhinged: An Insider's Account of the Trump White House*. The derogatory presidential comment occurred after multiple incendiary remarks toward women, Mexicans, those with disabilities, and more. The White House remark took place on January 11, 2018, in a bi-partisan Oval Office meeting on immigration reform and DACA. To determine the truth of the comment, during the Capitol Hill Senate Judiciary Committee hearing on January 16, 2018, Democratic Senator Richard Durbin grilled Department of Homeland Security Secretary, Kirstjen Nielsen, about the controversial comments of Trump.

Richard Durbin was in the Oval Office when President Trump made the comment, but Nielsen denied hearing the specific pejorative term, but she did admit "tough" and "impassioned" language was used. Republican Senator Lindsey Graham was also in the Oval Office conversation and confirmed the foul-mouthed comments of Mr. Trump. Democratic Senators Corey Booker and Kamala Harris interrogated Kirstjen Nielsen during the Senate Judiciary Committee hearing, but she held firm denying that she heard President Trump refer to Africa, Haiti, and El Salvador with the incendiary term. White House Press Secretary Sarah Huckabee Sanders said in her January 16, 2018, White House press briefing that "tough language" was used, but "no one is going to pretend like the President is always politically correct. He isn't."

Senator Booker said to Kirstjen Nielsen, "The commander in

chief in an Oval Office meeting referring to people from African countries and Haitians with the most vile and vulgar language, that language festers." He continued by saying, "When ignorance and bigotry is allied with power it is a dangerous force in our country. Your silence and your amnesia is complicity." In a prior interview about the comments of President Trump, Senator Richard Durbin said, "But I cannot believe that in the history of the White House, in that Oval Office, any president has ever spoken words that I personally heard our President speak yesterday." I applaud Richard Durbin for not being silent or complicit with the comments of the President, but it is clear that America has a distinct history of presidents who were major *slave owners*, starting with George Washington. I wonder how Mr. Durbin would classify Oval Office language of former presidents, such as James Madison who proposed the declaration of the *Three-Fifths Compromise*. This process resulted in enslaved Africans in America being counted and three-fifths of a person for taxation and legislative representation purposes.

James Cone and Two Americas

The evidence of silence in America toward racialized injustice continues to illustrate the reality of a duality within the American experience. On February 25, 2016, James Cone delivered an electric lecture at Union Theological Seminary, entitled "The Cry of Black Blood: The Rise of Black Liberation Theology." The lecture is one of the most riveting discourses I have ever encountered. I was uplifted, empowered, and mesmerized by his speech. To illustrate how divided America is, a question from the floor was posed by one of the white male participants. The alarming premise was the gigantic chasm between how he interpreted the message of Dr. Cone and what I heard and felt. The man asked Cone, "How much longer will your Black blood cry out from the ground? What will it take to satisfy this Black blood?" He said, "I feel a lot of talk on this subject is needlessly divisive." He added, "the talk would have been fine in the 1960s, but today things have turned around almost diametrically. A white person would not be able to come up there and talk about racism against Black people, the same way you are able to talk about whites. I find your talk needlessly divisive." He concluded by saying "I wonder also about this institution that gives audience or gives stage to these types of talks." I was aghast at the questions and statements, but he was pushing an agenda of silence in the face of oppression, race, and racism.

In response to the participant comments, Dr. Cone briefly paced on the stage, gathered himself, looked up at the man out in the audience and said, "You know… we live in different worlds." The racially diverse crowd erupted in applause. Although it is a reality that groups in America experience it differently, there should not be encounters that make it feel like there are two churches. While I was working on this literary project James Cone died on April 28, 2018 and he has left his mark on the world with theological, epistemological, and intellectual essays, books, and lectures that will take a lifetime for anyone to fully explore.

Michael Eric Dyson said in his 2017 book, *Tears We Cannot Stop: A Sermon to White America*, "Black and white people don't merely have different experiences; we seem to occupy different universes, with worldviews that are fatally opposed to one another" (p. 3). This polarization equates to the work that is necessary for conciliation and healing in America. Before American silence can be broken, there must first be psychological acknowledgment of the two worlds and oppressive historicity therein.

In addition to the spiritual and religious circumstances surrounding the deaths of my son and brother-in-law, the 2011 work of Dr. James Cone, *The Cross and the Lynching Tree*, also helped me understand the *why* of hypocritical silence and crystalized my understanding and approach to Christology and justice. The "Hellhounds" essay by Leon F. Litwack in *Without Sanctuary: Lynching Photography in America* says, "If white churches showed a relative indifference to lynching violence, there were some compelling reasons. The lynch mobs often included their parishioners" (p. 21).

About the silence and hypocrisy of white violence covered by the American church, Cone said:

> What I studied in graduate school ignored white supremacy and black resistance against it, as if they had nothing to do with the Christian gospel and discipline of theology. Silence on both white supremacy and black struggle against racial segregation made me angry with a fiery rage that had to find expression. How could any theologian explain the meaning of Christian identity in America and fail to engage white supremacy, its primary negation? (pp. xvi-xvii)

Cone was spiritually and emotionally forced to connect the cross and suffering of Christ with the brutal lynching of Black America. It is at this point that the spiritual ethos and psychology of white America and the church must be put on trial. Cone was disturbed at the silence directed at Black injustice and murder in America. How could the Bible be read and studied in the twentieth and twenty-first-centuries without it speaking a word to American violence, dehumanization, oppression, slavery, and discrimination? How could the silence of seminaries and Christian communities be so bold, cold, dismissive, and arrogant? We are still grappling with eerie silence today. As Baldwin highlighted, *The Cross and the Lynching Tree* points out as a critical premise made by Rabbi Joachim Prinz:

> When I was a rabbi of the Jewish community in Berlin under Hitler regime...the most important thing I learned under those tragic circumstances was that bigotry and hatred are not the most urgent problems. The most urgent and most disgraceful, the most shameful, the most tragic problem is silence. (p. 55)

The Divide Behind the Silence

Silence and racial division is still a condition the church has failed to comprehensively acknowledge and address. Because of that, it has even seeped into the schematic understanding and manifestation of Christian political intellectualism. The collective church, and especially that of America, has yet to implement the divine biblical spirit of *koinonia*, the sublime essence of sincere fellowship and community. As will be explored later, the genesis of Christianity in America was interlaced with racism and racist ideas. Whiteness espoused a version of colonized Christianity, rooted in white supremacy and Eurocentric hegemony. Ibram Kendi (2016) reports in *Stamped from the Beginning*, "As dissenters from the Church of England, Puritans believed themselves to be God's chosen piece of humanity, a special, superior people, and New England, their Israel, was to be exceptional land" (p. 16). This form of imperialistic thinking continues to haunt Christianity today. As captured by Bailey in *Paul Through Mediterranean Eyes*, D. T. Niles of Sri Lanka said:

> The only way to build love between two people or two groups of people is to be so related to each other as to stand in need of each other. The Christian community must serve. It must also be in position where it needs to be served. (p. 258)

Through the church and beyond its terrestrial borders, silence will not be holistically broken with sustained resolve until white America learns to see itself outside the role of superiority. From the beginning of church history in America, under the watch of slavers, Black folk still played a subservient role in the church. The church is called to be a body that functions under equity, equality, and liberation, but the church in America was baptized in white supremacy and white imperialism. That will be investigated later in this work, but historically, through chattel-slavery-America and previous forms of Eurocentric global dominance, European elites saw themselves as worthy of being served by Africans and other oppressed groups, claiming their acts of barbarism and religious totalitarianism was for the civilizing benefits of its enslaved and tortured victims. When white America, inside and outside the church, learns the lesson of human reciprocity, with mutual interdependence—without a thirst for dominance, classism, or racism—the true project of courageous love and justice will begin. Until then silence will continue to mask ill-conceived forms of righteousness and humility.

Once we determine that which is most salient in this life, we must strategically, assertively, and comprehensively confront and dismantle that which interrupts us from reaching and experiencing the goal. Understanding what is most important in life without addressing surrounding resistance is a flawed paradigm. Too many want the goal without the fight it takes and silence prevents the necessary fight. After almost one-hundred years later, the words, spirit, and advocacy of Du Bois are just as ripe today as they were in nineteenth and twentieth centuries. Manning Marble captured in the introduction of the 1999 edition of Du Bois' plea in *Darkwater:*

> In a sense, what Du Bois wants to achieve is the
> deconstruction of whiteness as a social category,
> and of its hierarchies of oppression. For this to
> be accomplished, Du Bois contends that white
> Americans must come to a new understanding and
> an appreciation of what it means to be black. (p. vi)

As a vocal international freedom fighter within Christendom and across the globe, Dr. King sat in a Birmingham jail for his acts of righteousness and sacrifice. He was initially offended at being labeled an extremist by some within the white power structure, but he soon changed his disposition about the negative overtone of the label. He said:

Though I was initially disappointed at being categorized as an extremist, as I continued to think about the matter I gradually gained a measure of satisfaction from the label. Was not Jesus an extremist for love: 'Love your enemies, bless them that curse you, do good to them that hate you, and pray for them which despitefully use you, and persecute you.' Was not Amos an extremist for justice: 'Let justice roll down like waters and righteousness like an ever flowing stream.

Dr. King concluded the above portion of his Birmingham Jail letter with a challenge that is presented to all of humanity:

So the question is not whether we will be extremists, but what kind of extremists we will be. Will we be extremists for hate or for love? Will we be extremists for the preservation of injustice or for the extension of justice? In that dramatic scene on Calvary's hill three men were crucified. We must never forget that all three were crucified for the same crime–the crime of extremism. Two were extremists for immorality, and thus fell below their environment. The other, Jesus Christ, was an extremist for love, truth and goodness, and thereby rose above his environment.

After the death of Dr. King and in hopes for the resurgence of prophetic voice, James Taylor penned in *Black Nationalism in the United States: From Malcolm X to Barack Obama:* "To the extent that pre-civil rights black Christian elites embraced an accommodationist social orientation, *they surrendered the prerogative of black Christian nationalism.* The black 'Christian heritage' of black nationalism would remain in abeyance until the arrival of James Cone, Albert Cleage Jr., and the black theology movement during the post-civil rights period"

(p. 83). Times are still critical, and the racially conscious prophetic voices cannot be silenced or operate in abeyance. Without breaking silence, the impact of Eurocentric hegemony on American and global epistemologies remain.

CHAPTER 3
EUROCENTRIC HEGEMONY AND ITS IMPACT ON AMERICAN EPISTEMOLOGY AND SILENCE

> The dialectic of theology and social existence is particularly obvious in its white American branch when that theology is related to the people of African descent on the American continent. While some white theologians in the twentieth century have emphasized the relativity of faith in history, they have seldom applied this insight to the problem of the color line. (Cone, 1997, p. 42)

Pigmentocracy Horror and the Creation Race

It is through the color line that American injustice and discrimination is traced and *pigmentocracy* and *colorism* are its basic components. It did not start under American constructs, but through the comprehensive thrust of European global dominance, authentic epistemology has been veiled and slanted, creating an element of paralysis in the face of injustice that manifests as silence and avoidance. Despite the depths of dehumanization for colorized people (people of color), the power structure of America is fascinated with color. Regardless of a person's belief or position within the dialectic process of racialized discussion, the 1970 essay of Frances Cress Welsing, "The Cress

Theory of Color-Confrontation and Racism (White Supremacy):
A Psycho-Genetic Theory and World Outlook," is worthy of an
investigative read. About "The Cress Theory" published essay and
later included in her book *The Isis Papers: The Keys to the Colors,*
Cress Welsing said: "The Color-Confrontation theory states that the
white or color-deficient Europeans responded psychologically, with
a profound sense of numerical inadequacy and color inferiority, in
their confrontations with the majority of the world's people – all of
whom possessed varying degrees of color-producing capacity" (2004,
p. 4). There is eerie silence regarding biological contributions of and
psychological reactions to melanin.

Ibram Kendi reveals suppressive elements and dehumanization
toward deeply pigmented people. He explained the 1787 sentiments
of Samuel Stanhope Smith in his lecture "An Essay on the Causes
of the Variety of Complexion and Figure in the Human Species."
Stanhope professed and believed, "Hot weather bred physical
disorders–like kinky hair, which was 'the farthest removed from the
ordinary laws of nature'" (Kendi, 2016, p. 113). This belief system was
a clear attack on African ontology and existence. Yet in the promotion
of the imperialism and empire of whiteness, the juxtaposed epistemic
advanced in support of Eurocentrism was captured by Kendi about
Samuel Stanhope Smith. He said, "Cold weather was 'followed by a
contrary effect': it cured ailments…" (2016, p. 113). Kendi goes deeper
with the following about the stamp of Blackness and the relentless
efforts repudiating African virtue. The theories went to the extent of
placing the biblical *Garden of Eden* in Europe:

> In addition to changing climate, a change in the
> state of society could remove the stamp of Blackness,
> Smith maintained. Just look at the house slaves. In
> their nearness to White society, they were acquiring
> 'the agreeable and regular features' of civilized
> society—light complexion, straight hair, thin lips.
> "Europeans, and Americans are, the most beautiful

people in the world, chiefly, because their state of society is the most improved." In the end, this assimilationist made sure to disassociate himself from Lord Kames and polygenesis. From only "one pair"—Adam and Eve in Europe—"all of the families of the earth [have] sprung," Smith closed. (2016, pp. 113-114)

Pigmentocracy deals with the structural system of power and categorical treatment based on skin-tone or phenotypic racial complexion. The darker the majestic hue, the more intense is the discrimination at the hands of implicit and explicit bias. This is parlayed in multiple encounters where darker skinned people are depicted as dangerous, aggressive, and prone to criminality. It is comprised of the racist pseudoscience constructions of *phrenology* and *physiognomy*. As will be discussed later, such thinking is rooted in white supremacy, an institution that refuses to diligently expose America and the world to the benefits of melanin, thus creating the racist idea of the *mythic savage*. Exposing the benefits of melanin and *Blackness* deflates the conception of white superiority. There is absolute silence about melanin in K-12 school settings unless Black entities privately operate them. The result is colorized self-hate. Derrick Bell discusses the depths of Black internal racism in *Faces at the Bottom of the Well: The Permanence of Racism*. Bell explained his racial Black psychology as a young person by saying, "We were a subordinate and mostly shunned portion of a society that managed to lay the onus of slavery neatly on those who were slaves while simultaneously exonerating those who were slaveholders. All things considered, it seemed a history best left alone" (1992, p. 2).

There are segments within the spectrum of Blackness that operate as if the racist and violent history and current status of American violence are still "best left alone." Thus *Colorism* functions as a type of within-group discrimination, also unconsciously influenced by white supremacy. It is the essence of a colorized group adopting the insidious belief that white skin is superior. Through the Black image and other people of color it works on two fronts: 1) those with lighter skin can ignorantly and arrogantly think they are better because their skin is closer to whiteness, and 2) people with a darker complexion may despise lighter-complexioned people within their group because they are perceived to have extra advantages and believed to be more accepted by whiteness. Marcus Thompson II highlights a portion of the *colorism* epistemic in his book *Golden: The Miraculous Rise of Steph Curry*. Thompson II said:

> Strike two against Curry: he's light-skinned. It may seem silly on the surface, but skin tone is a deep-seated issue in African American life. And many of the dignitaries, players, and fans who dissent from the popular opinion that Curry is amazing use the kind of coded language born of this intra-cultural phenomenon. (2017, p. 186)

Marcus Thompson II also chronicled the colorism Black psychology portrayed by former L.A. Laker Jordan Clarkson after a monstrous dunk on a Phoenix Suns center. Clarkson said, "All I remember was Kobe telling me that I've been going to the hole like a light skinned dude." He said "So I've got to start doing it like a dark skinned [dude]. So when I seen the lane open up, that's all I remember" (2017, p. 187). This kind of thinking is not possible without the influence of white imperialism and *coloniality*.

With reference to Eurocentric hegemony and its impact on American epistemology and silence, many people are not aware of the source of their ambivalence, silence, and denial. Walter D. Mignolo said about the effect of European "gnoseologic projects" and epistemological dominance in *The Darker Side of Western Modernity: Global Futures, Decolonial Options*, "...As was becoming clear by the end of the eighteenth century: every civilization or culture began to be perceived as stagnant and as falling behind 'modernity,' receding toward the past" (2011, p. 185). Mignolo also speaks of the "irrational epistemic exuberance of men like Ortelius and Kant, stating how the excess of information they encountered was ingested and then published within and from their limited schema saying, "...Therefore thy missed the fact that while they were 'seeing and conceiving the world,' the enunciated, they were doing so within the 'limits of their own subjectivities and places,' the enunciation" (2011, p. 188).

The spirit and influence of Eurocentric hegemony is so influential, it continues to operate without being explicitly taught or *declared*. Part of the silence is rooted in the epistemic package of creating colorized people as the *savage*. If a people can be categorized as the *savage*, then all their cultural, literary, religious, and academic contributions to the world can be abolished, omitted, and ignored. Under such constructions, the disregarded people would also not have to be acknowledged as the recipients of injustice. Thus, any time a people receive patterned and thematic mistreatment, it is imperative to check the historical impact of European dominance inflicted on that group. And tragically, the marginalized and oppressed people in America today, are the same groups that have been historically maligned on American soil. The 2012 work of Robert A. Williams Jr., *Savage Anxieties: The Invention of Western Civilization,* depicts a rationale to the genesis of the maligned and malignant treatment of colorized people, inclusive of Native Americans and Africans of the Trans-Atlantic Passage.

Robert Williams Jr. discusses the creation of Ancient Greek fiction literature and how they ultimately converted and superimposed their fictional literary antagonist characters onto actual non-European people across the globe. Williams wrote, "Here, at the very beginnings of written civilization in the West, in the first book of the Iliad, Nestor invokes the names of the immortal Greek warrior-heroes who defeated the savages tribes of half-human, half-horse creatures, the centaurs, the legendary battle of Centauromachy" (p. 11). He went on to say, "Fierce, savage monsters are encountered by Homer's most famous mythic hero, Odysseus, in several anxiety-producing scenes in the epic companion piece to the *Iliad*, the *Odyssey*" (p. 12). He continued by saying, "The ancient Greeks' conception of the savage as a fierce, lawless, irreconcilable enemy to civilization traces its earliest written point of emergence to Homer's two epic poems as well" (p. 13). The creation of a literary enemy started out as sport, but once the *other* was encountered, they labeled them *savages*. They moved their fictional blueprint into a psychological and literal murderous rampage that pillaged a world. Notice the continued scholarship of Robert Williams Jr. from *Savage Anxieties*:

> No longer confined to the realm of myths, legends, and fabulous tales of subhuman monsters and ennobled primitive tribes in far-off lands, the idea of the savage becomes an increasingly important part of the way the Greeks depict the "barbarian." For Classical Age Greeks, the "barbarian" referred to anyone who did not speak Greek. (p. 49)

This attack on humanity and control of contributed epistemologies was a vastly strategic package that continues to evoke silence. For many of the culprits, the purpose of modern-day silence cannot be explained. Without explicit command or teaching, white supremacy is unconsciously intuited, leaving the impacted person of privilege and power without the critical ability to explain their silence toward injustice, as experienced by those dehumanized and oppressed. It forces a continued and critical look at the plight of people of the African diaspora, those of ancient America, indigenous Aborigines of Australia, the *Maori* people of New Zeeland, and colorized people everywhere across the globe. Eurocentric hegemony has touched them, and a deep silence and insidious cognitive dissonance prevails, despite the truth of the mistreatment, rape, lynching, family separation, *Manifest Destiny*, and *Doctrine of Discovery*. In terms of the Grecian symposium Williams Jr. also said about the scandalous figment and creation of the colorized savage:

> Drinking vessels from the fifth century B.C., for
> example, show African Pygmies carrying a dead
> crane or being eaten by a crocodile. Such pictorial
> vignettes reminded the holder that the Pygmies of
> distant Africa lived in a savage, inhospitable world,
> far removed from the refinements in culture and
> civilization known to the Greeks. (p. 53)

Even though people today exist under less overt forms of racist language or racist ideas, the practices remain embedded. They are still in play and we must come to grips with the classic historical designs, models, and epistemologies that created a foundation for racist practices to exist and thrive. European domination and the current American project have their roots and genesis in racism and white supremacy. This must be examined and critiqued across multiple institutions such as schools and universities, religious centers, television and media outlets, literature, film, art, and music. It is this very issue that results in pervasive and predictable economic, educational, environmental, social, and sexual disparities, and oppression. Not to mention the issuance of aid and the determination of who is bombed in war (Epperson, 1995). Robert Williams Jr. also points out, "The problem is that most people in the West are not even aware of their habitual use of the idea of the savage to stereotype indigenous tribal peoples in nearly all domains of their daily life" (p. 223). We must continue to assess the lingering impact of the creation of the *savage*. What is the diagnosis for the European thirst for dominance?

Before moving forward, it is important to address the differentiated interplay between white supremacy and a white supremacist, and their nexus to hegemony, silence, denial, avoidance, and a biased embrace of knowledge. Some white people push away from the table when they hear the term, white supremacy. It speaks to the concept coined by Robin DiAngelo in her 2011 essay, *White Fragility* and her new critical 2018 book. She said, "White people in North America live in a social environment that protects and insulates them from race-based stress" (2011, p. 54). White protection from racial stress, when race and conversations dealing with racism are confronted, often results in heightened defenses, conversation deterioration, and people exiting the room. White supremacy is an American norm. America as we know it today was established on racial, discriminatory, and racist practices, policies, and ideas. It is that reality that makes America and many parts of the world ruled by an invisible spirit of white supremacy a fact. However, white supremacy as an institution that promotes seductive and subversive ideologies of Eurocentric privilege and power is not to be confused with the role, action, and ontology of a white supremacist.

Many white people are oblivious to the ways they benefit from white supremacy, and because of *White Fragility*, they may attempt to explain it away. Harlon Dalton said in *Racial Healing: Confronting the Fear Between Blacks & Whites* (1995), "Far and away the most troublesome consequence of race obliviousness is the failure of many to recognize the privileges our society confers on them because they have white skin" (p. 110). Despite this cognitive confusion, denial, and ignorance, white supremacists are keenly aware of their actions. They promote a form of white nationalism that includes a demeaning, dehumanizing, violent, and even murderous hatred for non-white and sometimes non-Christian people within society. For a white person to confess that they are not a white supremacist is one thing, but to deny the pervasive existence of white supremacy in America and beyond is blatantly dishonest, without integrity, and fully suspicious. The neo-Nazi, hooded Klan member, or emboldened *alt-right* nationalist clearly operates as a white supremacist, but it is white people who remain silent in the face of such racist activity that perpetuate and hold the system of white superiority in place, allowing those groups to act. In a racialized America, silence does not equal neutrality, it promotes the agenda of white superiority. This effort is so strong, even as men sought to be honest about the equality of humanity, their scholarship and epistemological contributions were vehemently challenged.

As discussed by Kendi in *Stamped from the Beginning,* Count Constantine Volney wrote *Travels in Syria and Egypt* and read the work of Thomas Jefferson, *Notes on the State of Virginia.* They eventually became friends. Based on the time Volney spent in Egypt, he developed an appreciation for ancient African and Kemetic scholarship, contributed epistemologies, and Egyptian global influences. As recorded by Kendi (2016), "When Volney first saw the Sphinx in Egypt, he remembered Herodotus—the foremost historian in ancient Greece—describing the 'black and frizzled hair' of the ancient Egyptians" (p. 112). Volney said because of his Kemetic explorations and African enlightenment, "To the race of negroes, at present our slaves, and the objects of our extreme contempt, we owe our arts, sciences, and even the use of speech itself" (p. 112). Although not Thomas Jefferson, "American racists ridiculed Volney as an ignorant worshiper of Black people when he visited the United States in 1796" (p. 112). This classic and vitriolic denial of Black thought and contribution remains as the current American underbelly. The denial and erasure of Blackness continue through standards of beauty, promoted through *phrenology* and *physiognomy.*

Samuel Stanhope Smith continued his racist and racial maligning of Black people compared to white, and moved forward with the type of racist rhetoric that accentuates the spark of *colorism.* It was customary for those who professed an antislavery position to still hold some racist views about Black people compared to white, but Stanhope was set in his dehumanizing beliefs about those dwelling on the other side of the Mediterranean shores in Africa. Again, as captured in *Stamped from the Beginning,* Kendi said about the launched epistemic of Samuel Stanhope Smith, "Using European features as the standard of measurement, Smith judged light skin and thin lips on Blacks to be more beautiful than dark skin and full lips." According to Smith, "He also distinguished between 'good hair'—the straighter and longer the better—and 'bad hair,' the kinkier and shorter the worse" (2016, p.

114). This perverted epistemic or belief system traverses the milieu of all groups of color today, with the most dehumanized victims being those of the African diaspora in America. There is a lingering impact from these published and promoted racist ideas. We have not escaped or outgrown them in America or globally; the sentiments are deeply present today.

In *Pedagogy of the Oppressed* Palou Freire said, "It is only when the oppressed find the oppressor out and become involved in the organized struggle for their liberation that they begin to believe in themselves" (p. 65). Intellectually and under epistemic constructions, Eurocentrism has attempted to snuff out Afrocentric and colorized forms of cerebral contributions to global development and schema. From an American perspective this has happened religiously, academically, and culturally. In "The Hands of Ethiopia," a Du Bois essay within his *Darkwater: Voices from Within the Veil,* he exclaimed: "As Mommsen says: 'It was through Africa that Christianity became the religion of the world'" (p. 32).

The white academy and seminaries have silenced the reality of African scholarship and contribution and it has resulted in many Black people dismissing Christianity without critical investigation. African presence in the Scriptures is deeply and critically influential. African Christian influences will be explored on deeper levels later, but Walter D. Mignolo said in his essay, "Preamble: The Historical Foundation of Modernity/Coloniality and the Emergence of Decolonial Thinking" in *A Companion to Latin American Literature and Culture*: "Modernity/coloniality is an imperial package that, of necessity, generates decolonial thinking and action. But actions themselves cannot be decolonial if they are not conceptualized as such" (p. 17).

Mignolo acknowledges the force and pervasiveness behind Eurocentric erasure of colorized intellectualism, stating: "Indigenous production coexisted and was mixed up with the cultural production (texts, architecture, music, painting, etc.) of the Spanish and Portuguese invaders. However, the same logic that made 'modernity' visible (and modernity meant European history in all its manifestations) at the same time also made non-European histories and ways of thinking invisible" (p. 24). The continued impact of this hegemonic behavior must be continually assessed and critiqued for twenty-first century implications and applications. This continues to be true on academic, cultural, and religious levels. The centuries that have elapsed since the genesis and zenith of white imperialism have created forms of ignorance, intellectual blindness, and cognitive dissonance toward the lingering treatment and injustice of marginalized people. It arrives as silence. Despite the force to suppress colorized thought, creation, and contribution, Walter also said:

> From the beginning of the 1980s, the situation started to change and art historians, anthropologists, ethno-historians, and literary and cultural critics contested previous history. In their contestations, they helped make visible one of the consequences of coloniality of knowledge and of being – to relegate, silence, and dismiss the knowledge and subjective formations of indigenous people throughout the Americas. The situation is similar with people of African descent, and today – although on a different scale – with Latinos and Latinas in the United States. (p. 25)

Something must be said about the level of force and intentional mendacity that has to be solidified for authentic epistemology to be suppressed, and that of the *other* erased. Although more will be said about this in later chapters, even the true intent of the biblical record was misapplied under Eurocentric hegemony and dominance. James Taylor said of Du Bois and through a Christian ethos, "When it came to the dealing of Christian and heathen, however, the century saw nothing wrong in slavery...The slaves were to be brought from heathenism to Christianity, and through slavery the benighted Indian and African were to find their passport to the kingdom of God" (p.

87). On display here is the deep level of cognitive dissonance that refuses to see the humanity, worth, and merit of every human. When knowledge is suppressed, erased, twisted, or commandeered across centuries, some people are rendered helpless in their ability to resist. However, this is not an excuse.

The Bible says, "Again I say, don't get involved in foolish, ignorant arguments that only start fights" (2 Timothy 2:23 NLT). Despite the saying, the biblical premise cannot be used to justify silence. Under the construction of whiteness, when wise, sincere, and generative questions are posed about historic and current injustices, silence or avoidant behaviors are rendered. Because of the critical nature and time of this twenty-first century epoch, honest dialogue and teaching are imperative. Joy DeGruy in her 2005 book, *Post Traumatic Slave Syndrome: America's Legacy of Enduring Injury and Healing,* expresses the urgency of necessary dialogue for adults and children. DeGruy said, "We need to tell our children the truth and prepare them to thrive in the real America. We need to replace America's racist socialization with racial socialization" (p. 193). She went on to say, "So we should do ourselves and our children a favor by not pretending that the problem of racism no longer exists. We should not send them unprepared onto a racially charged battlefield ignorant of the mental, emotional and social landmines that await them" (p. 197). The sharpened sword of her discourse was profoundly introduced when she said, "Continual education is at the heart of racial socialization. For young children, education is the elders' responsibility. For us adults, the responsibility is our own" (p. 194).

Without any explicit teaching, *racist socialization* is the going rate in America and the development of an antiracist schema and praxis in the children is the responsibility of adults, but the development of an antiracist adult lens and disposition is the responsibility of each individual adult. This duty cannot be placed on anyone other than self. In this epistemically rich age and era, silence cannot mask the responsibility of people on American soil, or across the globe, from being effective advocates for a radical love, equity, social, and racial justice. The grip of Eurocentric dominance must be confronted and overcome, one person at a time, and the education of the children and young people must be transformed.

The 2018 Spring issue of *Teaching Tolerance Magazine* addresses critical teaching strategies related to "Teaching Hard History," which includes American chattel slavery. The 2018 Spring edition focuses on how to engage in culturally relevant instruction, pedagogy, and dialogue about the racial history of America. It is a strategic attempt to implement platforms across educational settings that allow for silence to be broken. Similar to the efforts of DeGruy, the issue focuses on providing students with honest and forthright spaces to process and confront a racist past, assessing the lingering impact today. In the *Teaching Tolerance* essay "Debunking the Mobility Myth," Reece says:

> One of the first steps toward changing an unfair system is to recognize its existence, and to share that recognition with students. It may feel harsh or unkind to tell black students that they won't be afforded the same opportunities as some of their fellow citizens. But honestly engaging them about the limitations of their social positions can help them understand that the barriers they face are real. More importantly, it shows that these barriers are not of their own construction. And evidence shows that addressing these issues with students can make a difference for them in the classroom and beyond. (p. 24)

Eurocentric hegemony and allegiance to a white power structure has made social justice allyship an awkward and clumsy process for white people and some people of color. The grasp of the hegemon is tight, and it forces people to question their stance of advocacy because they know it comes with a price. To express the difficulty Cornell West said in a speech entitled, "Struggle for Honesty, Decency and

Integrity in Modern America," delivered as the Ware Lecture to the 2015 General Assembly of the Unitarian Universalist Association. He said:

> Integrity has to do with what is the quality of your courage and your willingness to bear witness radically against the grain, even if you have to sacrifice something precious, including your popularity, in the name of integrity? That's what Du Bois was talking about. And let us be very clear, that to be fundamentally committed to integrity makes you counter-cultural in an age of mendacity.

Being counter-cultural in an age of hypocrisy and imperialism is a thorny balance for most and the proper teaching of our children is germane. The focus must be sharp or else people begin to slip into a half-baked form of advocacy and racial justice. The default to everyone is comfort, but there is no physical comfort through a quest to part with or break from the clutch and actions that unconsciously reinforce white supremacy. In the *Teaching Tolerance* article, "Teaching Hard History: Educators Talk about How to Teach American Slavery" an interesting scenario and approach is captured by Van Der Valk:

> Because we have such a large white population and such a small black population, oftentimes I have one or maybe two black students in my class. There's always a difficult moment where I have to pull the student aside and be like 'Look. We're going to be talking about some issues and everybody's going to look to you, and you don't have to speak on behalf of everybody else. (p. 53)

Despite the good intentions of the teacher, a prime opportunity was missed, and it is symbolically reminiscent of the way silence and blind spots work under the invisible grip and pressure of Eurocentric hegemony. In the provided teacher scenario, the picture is painted that the Black student needed to be cared for, but the reverse was at play. In teaching and discussing the concept of slavery, especially in a predominantly white class, the focus should be on the role, mindset, and horror of the *slaver* and not the *enslaved*. White students need to grapple with and come to terms with why whiteness was so dastardly fixated on domination and barbaric treatment of segments of humanity. The conversation of chattel slavery in America is not just about the torture, rape, dehumanization, family separation, and murder of Black people, it is also about the demented psychology of a European epistemic and population that supported the institution in every way. If someone is really concerned about Black empathy, the best way to care for the Black child or student during conversations about race is to put the white mind of American slavery, *reconstruction*, Jim Crow, and the civil rights era on trial and display. Why was the white thirst so strong and set to destroy and dehumanize *Blackness?* Let the white student grapple with that in every twenty-first century classroom, church, at the dinner table, and in any space dominated by white supremacy.

To further emphasize the European hegemonic impact on American epistemology and silence, in *Yurugu: An African-Centered Critique of European Cultural Thought and Behavior,* by Marimba Ani, the Late John Henrik Clarke said in the introduction, "In the 15th and 16th century Europeans not only colonized most of the world, they colonized information about the world. They developed monopoly control over concepts and images" (pp. xv-xvi). The Eurocentric control over not just information and knowledge, but also images is what gave *physiognomy* and *phrenology* their pseudo-science power and ill-gained legitimacy. One of the most dominant and influential images is the depiction of a Europeanized *Jesus Christ.*

Hegemony comes with the benefit of power and privilege, thus to speak against it is to call into question the ownership and maneuverings of whiteness. Because of that many remain silent, refusing to articulate or confess to their possessed power. In the 2017 work of Michael Eric Dyson, *Tears We Cannot Stop: A Sermon to White America*, he calls the creation and possession of whiteness on the carpet. We will discuss the conception and social creation of race later, but Dyson said, "Race has no meaning outside the cultures we live in and the worlds we fashion out of its force of energy. Whiteness is an advantage and privilege because you have made it so, not because the universe demands it" (p. 44). He went on to say, "...I want to tell you right off the bat that whiteness is made up, and that white history disguised as American history is a fantasy, as much a fantasy as white superiority and white purity" (pp. 44-45).

Under the scope of *White Fragility*, the power and benefits of whiteness are denied. The denial prevents the privileged from being able to advocate for underprivileged groups. Dyson analyzes it this way, "Until you make whiteness give up its secrets none of us will get very far. Whiteness has privilege and power connected to it, no matter how poor you are. Of course, the paradox is that even though whiteness is not real, it is still true" (p. 46). Joy DeGruy (2005) said, "Unfortunately, while race is illusory, the fact of racism is not" (p. 22).

The sooner the conceptualization of Dyson and others traverses from theory to praxis, America will be suspended in an ethereal vacuum of toxic denial and duplicity. Eurocentric imperialism is the force that created the concept of American whiteness that is now a globalized racial brand. Any person, regardless of race, seeking acceptance by the dominant power structure in America, must somehow conform to the cultural formations of whiteness. Dyson says:

> Whiteness forged togetherness among groups
> in reverse, breaking down or, at least to a degree,
> breaking up ethnicity, and then building up an
> identity that was cut off from the old tongue and
> connected to a new land. So groups that were often
> at each other's throats learned to team up in the

new world around whiteness. The battle to become
American forced groups to cheat on their old selves
and romance new selves. (p. 45)

In the book *off white: Readings on Power, Privilege, and Resistance*,
Howard Winant discusses the entrenchment of whiteness in his
essay, "Behind Blue Eyes: Whiteness and Contemporary U.S.
Racial Politics." Winant said, "Like any other complex of beliefs
and practices, 'whiteness' is imbedded in a highly articulated social
structure and system of signification; rather than trying to repudiate
it, we shall have to rearticulate it" (p. 11). The silence is so pervasive;
all racial groups are impacted and practice the behavior to some
extent. While studying and preparing for my 2017 October-December
lecture series that led to this project, I was mystified by some of the
comments I read. I was unsure of what to do with quotes that appeared
to exemplify a form of *double consciousness*. Although I codified the
remarks, they were never used for the lecture series because they
spoke of Black liberation and Black inferiority within the same breath.
I was puzzled by the words, so I remained silent. The work of Dr.
Kendi, *Stamped from the Beginning*, helped me understand what was
happening. We are all impacted by racist ideas and a person does not
have to be racist to speak or promote a racist idea. It is also important
to note that the aforementioned statement is not synonymous with
someone postulating that all people are or can be racist. Racism is a
white supremacist ideology, reserved for those in power. Any person
can float or adopt a racist idea, but to be racist, the person must be
connected to the group that has the power to oppress.

W.E.B. Du Bois is an international giant in the intellectual world
of social justice, advanced epistemologies, classical and transformative
literature, and racial liberation. Despite that fact, the schema,
intellectualism, and scholarship of Du Bois were impacted by the
racist ideas of his day. This is the pervasive result of white supremacy
and the flooding of racist ideas across global epistemologies and
constructions of knowledge. As an example, Kendi reported, "Black

resistance caused lynchings to spike in the early 1890s. However, the White lynchers justified the spike in lynchings as corresponding to a spike in Black crime." He went on to say, "This justification was accepted by a young W. E. B. Du Bois, by the middle-aged, ambitious principal of Alabama's Tuskegee Institute, Booker T. Washington, and by a dying Frederick Douglas" (2016, p. 274).

Even more emphatic was the impact of Eurocentric hegemony and intellectual dominance on the mind of Booker T. Washington. He was praised and financially supported by the white power structure because of his disposition of racial inferiority and white appeasement. The American assimilationist project is rooted in the attempt of people striving to become white or accepted by formations of whiteness. To do such, a person must divorce themselves from their non-white cultures, customs, and ways of being. Booker T. Washington presented at the Cotton State International Exposition on September 18, 1895. His speech was the "Atlanta Compromise" and as detailed by Kendi, Washington "asked southern Whites to stop trying to push Blacks out of the house of America, and allow them to reside comfortably in the basement—to help them rise up, knowing that when they rose, the whole house would rise" (2016, p. 277). White people praised his speech as well as Du Bois.

Du Bois was hardly as racially accommodating and compromising as Washington, but it again illustrates the psychological and historical impact and influence of Eurocentric hegemony. A more subtle example is found in the 1829 four-essay-collection, *David Walker's Appeal*. More will be shared later about David Walker and his brilliant *resistance* and critique of the role of Christianity and the Bible in American slavery and brutality. However, David Walker pinned in his appeal:

> When we take a retrospective view of the arts and
> sciences—the wise legislators—the Pyramids, and
> other magnificent buildings—the turning of the
> channel of the river Nile, by the sons of Africa or

of Ham, among whom learning originated, and was carried thence into Greece, where it was improved upon and refined. (p. 19)

David Walker consents to the deep layers of African epistemologies, sciences, artistry, miraculous building of the pyramids, and more, but he then hands them off, attributing their *refinement* and *improvement* to Eurocentric and Grecian influences. Because of the overwhelming resistance and fight for social justice by Walker, I cannot classify this comment as being impacted by racist ideas, but the work of Kendi provides the model for understanding and processing ways in which someone can be a staunch advocate for racial, economic, environmental, democratic, relational, and educational justice, while at the same time advancing a comment that appears to be antithetical to the cause. I heard Robin DiAngelo say in a speech or interview, something to the effect of, "We are all swimming in the waters of white supremacy." We can add that we also are all trying to navigate ourselves through the engulfing waters of racist ideas.

Why did Booker T. Washington assume his role of relegating Black people to the basement? Why did he say, "...The wisest among my race understand that agitation of questions of social equality is the extremist of folly" (Kendi, 2016, p. 277)? Why was Ida B. Wells different, like Prophet Jeremiah she had fire shut up in her bones, refused the chains of silence, and wrote the 1892 pamphlet, *Southern Horrors: Lynch Law in All Its Phases?* What prevents some white people and assimilationists from breaking silence toward blatant racial oppression and disparate treatment? What is the psychological pressure that results in a denied oration of truth while personally witnessing injustice?

The formation of double consciousness, implicit-bias, or bigotry was also embedded within the psychology and schema of Dr. Blumenbach who "...Campaigned for the abolition of slavery (a view not popular in his day) and, interestingly, asserted the moral superiority of slaves to their captors" (Gould 1996). Nevertheless, in the end, Blumenbach ended up with a system with one single race, Caucasian, at the top" (Sussman, 2016, p. 20). Thus, Blumenbach was against slavery but persistently promoted the overall racist idea of white supremacy.

Introduced to me by Dr. Fred Brill, *The Small Big: Small Changes that Spark Big Influence* (2014), is based on multiple research studies. Martin, Goldstein, and Cialdini concluded "...That going against the pull of the crowd is not only emotionally distressing but, according to recent neuroscience research, it can even be painful" (p. 8). Although the studies explored in the *Small Big* were business organizations and institutions, white supremacy is an institution that presents with a similar pressure and "pull of the crowd," but this crowd is whiteness. Studies also evidenced that when there was "independent judgment that went against the consensus of the group, the areas of the brain associated with emotion were activated, suggesting that there is a real emotional cost to going against the group and the price we pay is a painful one" (p. 9).

The dominant thread of America promotes an ethos of European superiority, thus from a simplified paradigm, to go against that epistemic force, even when it is the socially righteous thing to do, for many, the emotional cost and psychological pain is too great to endure. As has been the historical indictment against the American hegemon and devotees, racial groups outside of Eurocentrism are treated as not being *worthy* of the sacrifice it takes to stand for racial justice, despite blatant acts of institutional racism and Black subjugation.

We need more people with the spirit, willingness, and vulnerability of Ida B. Wells. In the end, Eurocentric hegemony and its impact on American epistemology and silence is, at least in-part, due to an unwillingness to speak truth to power because of the discomfort and psychological angst it causes those with racial power and privilege. All of this is a result because of the role and creation of race in America, which shall now be further investigated.

CHAPTER 4

PERSONAL ENCOUNTERS: CONSTRUCTIONS, FORMATIONS, AND THE IMPACT OF RACE IN AMERICA AND BEYOND

> In buying this New South, Americans had adopted a new tool for blaming racial disparities on Black people: faith in racial progress (and ignoring the simultaneous progression of racism). It was being taught that American slavery had developed those backward people who had been brought over from the wilds of Africa. (Kendi, 2016, p. 266)

As discussed by Chancellor Williams (1987) in *The Destruction of Black Civilization: Great Issues of Race from 4500 B.C. to 2000 A.D.*, Mamelukes were white people enslaved by Arabs during a time when race was not a divisive factor, as in modern and postmodern times. According to Williams, during the fourteenth-century, "Whites, blacks, browns or yellows, all were made slaves if captured" (p. 153). Captured and enslaved by the Arabs, the Mamelukes developed into a fierce white slave army, revolted, defeated the government, and established their own rule. Williams said, "The white ex-slaves hated their former masters.... This white slave revolt and its historical significance are underplayed. Yet its impact was such that it influenced the course of modern history in black-white relations" (p. 153). The murderous revolt by the white slaves or Mamelukes against the Arabs was so vicious that whites were never enslaved again. "On this the record is clear: White slavery ended after the Mameluke rebellion. After that Black Africa became the exclusive hunting ground for slaves... (Williams, p. 153). With this extensive development, "since black populations were everywhere under white control, they could actually be forced into inferiority by a dehumanizing program 'silently' structured in all institutions and phases of white national life" (Williams, p. 154). Discussing the development of race and the onslaught of global European hegemony and the specific attack on Africans, this historical epoch is rarely referenced. It is this historical frame that set the table for racial constructions to be developed and systemized.

America must comprehensively revisit the depths with which whiteness historically operated and continues to demonize, dehumanize, and suppress Blackness. The role, place, and creation of race require continued analysis and critique. There are different theories connected to when the conception of race was created, but what is clear is that it is a sociological construct, rooted in hegemony, toxic hierarchy, and white supremacy. Related to race Joy DeGruy (2005) said "We need to notice because the overarching problem of this millennium continues to be the problem of the color line." She went on to say, "Issues of race and diversity are so critical because they remain at the root of the most pervasive problems facing this nation" (p. 24). Robin DiAngelo (2018) said in *White Fragility: Why It's So Hard for White People to Talk About Racism*:

> Freedom and equality—regardless of religion or class status—were radical new ideas when the United States was formed. At the same time, the US economy was based on the abduction and enslavement of African people, the displacement and genocide of indigenous people, and the annexation

of Mexican lands. Further, the colonizers who came were not free of their own cultural conditioning; they brought with them deeply internalized patterns of domination and submission. (pp. 15-16)

White colonizer-conditioning contributed to toxic hierarchy entrenchment of racial formulas. Hope is needed under American racialized structures, but hopelessness around comprehensive change is more of a reality. About the initial hope and racial epistemic of France Fanon, Derrick Bell captured the sentiments in *Faces at the Bottom of the Well* (1992) saying, "On one hand, he believed racist structures to be permanently embedded in the psychology, economy, society, and culture of the modern world—so much so that he expressed the belief 'that a true culture cannot come to life under present conditions'" (p. x).

According to the research of Browder "The concept of race was created by scientists and scholars at Gottingen University in Germany between 1775 and 1800. During this twenty-five-year period, these 'scholars' invented the word Caucasian, divided humanity into races, and contended that the white race was superior" (p. 4). Despite the sociological and non-biological essence of race, the institution of race wreaks havoc across the globe. Race was not created to simply express and codify difference; it was concocted to perceptually juxtapose superiority with inferiority, power with weakness, beauty with ugliness, and intelligence with stupidity. All of this was to be instantaneously declared through the quick-glance of a phenotypic racial prism.

Without the creation of race there could be no racism. Anthony Browder said in *Survival Strategies for Africans in America: 13 Steps to Freedom*, "Contrary to popular belief, there is no such thing as race. Race is a false construct which was created by Europeans, hundreds of years ago, to differentiate themselves from people of African descent and other people of color throughout the world" (pp. 3-4). About the initial constructions of race, *physiognomy*, and phenotypic difference,

J. A. Rogers said in the classic work *Nature Knows No Color-Line,*
"This pseudo-science probably originated in the East...But the work
to which it owes development and power in the West was Aristotle's
Physiognomica of the fourth century B. C." (p. 17). Rogers also offers
an explanation to the development of racial structures within the
isolated context of whiteness:

> It is quite possible also that the color prejudice of
> white for black began in the prejudice among the
> whites for shades of their own color. I refer to the
> so-called science of Physiognomy, which rates
> individuals as good or bad, desirable or undesirable,
> on their physical traits. (p. 17)

Destructive and humiliating racial and racist encounters occur
daily because of the globally systemic creation of race. As documented
by Robert W. Sussman (2016), in *The Myth of Race: The Troubling
Persistence of an Unscientific Idea,* it was John Friedrich Blumenbach,
University of Göttingen (1795) that "...Coined the term Caucasian
to refer to people of European descent and in doing so defined them
as the most beautiful, the closest to representing God's image, and
'original' humans from which other varieties degenerated" (p. 19).
The creation of the premise and international institution of white
supremacy must be navigated daily. Race and its effects are pervasive,
unrelenting, and far from resolved. The day must arrive where the
racialized experiences of Black people and other people of color are
no longer denied or explained away through victim-blame rhetoric.
Before going deeper into the constructions, formations, and influence
of race in America and beyond, I have elected to share a few personal
stories that were all manifestations of racial dynamics and encounters.

Summer School in Seoul City Korea

In 1996 I spent thirty days in Seoul Korea for a summer school
program at Seoul City University. I linked up with six other African

American students from San Francisco State University, through a study-abroad program, sponsored through the office of then-Mayor Willie Brown. Upon arrival in Seoul, we joined with groups of students from Vietnam, Mongolia, China, and Korea. Totaling about thirty students, we immersed ourselves in the study of Korean language, culture, art, government, and history. The experience was invaluable and one that I will forever cherish.

It was a straight flight (eleven hours) from San Francisco into Seoul and my first international flight. I was excited about the entire process. The team of seven students from San Francisco consisted of four women and three men. Soon after landing, Mark, Zachary, and I walked into what was said to be *college town*, escorted and chaperoned by a male Korean native who was also a student at Georgetown University. I cannot recall his name, but he was slightly younger than us, but also had his own level of Korean swag. Embarrassingly, but of our own American volition, our first meal in Seoul was Burger King. The three of us laughed at the fact that we flew eleven hours into another country, and our first meal was American fast food. We vowed to not have that happen again, but I do recall us also eating Kentucky Fried Chicken; it was very popular in Seoul.

College town was bustling with energy, it was dark and the city lights were bright. The weather was warm and slightly muggy, but it felt good walking the city streets of Korea. Although I did not have the formal terminology at the time, I was amazed at the prominence and popularity of *whiteness* in Korea. The pictures of white male movie stars like Brad Pitt and Val Kilmer were gigantically displayed. Whiteness had elevated and appreciative value, at least in Seoul. This was our first night in Seoul and we had been in town for approximately four hours. We looked in stores, admiring and pricing watches, shoes, and clothes. My eye was on a silver *FILA* watch, based on money conversion, I was attempting to determine if it was affordable. I went back and looked at the watch several times and finally realized it was too expensive.

We continued to walk the town and the people often thought

we were professional athletes. Perhaps because of my height, this was a daily occurrence for me. I could have played along and signed autographs; many were so convinced I was a professional basketball player. We took it in stride and in good fun. I felt great walking through Seoul as a young-adult, in another country for study and immersing myself into the culture. Suddenly two men ran up to Zach, Mark, and I, and yelled something to us in their native language, started laughing, and ran off.

We were not startled or surprised, thinking the encounter was similar to those who thought we were celebrities or athletes. We looked to our chaperone, but his countenance changed. We asked him what the two men said, but he shook his head and declined to share. We pressed him to share their comments, but he still refused. We pressed harder. Based on this incident and being American in Korea—gave me immediate insight into American arrogance. I pressed our chaperone to respond and I could later detect my American arrogance. I had no way of knowing the two men said something derogatory, so I pressed: "What did they say?" Our chaperon shook his head and dropped it, but we kept asking. After continued pressure as we walked through the town, he finally relented and informed us that the two men called us *black monkeys*. In Korea for only two hours, from distant San Francisco, and we had already been racially profiled with incendiary language.

We processed many emotions and I also felt bad for the chaperon who did not want to reveal the details of the bigoted encounter. He was a native Korean and watched two men shamelessly insult his guests. We did not allow the racist episode to ruin our trip, but we did share the encounter with our four American schoolmates. They were appalled. I do not recall us sharing the story with anyone else while in Korea. However, it was clear, racism and Black marginalization was not limited to America; it was international, and I witnessed its influence and grip in real-time. Some people attempt to downplay racist encounters and bigotry, but this incident of racial insult is forever etched in my psyche.

Probably Not a Good Idea

One Friday night of the latter part of 2017 my family and I travelled from San Leandro, which is one city over from Oakland, to Dublin for a visit to our favorite pizza restaurant, *Amici's East Coast Pizzeria*. It was after 8:00 PM so it was dark. As I pulled up I let my wife and four children out at the restaurant entrance and then found a place to park. The restaurant is in a large shopping mall complex with a grocery store, multiple restaurants, and a few smaller shops and businesses. As I pulled into a parking stall, I noticed that the hatch of the *Range Rover* in front of me was fully open. The front of the vehicle faced me, but it was clear that the hatch was open. I assumed someone may have been at the rear of the car, loading or unloading something, either about to go into a store or drive away.

I remained in my car longer than normal, assessing the situation of the *Range Rover*. I wanted to know if someone was still in the SUV. It was soon clear that no one was in the vehicle or at the rear, despite the hatch being fully open. I exited my vehicle and looked around for a moment, contemplating as to whether or not I should close it. I wanted to close the hatch, thinking the driver may have accidentally opened it remotely. However, for me to close the hatch of the car in a dark parking lot, I would have to walk completely around the SUV, reach up, and manually close the door.

As a tall inner-city African American man, every stereotype infiltrated my racial psyche. I had no idea what I would see after walking to the rear of the open vehicle. There could have been a purse, luggage, groceries, or other valuable items. I envisioned myself walking to the rear of the SUV to perform a good deed, just in time for the owner or the entire family to move within sight of the vehicle, yelling, "Hey, get away from my car! You broke into my car. Security!" I thought, "If I close it fast enough, no one would detect my actions." I soon cancelled that thought, knowing a Black man cannot move suspiciously and quickly around cars in a dark parking lot. In addition, someone could have been watching my actions the entire time. Instead of scoping out the car to see if I could safely close it, someone could have perceived my actions as having criminal intent. I soon decided it was too risky for me to close the hatch of the vehicle, so I turned and walked to the restaurant. Because of race and racism, I could not perform a good deed.

As I sat down with my family I replayed the scenario with my wife—without hesitation she leveled her opinion, emphatically stating that it was in my best interest not to touch or go near the car. Because of race and racism there are certain things some racial groups have to contemplate that others do not. Experientially, this racial reality is reinforced over time.

Police Encounter: Black and Voiceless

At the age of 29 (1999), in San Francisco, I worked as a clinician and therapist for the *Westside Community Mental Health Assertive Community Treatment Program*, serving one-hundred of the city's top four-hundred residents suffering from extreme forms of mental health conditions. I had already graduated with my Master of Science degree in Counseling, with specializations in Marriage and Family Therapy and School Counseling, and I was working on my doctorate at the University of San Francisco. Additionally, I was preaching twice a week at my then-home church, Uptown church of Christ, and the other two weeks preached somewhere in the Bay Area or California.

While at work on a bright sunny day, one of our African American male clients was having a psychotic episode and we received information that he physically assaulted and battered the church custodian behind the clinic and was headed our way. Although the clinic and program are no longer in the same location, at that time it was located at the corner of 888 Turk street, intersecting with Gough Street. The police were contacted to initiate a 5150 assessment, the beginning stages of an involuntary psychiatric hold, for the safety of my client and others. I was concerned about the safety of my coworker that was pregnant, so once the client arrived, I casually took him

84

outside. The client and I had a great relationship; we were close in age, grew up in the same *Fillmoe* neighborhood, and knew some of the same people. We walked outside and relaxingly leaned against the wall of the clinic on the Gough street side. We engaged in our typical conversation and he did not indicate anything about previously assaulting the church custodian. I was outside alone with him while my coworkers remained inside, working on the 5150 dispatch.

I knew the police and paramedics would arrive soon, but I did not share that with my client. He was outwardly calm at the time, but inward pensiveness was apparent, and he was still processing through psychotic ideations. Considering my healthy relationship with him, it was important for me to be present for the encounter to help deescalate and prevent harm to my client, should he attempt to run or manifest psychotic behaviors that might trigger an injurious or fatal reaction from a San Francisco police officer. Again, for his protection and safety, I did not inform him the police were in-route, fearing the situation would result in a foot chase. I knew the adrenaline of a foot-pursuit could result in life-threatening outcomes. I strongly believed my presence would serve as the mediated buffer to ensure the safety of my client and others, considering his labile disposition.

As we stood outside the clinic talking, a solo white police officer pulled up in his patrol car. My client was still calm and unaware the police were there to assess him; not for an arrest, but for the 5150. I wanted the encounter to be smooth and without further violence or agitation. My client was one of the nicest men anyone could meet and while struggling through psychosis, I never observed him act in violence or aggression. Out of fear for his safety I did not want him to run. At this point he was externally subdued, presenting with a flat affect, yet struggling through internal psychosis and anxiety. I had to figure out how to communicate with the white officer in a way that would not exacerbate the situation. Suddenly I allowed my racial consciousness to slip.

Just before the officer exited his vehicle, I strategically made direct eye contact with him and nodded or motioned my head twice in the direction of my client, attempting to non-verbally inform him that the man to my right needed assistance. I did not want to shout it or say it mildly, fearing my client would run. I thought my non-verbal communications were clear and understood by the officer.

The tall white police officer exited his vehicle and immediately moved toward me. Stunned and in disbelief, I started slowly backing away as he moved closer, asking for my name and identification. Suddenly I was in the perplexing situation of not wanting to run and be tackled by the officer. The situation changed instantaneously; in the blink of an eye I was trying to find balance between self-advocacy, self-protection, respect, and compliance. For *goodness sake*, I was at work. Although the officer asked for my "ID," I was hesitant to reach for my wallet, but I did. Within seconds I was cuffed and tossed in the back of his tight and cramped police car. My client never moved from the wall, did not utter any words, and was now watching me detained in the drivers-side backseat of the squad car.

At this point, from the back seat of the police car, I continually told the officer, "It's not me, why am I in the back of the car handcuffed?" Although speaking, in that moment I was *voiceless*, my voice meant nothing to the white officer. I drove to work that morning to find myself in the back of a police car handcuffed tightly, ninety minutes later. It was not until my white female co-worker and white male clinical supervisor urgently came outside screaming at the officer, "Why is he in the car?" that he opened the door, released the cuffs, and eventually returned my wallet. Aside from him asking for my name and *ID*, I do not recall him saying one word, and clearly he offered no apology. I do not recall what ultimately happened to my client that day. I was so humiliated and upset; I ended up in tears of frustration. My voice and self-advocacy had no meaning or relevance to the white police officer. My co-worker and friend Keidra tried to calm me and eventually, I just got in my car and drove home.

Although decades old, this racialized encounter remains at the forefront of my racial psyche. It is a result of the sociological construction of race. I must assume that the white police officer knew he was looking for a Black man. He saw two and for whatever reason selected me. On several occasions I have shared this experience in educational trainings, professional developments, and lectures, evoking various reactions and responses. I recall sharing it for the first time in a 2003 presentation, while working at a Bay Area High School. At the end of sharing my experience and vulnerable story, one veteran white male teacher raised his hand, chuckled, and said something to the effect of, "I am sure you eventually had to laugh at this situation." I was mortified at the insensitive response, but this is the risk a person takes when venturing into racialized discussion. Nothing about the encounter was comedic and I do not share it for laughs. If I have ever laughed at the fact that my *in-crisis* client was totally calm while I was in the police car, it is simply to momentarily mask the pain and insult of Black denial, marginalization, and rage. Not only do I wish this encounter never occurred, I also wish it was the only racially negative encounter I ever had with law enforcement at work, while professionally and expertly doing my job. It is not. I could write a separate book on *Police Encounters* as depicted in my Sahealing.org blog.

Tell Me You Are Not With Them

As mentioned in the encounter above, as an African American male reared in San Francisco and East Oakland, I experienced many racially negative episodes with police. I do not classify all my police encounters as racial, but some have contained an explicit racial nexus. Some of these encounters occurred while I was a teenager and others at various stages of adulthood.

I graduated from J Eugene McAteer High School in 1989 after spending my ninth, tenth, and eleventh grade years at George Washington High School, both of San Francisco. I was in the seventh grade when the introduction of crack cocaine made its way into inner-city San Francisco neighborhoods and across America. By the time I was in high school, its melodic devastation was apparent, but its future destruction was unforeseen. During my high school years, the 1988 movie *Colors* landed, and although it depicted police interactions between Black and Brown youth and young-adults in Los Angeles, it documented a dynamic happening across American cities where crack, gangster rap, formations of violence, and increased homicides were thematic. After graduating high school and moving to East Oakland (August 1989) the epic 1991 film *Boyz in the Hood* took America by storm, followed by the emotionally raw 1993 movie, *Menace II Society*. I lived and navigated the streets of East Oakland from August, 1989 to 1994, before moving to Hayward, California and then back to San Francisco. During my days in Oakland, both films, *Boyz in the Hood* and *Menace II Society* captured inner-city emotion, anxiety, danger, joy, and toxic relationships with law enforcement with precision. The raw image of the *Black* and *Brown* experience made it to the cinematic big screen.

The 1992 film, *South Central,* hit the market before *Menace II Society* and *New Jack City* provided a breathtaking 1991 testimony and gaze into New York inner-city *gangsterism*, crack cocaine empire, violence, and police corruption in neighborhoods, months before *Boyz in the Hood* landed. Still, one of the first influential movies, while I was in high school, was *Colors*. *Colors* depicted racial happenings across American inner-city neighborhoods between Black and Brown young people and the police. The industry shattering N.W.A. album, *Straight Outta Compton* emerged from the ether of Hip-Hop energy on August 8, 1988, just before the start of my senior year of high school and three months after the movie *Colors*. The second N.W.A. rap album dropped on May 28, 1991 and unapologetically reinforced elements of *Black* and *Brown* inner-city living.

Before and during this epoch, it was open season on inner-city residents. Insults, brutality, and legal breaches rapped about in *Straight Outta Compton* and their second album were daily occurrences. While walking or standing with friends in my San Francisco neighborhood, it was common for police to jump out of their cars, make people line up against the wall, and conduct body searches without reason, probable cause, or rationale. Alleged teenage crimes were simply walking or standing while Black. On one occasion, about ten of us were forced against a wall on the corner of Divisadero and McAllister, and one of the officers said, "If any of you have a check stub I will let you go." In typical fashion they would run their hands through our pockets and then drive away. During this search I was a high school student, working as a dishwasher at Firehouse BBQ, and ironically, I was in possession of a check stub for $32 in my back pocket. The officer was launching a racist idea, assuming none of us had a job, making their illegal search justifiable.

Being searched by police was always a deeply anxiety-provoking experience because I often involuntarily twitched while being searched. I would try my best not to move, knowing it startled the searching officer, causing them to think I was resisting or reaching for a weapon. There were times when extra force was used because of this misperception. I recall me and a group of friends being forced against a wall, as depicted in *Colors*, and my best friend who suffered from a leg disability from early childhood, causing one leg to grow longer than the other, was also present. About eight of us were against the wall and I was next to Nate. The officers told us to put our hands on the wall and spread our legs. We all complied, but the officer did not think the legs of Nate were spread wide enough. Without warning, the officer kicked Nate in the leg and yelled, "I said spread your legs." The sight and sound of the kick sent shocks through my body and, with hands up and legs spread, I yelled back to the officer, "He has a disability; his legs is are spread!" The officer did not say another word, continued his searches, and Nate remained speechless. After they searched all of us we continued with our day.

During this era, relevant music and films existed, depicting the condition of governmentally and CIA designed crack-infested, police corrupted, urban American neighborhoods. It was my daily reality and the above information was shared to set the stage for this next episode.

It was the same process, same corner, and virtually the same group of friends, but this time Jessie, who now goes by his Jewish name, Yishay Ben Levy, was present. To racialize the story, Jessie is white but just as *Fillmoe* as any of the other neighborhood natives. Although Jessie and I knew the same people and lived in the same neighborhood, we formally met in our ninth grade George Washington High School English class of Ms. Riley. Ms. Riley constantly separated us in class because every day we incessantly talked basketball, football, and life. The only thing I remember about that English class is Jessie and I always talking, Ms. Riley admiring my use of the term *fresh* to describe my light blue and yellow low-top *Etonics* sneakers in my essay, and the reading of Richard Wright's *Native Son*.

We were in our neighborhood and in routine fashion the police pulled up and asked all of us to put our hands on the wall and spread our legs. This was in 1987 or 1988. Jessie was always the only white male in the group. During this encounter he was standing next to me with his hands and legs spread when one of the white officers approached him and said, "Tell me you are not with them, and I will let you go." Jessie responded with a few expletives and the officer did not reply. The police officer appeared to have no concern that I heard his racist comment.

Ghana and Racial Exploration

In 2005 I made my first trip to Ghana. We landed in Accra, stayed overnight, and the next day travelled two hours through red-clay roads to Akwatia, where we lodged for seven days. Decades before I was ordained as the preacher of the West Oakland church of Christ, they began financially supporting the preacher, family, and church in Akwatia. Despite the financial support, no one from the congregation had visited the church. The primary goal of this visit was to participate in the inaugural ceremony for the opening of the churches school computer learning center that we financed the year prior. Traveling with me was a former church member, Dwight Gray. It was during my second trip in 2007 that I traveled with Dwight Gray and Rodney Stovall Sr., ten-plus days and it included a visit to the Ivory Coasts' *Elmina Castle* slave dungeon. *Elmina Castle* was operated by the Portuguese, followed by the Dutch, and lastly the British.

Both Dwight and I are of the African diaspora, but of different phenotypic racial complexions within the ebony continuum. Dwight is lighter in complexion. We did not have this experience in Accra, but while walking in Akwatia or a nearby town, some men yelled and pointed at us from the window of a bus, "Oburoni, Oburoni!" Ecstatic and in awe of being in *Africa* for the first time, I smiled at the acknowledgement, but ignored the inhospitable tone and spirit behind the greeting. The first time I heard the term I did not question it, but it soon became a pattern. It was never said within close proximity, "Oburoni" was always directed to us from afar.

Finally, I asked, "What does *Oburoni* mean?" Reluctantly and embarrassingly, like my chaperone in Korea, our Ghanaian host and then-preacher of the Akwatia church of Christ said, "it means white man." Dwight and I were aghast. As an inner-city Black man who struggles through dehumanization and American oppressions of whiteness, studied the traumatic legacy of the *Trans-Atlantic Passage*, feels the reverberations of the African *Maafa*, and lynching on American soil—how could we be called *"white man"* in Africa? How could this unexpected encounter manifest? I was in Africa to reconnect with my *West African* roots, but ended up racially outcast and confronted with a complex and contradictory consortium of *racial ideas*. Were Dwight and I foreigners to Africa and declared the *other*?

The experience of colorism and pigmentocracy in Africa resulted in immediate dialogue with the young and old Ghanaian men in Akwatia. With heartfelt emotion, I explained to them the condition of Black people in America who are descendants of Ghanaians, and the constant pain, racism, and discrimination we experience daily. Some of the younger Ghanaian's who spent more time in Accra and had a broader awareness of American customs, racial history, and Hip-Hop, were embarrassed at the encounter. They described the label-launching of *Oburoni* as the result of some people not being exposed to information on international levels. The men that hosted and accompanied us were from the two *Akan* Ghanaian tribes of *Fante,* and *Ashanti.* By the time the conversations were complete they understood us as brothers.

Because race lacks comprehensive certainties and functions as a sociological construct, created to establish white and Eurocentric imperialism, it produces clumsy results when homogeneous populations encounter someone who is phenotypically different. As I said, racially, Dwight is lighter than I am, thus days after we had the conversation about *Oburoni,* the preacher walked with me outside after a church service and said about Dwight once we were alone: "Is he Black? Is he Black?" Minister Brantuoh was trying to make sense of Blackness, Pan-Africanism, and Afrocentrism within an American prism. "Yes he is Black," I responded. It took some additional explaining, but his initial inquiry illuminated a racial dynamic that developed soon after we arrived in Akwatia.

After arriving in Akwatia I was typically called *brother Saheli* and Dwight was *"brother Gray."* However, over time, the men referred to Dwight as *honorable Gray.* Because of his lighter skin, he was given a title depicting more honor. Although unexpected, this was a clear case of *pigmentocracy,* influenced by the creation of race. We shall now explore racial dynamics of my 2007 visit to Ghana.

Ghana 2007

After my first trip to Ghana, I was consumed with emotion and destined for a return visit. During the first excursion to Africa, we participated in the opening of the computer learning center, and for the second visit, we prepared for the ceremony to celebrate the establishment of their new borehole for fresh running water that our congregation financed. The third project was the financing of a restroom project which was completed, but we have not returned to Akwatia since the 2007 visit. During our 2005 visit, we did not tour any of the slave dungeons. Before our second trip, Joseph Brantuoh, our host and the minister of the Akwatia Church of Christ died from Malaria. He was an amazing and profoundly spiritual man. Before he died, I communicated with him about a conditional arrangement that would be required for me to return to Ghana. Tragically while writing this chapter, their second preacher, Gideon Torku, his wife, and others from Akwatia died in a horrible car accident while traveling the Accra-Cape Coast Highway

I was ecstatic about the possibility of returning to Ghana, but I said I would not return if they did not include, in the second trip, a visit to one of the slave dungeons. I had already been introduced to the concept of the *Maafa* by Dr. Kobi Kambon through his 1998 work, *African/Black Psychology in the American Context: An African Centered Approach*. Thus, in addition to preaching and sharing the gospel in Ghana and participating in the borehole ceremony, the second pilgrimage was also connected to working through my *Maafa*. As stated by Kambon and related to the *Maafa*, "It is a 'Kiswahili' term meaning a (prolonged) period of great disaster. It usually refers to the African Holocaust of Eurasian-European enslavement beginning in Africa under the Arabs and continuing through the so-called Western Europeans" (p. 530). Since many involuntary immigrants in America, of the African diaspora, trace elements of their roots to West Africa, *Maafa* identification, and mental processing are essential. Without this process, self-hate, the byproduct of racial dehumanization, fraudulently results in unconscious and deeply entrenched formulas of internal racism. Because of global and Eurocentric formulated constructions of race under hegemonic systems, psychological and sociological processing are required for delinking and healing the Black condition. In describing the nexus, link, and criticality of engaging the *Maafa*, Kambon (1998) said the following:

> The African Holocaust of European enslavement, [this] is a critical psycho-educational period for comprehending the full nature of African reality

in the American hemisphere. It is foundational in
that it provides the vital historical link between the
African past and the African present which is seeking
to reclaim its wholeness on this side of the Atlantic.
(p. 103)

Africans must re-travel this painful path both
psychologically and spiritually (as the feature film
Sankofa attempts to portray in a sense) in order to heal
the African psyche and ultimately become victorious
over European/White supremacy domination.
Going back through the Maafa on a psychological-
spiritual level is the only way (in my view) that
Africans can reclaim their true Africanity and fully
complete their physical and, most importantly, their
spiritual return to Africa. (p. 106)

The second trip to Africa was partially designed for me to re-
travel my painful racial, traumatic, ethnic, cultural, and ancestral
past. As a result, I told the men of Akwatia I would not return if
they would not schedule a trip to one of the slave dungeons. They
attempted to talk me out of it, but I remained firm. It was a non-
negotiable aspect of my return to Africa. I needed to visit at least one
of the locations my ancestors tragically occupied before boarding *slave
ships*, beginning the *Trans-Atlantic Passage*. It was difficult for them
to locate the source and cause of my unwavering request; it was the
racialized confrontation between the native West African who had
not been kidnapped versus me (the involuntary African immigrant
in America). It was about the lingering legacy and representation of
horrible and murderous transactions that resulted in African slavery
across the globe, and in my case America. The visit was essential to my
racial, religious, and spiritual identity development and restoration.

It was the summer of 2007 and although we were flying to West
Africa from the San Francisco International airport, on my lap was

the 1992 work of Anthony Browder, *Nile Valley Contributions to Civilization: Exploding the Myths Vol 1*. Knowing a slave dungeon would be visited, I was in tears as soon as the airplane lifted off the runway. I was unsure of what would be experienced but confident it would be an extension of my ontology.

The second Ghana visit was filled with deeper purpose and conviction. This time the landscape, food, and cultural customs were more familiar. I was there under a Christian context, but also for racial development and a cosmic connection with the pain and suffrage of chained West Africans—my ancestors, as they remained arrested at the shores of the Gold Coast. During this visit, I was accompanied again by Dwight Gray and also one of our soon to be church Elders, Rodney Stovall Sr. It was close to five days into the trip that we made the drive up the Ivory Coast. What I encountered was unexpected. Involuntary African immigrants in America might typically view Africa as a homogeneous continent where Blackness exists as one unified family. That is a phenotypic figment from afar, but on the continental grounds of Africa, identity is not rooted in race, but tribe, ethnicity, and language. Before formations of colonialism and coloniality, everyone is African, and everyone is Black, but not everyone is from the same tribe, even within the same country, village, or town.

My racial psychology of Africa was such that upon arrival, I would reconnect with my West African brothers and sisters, whom I postulated, viewed themselves as one united brotherhood and sisterhood. Ethnically, the beloved West African men and women we communed with were of the Akan people, represented by two tribes, *Fante* and *Ashanti*. We will return to the specifics of this context, but understand that race is an assimilation project that is incapable of providing for identifiable variation, ethnicity, or culture. The creation of race is designed to erase culture and ethnicity, forming one melded unit of imperial power and the other of inferiority. In America, Eurocentric ethnicity is sacrificed for whiteness, and this distorts how people view race globally. Because of that reality, some white Americans struggle to identify an explicit culture related to whiteness. The concept of whiteness was an intentional amalgamation, and without the concept of whiteness, the modern version of Blackness could not exist. The concept of whiteness erases Eurocentric ethnicity, and when viewing the continental conception of Africa existentially, it would appear that every person is merely African. Under phenotypic paradigms, Africa appears homogeneous, but ethnically, culturally, and tribally, it is incredibly diverse. It is in America where the conception of racial Blackness is viewed without diversity or distinction, assuming American Africanity equates to one holistic tribe.

With the men of Akwatia, we traveled to Elmina Castle and shortly after we walked out of the building I asked, "How were you able to help the Europeans capture the people of West Africa. How were you able to sell each other into slavery?" It was also the first time my Akwatia *Fante* and *Ashanti* brothers visited the slave dungeon. Through this visit I observed their covered shame and sadness and suddenly understood the complexities of why they never visited the site and tried to convince me not to go. It was an embarrassing reminder of a traumatic history. They wanted to forget the atrocity and definitely did not want to escort their American guests to that horrible place. At the time I did not have the schema to contemplate their feelings; I assumed they would be just as passionate as I in sharing the historical healing process together. I was there to work through my *Maafa*, they were not; at least not at that moment. I was ignorant and blind to the emotions native Ghanaians would experience visiting the dungeons where our ancestors were sold, tortured, starved, murdered, and raped—before most walked through the *gate of no return*, packed into ships to begin the unbearable Trans-Atlantic voyages and life as enslaved Africans. I knew multiple tribes existed across the various nations of Africa, but my American lens of race and the horrific and torturous impact forced me to view West Africa as one tribal family. Ethnicity and culture existed long before the sociological construction of race, and it is the formation of race that attempts to blur, distort, and erase ethnicity and culture. Kivel said "We have been given a distorted and inaccurate picture of history and politics because the truth about racism has been excluded, the contributions of people of color left out and the role of white people cleaned up and modified" (p. 36).

Their response to my question about participating in the capturing and selling of the eventual enslaved was something like, "We did not sell off our own, we sold other tribes." I will share more about the actual visit to the Elmina slave dungeon later, but this statement floored me, but with teary eyes, this was the honest explanation I unknowingly pressured them to reveal. Before this moment and knowing about some Ashanti and Fante tribal distinctions, I still viewed them through a single racial prism, as one African family. The global African slave-trade was an evil exploitation of tribalism. I did not delve deeper into who sold who, that can be researched, but it was a vile concept and context of white supremacy, racism, imperialism, and coloniality that resulted in the most heinous crime against a people that the world has ever seen. When the Portuguese first established Elmina Castle in 1482, it was purposed for trading, but once they discovered money could be acquired by selling people, they moved out the material items from the castle dungeon, restocking it with African people: Men and women in separate quarters, some naked and some clothed, no restroom facility, minimal food, and up to three months before being escorted in shackles onto ships destined for India, the Caribbean, Americas, and more. The entire time I walked through the dungeon I was in tears. My Akwatia brothers viewed our American tears as weakness, but we were working through our *Maafa* and various forms of dehumanization.

Remove the Eurocentric hegemonic creation of race and the globalized institution of white supremacy domination and racialized strongholds could not be realized. Despite the multiple maladies and typologies of injustice, they all have an eerie way of being traced to a racial epicenter that includes class, caste, colorism, pigmentocracy, phrenology, physiognomy, implicit-bias, micro-aggressions, and insinuations—cloaked under racist policies and held in play by insidiously violent racist ideas. In Africa the grip of white supremacy is present; even in some towns or village where no white people exist.

Blackness, Race, and Employment

Because of colorism, pigmentocracy, and phrenology race and racism are always contemplated factors, especially amongst people of the African diaspora. Despite racial silence and the illusory colorblind façade, race is always at play, but some attempt to diminish its pervasive impact, labeling people who vocalize the strain as racially obsessed or neurotic. The basis and purpose for the creation of race was the perpetuation of racism, through which colorized and *melanated* spectrums exist—under a white supremacy system and world. The less melanin a person has the safer and more honorable they are erroneously perceived. Conversely, the darker the complexion, the more sinister, dangerous, and prone to criminality the person is deemed. Both postures are rooted in racial myths, but they continue to float through the unspoken racial ether. People of the African diaspora cannot hide phenotype; thus every encounter is processed through a racial prism. Navigating the landscape of racist and racial socialization is not racial paranoia, fixation, or neurosis; it is part of the survival strategy of Pan-Africanism. People who exist in the category of the racial hegemon rarely, if ever, consider how their race privileges them. "It has been said that a fish would be the last creature on earth to discover water, so totally and continually immersed in it is he" (Barth, 2007, p. 161). This is how white supremacy works; it does not have to worry about the waters in which it swims because the Eurocentrism therein controls the tides.

As examples, when Black people are followed in a store, not greeted when entering a school building or office, pulled over by the police, not served swiftly in a restaurant, or overlooked for job opportunities after an interview, they are compelled to consider the racial element. Unless we elect to act in denial, Black people do not have any reliable data to prove that racial bias and discriminations are a thing of the past, and ostensibly we have many personal experiences to confirm the opposite. Racism does not decline as a Black people, and people of color garner educational or financial success; the higher a person moves, the more intense the racism and potential desire to remain silent. Notice the commentary in the Jay-Z, November 2017, interview by *New York Times* Executive Editor, Dean Baquet:

> Dean Baquet asked, "Are their incidents even at this stage in your life (so you are famous, you are rich, you own stuff) where you run into racism that is evident to you that is easy to recognize at this stage of your life?
>
> Jay-Z responded: "Yeah, yes, yeah. It mostly comes when you try to challenge the status-quo. If I am being quiet and entertaining everyone it's cool. It's great. You don't feel racism. But when you try to challenge the club...Then it gets into a weird space.

Despite training and educational level, my last three jobs included racial and racist implications. Axiologically, my first responsibility is to God, followed by my wife, and children. Spiritually, my first vocation exists pastorally, then that of an educator and business owner. Because my first allegiance is to ministry, I am protective of job-type and the culture and climate surrounding it, so as to not cast ministry into disequilibrium. Personally, my ministerial, familial, and educational balance is under constant assessment. I received my doctorate from the University of San Francisco in 2003 and worked in two educational positions for seven years; I was over-qualified for both positions but the balance was appropriate. At this point, I am introducing three employment and career scenarios, all influenced by race and racism. Racist encounters do not require malice or intent to hurt or harm. Some people unconsciously foster behaviors stimulated by race and racism. Under the guise of employment and because of institutional racism, doing the right thing educationally and having the appropriate experience is not always enough for people who exist outside the structure of whiteness and the European imperialism package.

Educational Encounter #1: During this time in my educational career, I served as a high school coordinator. The job was a mixture between school counseling and school administration. The position was thoroughly enjoyable, and our leadership team engaged in cutting-edge practices, ripe for another book. In my fourth year in that position, I randomly received a call from the district office, asking me to apply for an Assistant Director position. I was dedicated to the coordinator position and committed to the school principal who became a mentor and close friend. I eventually applied for the position and submitted my application documents directly into the hands of the Assistant Superintendent of Human Resources, who was elated to receive my application. I went through the first and second interviews and after the second interview, while driving home, I received a call from the Director of Student Services, offering me the position. He seemed rushed and I was being pressed to say yes, but due to my loyalty to the school principal I said yes but, "Out of respect for the school principal, I need to speak with her first thing tomorrow." The Director offered another element to sweeten the deal and said, "Will you accept the position now?" Again, I said "Yes, but I still need to speak with the principal in the morning before I can fully confirm." The next morning, I informed the principal who supported the career opportunity, so I confirmed my acceptance. He was pleased. I was asked to apply; I applied, was offered the position, and ultimately accepted.

Later in the day and shortly before lunch supervision, I received a call from the Assistant Superintendent of Human Resources. She said she needed to speak with me and asked if we could meet at the school. I told her it would be best to meet after the conclusion of the student lunch period. At the end of lunch, we connected and walked to my office. It was a gloomy and rainy day and I recall having on my large green puff-coat. Once we sat in my office, I noticed her eyes were swelled with tears and I was unsure what to make of it. We were friends, and she was a great lady and still is. I assumed we were convening to discuss salary and logistics of the new position, but her watery eyes and repressed countenance was puzzling. The countenance was different from the expression I observed when I submitted the job application and packet. Finally, she said, "I am sorry Ammar; the position can no longer be offered to you." I had already been offered and accepted the position, thus the encounter was peculiar. She could not share why the offer was rescinded, but her tears spoke volumes. I did not press her for a rationale. It was clear that she was the one selected to deliver the injurious news, but was not in agreement. I was embarrassed. I had already called my wife and shared with her the good news about my new job. Shamefully, I had to call her again. I never received clarity about that humiliating fiasco. If they could no longer offer the position, why did they ask me to apply? I had no initial intention of applying.

It was soon apparent that someone above her made the call and she was the scapegoat assigned to deliver the news, with which even she disagreed. The only later rationale reported to me was that a white woman wanted her position back and threatened to make a fuss about me moving into the position. Apparently, I was not worth the advocacy. The white woman who left ended up back in the position they asked me to occupy. According to Derrick Bell, "More often, management would prefer to hire the white man [or woman] than the black applicant. As one economist has argued, 'racial nepotism' rather than 'racial animus' is the major motivation for much of the discrimination blacks experience" (1992, p. 56). Race and racism was a factor, despite my educational level and experience. Because of my deep respect for the Black people who were in District leadership at the time, I accepted the decision silently, but trust and my heart were broken. I left the school district one year later.

Educational Encounter #2: As discussed with the previous school, trust had been broken and I decided not to seek additional opportunities or promotions with that district. I was told that I would eventually be promoted to a principal position, but after my experience of having a job offered and rescinded, I felt it would be irresponsible to believe such. I knew I would eventually leave the school district, but I was not sure when. My wife and I became pregnant with our fourth child and we learned on November 21, 2005 that in-utero he had a severe heart condition. Three days after his birth he died. My wife wrote in her 2013 book, *The Memoirs of a Young Millennium Preacher's Wife: A Story of Life, Love and the Testing of Faith*, "A numbing feeling quickly came over me as I tried to process what he was telling me. He proceeded, 'This is a fatal congenital heart defect in which the left part of the heart is small or not visible at all" (p. 72).

While I was on my way to Sacramento to investigate a gang intervention program, along with the Director of Student Services and two colleagues from the high school, my wife called my cell phone and exclaimed hysterically about our son. I was trapped in a car and on the other end of the phone my wife said: "...He has a hole in his heart" (p. 73). I spent the rest of that year bracing for the birth of our son, followed by grieving his death. I became claustrophobic with the job and knew it would be my last year.

I was not sure where I would find another job, but knew I would not return. Toward the end of the school year our high school took a team of educators and staff to a Stanford University equity conference. Two of the main speakers were Noma LeMoine and San Francisco State University professor, Wade Nobles. The one-day conference was powerful and my son Zion accompanied me. Part of the day included school districts demonstrating their equity spirit on stage. The high school in my city performed a rap and at the end said they were hiring. After that was said my colleagues looked at me with eyes that said, "Oh no." The Assistant Superintendent of Human Resources was present, and I gave him my card. He approached me a few minutes later, told me to apply and gave me a date for an interview. When I arrived home, I started the application process, but realized I had already applied for the position. It was an Assistant Principal position in a local high school. I was overqualified for the job, but I knew I could balance it with ministry and it was very close to my home.

I walked into the interview and I remember one of the interview panelists later saying, "You had me at hello." I was also informed that they attempted to hire someone with a first round of interviews, but were not satisfied with the candidates. The position reopened for additional interviews and I was included. After the conclusion of interviews, it was stated that I was the best candidate. I appreciated the compliment, but it was also troubling. I was given an opportunity to interview, only after they reopened the process. My application was submitted before the original closing date, but why did I not receive an initial interview invite? I was only selected to interview for the reopened process after introducing myself at the Stanford University conference. Racial contemplation is always an embedded reality. They shared with me their dissatisfaction with the first pool of candidates; the mystifying notion is that my original application was in that pool, but I did not receive an interview offer. How does a person racially and psychologically rectify such occurrences? Was my application packet not good enough? At the time of applying for the position, I had worked as a therapist (three years), middle school counselor (three years), middle school dean (one, year), and high school administrator (4 years), held all appropriate position credentials, and had a doctorate in education. Toward the end of the interview, one of the interviewers asked me why I wanted the position with my credentials and if I would commit to staying for at least two years. I explained why and said yes.

In the previous district I was offered a position and it was removed. In this case I was not called for an interview initially, but was then told I was the best candidate. Some seek to deemphasize racial influences, but when a Black person experiences repetitive encounters in America, we are often compelled to contemplate racial implications and rationales. From my perspective, the next encounter is even more racially insidious—I finally attempted to push the envelope with the balance of my secular profession and ministerial responsibilities.

Educational Encounter #3: As I promised in the previous interview scenario, I remained at the high school for two years. After yet another deeply racialized encounter that involved the police, I was ready to apply for a position that matched my experience, credentials, and education. As a result, I applied for three positions and said I would accept whichever opportunity was offered first. I applied for a Director position in a neighboring school district, a Principalship in Oakland Unified, and Dean of Student Services for the Peralta Community College District. I am not sure how much time elapsed, but one day after work I went home, changed my clothes, and began relaxing for the evening. Suddenly I received a call from the Human Resources Assistant Superintendent of my then-district, stating the Superintendent of the neighboring district, for which I applied, wanted me to call him. It was after 5:00 PM and I made the call; to my surprise the Superintendent asked me if I could come in for an interview immediately. I said yes, put my suit back on and drove to the neighboring district for an evening interview in the Superintendent's office.

As I entered the Superintendent's office, two other people were present, then-Assistant Superintendent of Human Resources, and then-Assistant-Superintendent of Business Services. The interview took place during the midst of the Spring 2007-2008 school-year and at the end of the lengthy interview they asked me if I wanted the job. I said yes, knowing the job would go into effect the summer of July 1. What I learned later was that, similar to the last position, they had wrestled through one or two phases of interviews, but I never received a call. I was informed that someone flagged my file under the no-interview category. The superintendent asked why, but no one had an answer. I was told that out of all the interviews I was the strongest candidate; yet I guess not strong enough to get an interview without the Superintendent making a special request.

I remember when I walked my application into the district and placed it in the hands of a white lady with blondish hair and blue eyes. When I told her what position it was for, her eyes enlarged as if she had seen a ghost. I did not know what to make of it, so I said thank you, turned, and walked away. Ironically the next day, and after having accepted the Student Support Services position, I received a call from Oakland Unified asking me if I was interested in the McClymond's High School Principal position. The offer was just a few hours too short, but I continue to wonder what that would have been like, considering the high school is in West Oakland, not far from my West Oakland church building and office. As with the other educational employment encounters I have shared, I was forced to contemplate racialized factors. This is the climate that race has created. People of the African diaspora in America, especially those who are in America as an extension of chattel slavery, cannot help but ponder if the marginalized or differentiated treatment we receive is a result of our Blackness.

The Creation of Race

The creation of race has produced an eerie scene in America and internationally. Because of race I was called "black monkey" in Korea, *Oburoni* or *white man* in Ghana, and handcuffed while at work in San Francisco. And these are just some of the racialized episodes I have decided to share for this literary project. The creative forces behind racial constructions require more analysis to help move to a place of addressing toxic and eerie forms of racial blindness, denial, and avoidance. Now that I have shared a few personal examples of how race and racism intersect with employment and education, we shall return to developmental constructs and the creation of race.

Anthony Browder and others place the creation of race within the range of 1775-1800, but its informal conception began much earlier. Jacqueline Battalora reveals in her 2013 book, *Birth of a White Nation: The Invention of White People and Its Relevance Today,* "The history of the invention of white people exposes the 'white race' for what it is: a historical creation to serve the interests of the wealthiest capitalists and provide unearned advantages for those labeled white, and unearned disadvantages to those labeled other-than-white" (pp. 89-90). About racial superiority she said, "This is not to say that members of the group are in fact superior intellectually, physically or otherwise, but rather, the superiority served as the reason to justify the creation of the group" (pp. 90-91). She went on to reveal, "This was true in 1681, when 'white' first appeared in law and assumed ideas about the British as those deserving of rights and privileges from which others can be denied" (p. 91). This type of *othering* was consistently used to justify brutality, especially on American soil. David Stannard (1992), said in *The Conquest of the New World: American Holocaust:*

> A traditional Eurocentric bias that lumps undifferentiated masses of 'Africans' into one single category and undifferentiated masses of 'Indians' into another, while making fine distinctions among the different populations of Europe, permits the ignoring of cases in which genocide against Africans and American Indians has resulted in the total extermination—purposefully carried out—of entire cultural, social, religious, and ethnic groups. (p. 151)

"...'White' people as a designation of a group of humanity, much less a race, never existed until late in the seventeenth century" (Battalora, 2013, p. 1). Even though Aristotle lived from 384-322 BC, he codified and postulated conceptions of Eurocentric superiority, even from a within-group frame. The tracking and categorizing of European phenotypic differences set in motion the continuum for racial hierarchy to be advanced. In literature the Greeks established the concept of a *fictional villainized other* that was later affixed to non-European groups, and the same was the case for the development of a racialized European axiology. Race as a European construct did not start with the *othering* of existential groups; it first started with the differentiation of people within Europe. In *Nature Knows No Color-Line*, J. A. Rogers captured the sentiments of one of the world's most popular philosophers: "Soft, silky hair, said Aristotle, was a sign of cowardice. Coarse one meant courage provided it curled gently at the ends. If it curled too much, or was 'wooly like that of the Ethiopians' then it signified the same as the soft, silky one" (p. 17).

Although the concept of race had not been fully developed, for Aristotle a schematic foundation for racial superiority was being established and in some ways was already entrenched. To assess internal and within-group Eurocentric value, Aristotle was forced to advance a comparison with African people. The original depiction of phenotypic or bodily value for Aristotle has changed today. He codified and valued curly hair over "silky" hair. In current United States depictions of beauty, this is reversed. The problem is, once a value was constructed based on appearance; the door was open for concepts like *phrenology* and *physiognomy* to amplify a compromising, dominating, and hegemonic social stronghold over humanity. Aristotle did not stop with hair. Rogers (1952) also captured the following regarding the thoughts and racial philosophy of Aristotle:

> A full voice, deep and round, indicated courage: a languid or high-pitched one, cowardice. Short arms showed addiction to gambling and dancing. A pale complexion, small eyes, and thick black hair on the body showed lasciviousness. Big feet meant strength of character, provided the toes did not curve at the ends in which case it indicated impudence. Bony buttocks showed strong character; fat ones a weak mind. A large head was quickness; a small forehead, stupidity; grey eyes, cowardice. (Rogers, p. 17)

Much of *western tradition* and American epistemology is established through Grecian and Athenian customs and the dialectic process of Socrates, Plato, and Aristotle. In addition to logic and metaphysics, Aristotle functioned as a type of scientist. His system of classification and categorization assisted in opening the door for racist ideas to flourish beyond the boundaries of isolated Eurocentrism.

Although the racial and ethnic stereotypes declined in Europe, the treacherous, eerie, and toxic ideas were emboldened in America, especially toward Black people. The influence of race transformed into racism is a deeply seductive vestige that victimizes the hearts and minds of humanity before conscious detection. For individualized and sustained community praxis to emerge racially, the destructive remnants of race and racism require all people to assess its impact. Rogers continued his Aristotle influential tracking by stating:

> These laws lessened this pseudo-science in Europe.
> But it had been developing meanwhile in the
> American colonies where difference in skin color was
> much more marked. With no restraining hand there,
> Physiognomy mounted the throne. What whites had
> been saying about one another's color and features
> they now applied with double force to the blacks.
> (1952, p. 19)

With the documented racial epistemological shaping of the mind, it must be asked: Despite the ancient foundation of the creation of race, how are people impacted today? Additionally, how are people unconsciously advancing racist ideas, practices, and policies across modern educational, religious, and cultural systems? There is more that is included in the continuum of discrimination, but after sifting through all the non-racial disaggregated data, remaining with an unavoidable glare is a racialized problem. Some people prefer to remain silent and skip or remove the malady of race, jumping to less-potent benchmarks of class, socio-economic levels, and educational attainment, but because race is rooted in a system of institutional hierarchy—wealth and education do not excuse Black people and non-white people from racist encounters and bigoted treatment. Regardless of income, education level, criminal history, or neighborhood, "...All whites share to some degree in the overall package of advantages conferred upon them at any given historical moment on the basis of their being viewed as white" (Battalora, 2013, p. 90). The opposite is true for Black people and those who cannot racially pass for white. As stated about white racial epistemology connected to race in the 2004 work, *Off White,* and the essay "We Didn't see Color: The Salience of Color Blindness in Desegregated Schools," the following was shared:

> On one hand, white Americans want to think about race only on the individual level—how individuals treat each other—but on the other hand, they lack any broader, societal level explanations for ongoing racial inequality. Thus, they try to explain away this inequality by blaming the victims of it for not acting white, while simultaneously swearing we are all the same in this, our color–blind society. (Revilla, A. T., Stuart Well, A., & Jellison Holme, J., p. 285)

The creation of race established a structure of dominance, power, and privilege, especially in America, that many groups hustled to manipulate and join. As explained in *The Myth of Race,* Europeans were considered supreme and other groups or "...Degenerates could be remediated by giving them the benefits of European education and 'culture,' especially by missionizing them to Christianity" (Sussman, 2014, p. 14). In addition to the construction of the multiple racial categories as developed by Carl Linnaeus (1707-1778), "founder of modern biology and the person who developed the system of zoological classification of species....Linnaeus then classified varieties of humans in relationship to their supposed education and climatic situation" (Sussman, 2014, pp. 15-16). Building from the work of Carl Linnaeus, German physician Johann Friedrich Blumenbach (1752-1840), ultimately arrived at five racial varieties or categories. "His five varieties—Caucasian, Mongoloid, Ethiopian, American, and Malay—became widely accepted by the educated community, and with some slight variations they are still in use today" (Sussman, 2014, p. 19). Just a few decades later from the influence of Linnaeus and

Blumenbach, still spewing racist theology, "The Reverend Robert L. Dabney, one of southern Presbyterianism's most influential intellectuals and an old Confederate Army chaplain, argued that only enslavement could provide Black people with a civilizing education" (Kendi, 2016, p. 266).

Through the *morphing* of Europeanism in America, the tag of whiteness became a prized commodity; it forced many Europeans to throw away their ethnicity, while many non-white groups also maneuvered to join the ranks of *whiteness*. Because race is a hierarchical system, there was no way to attempt joining the club of *whiteness* without castigating and shunning Blackness. The initial construction of whiteness did not include all European ethnicities; it was relegated to Northwestern Europeans. Jewish people of European descent in America were originally excluded from the categorical privileges of whiteness. In her 2004 *Off White* essay, "How Did Jews Become White Folks?," Karen Brodkin said, "American anti-Semitism was part of a broader pattern of the late 19th-century racism against all southern and eastern European immigrants, as well as against Asian immigrants, not to mention African Americans, Native Americans, and Mexicans" (p. 17). Additionally, she said, "By the 1920s, scientific racism sanctified the notion that real Americans were white and that real whites came from northwest Europe" (p. 19).

Paul Kivel said in *Uprooting Racism,* "It is not necessarily a privilege to be white, but it certainly has its benefits. That's why so many of us gave up our unique histories, primary languages, accents, distinctive dress, family names and cultural expressions" (p. 28). European Jews were not the only group in America that sought to break free from non-white status. Whiteness today is viewed through a singular prism and spectrum, as if all European people in America were always declared white, privileged, and empowered. Neil Irvin Painter (2010) illustrates the struggle and sacrifice of those who fought to assimilate into whiteness in her book, *The History of White People.* She said, "One group, however, utterly repudiated the notion of black-Irish similarity, and that was the Irish in the United States. Irish immigrants quickly recognized how to use the American color line to elevate white—no matter how wretched—over black" (p. 143). To access the status of whiteness, two things were required: 1) Phenotypically white skin and 2) A vocal castigation and subversion of Blackness. Racial groups in America went to great extremes to disconnect from categories that included those of the African diaspora, especially in America. Neil Irvin Painter also said:

> Anti-Semitism was already well established in the United States but grew increasingly abusive in the early twentieth century. Before the war Jews had figured as only one in a list of inferior Europeans, along with Slavs and Italians. Now Jews moved to the top, personifying the menace of immigration and bolshevism in racial terms. (p. 304)

Richard Delgado and Jean Stefancic, in their 2001 work, *Critical Race Theory: An Introduction* indicates, "Another aspect to the construction of whiteness is the way certain groups have moved into the white race. For example, early on in our history Irish, Jews, and Italians were considered nonwhite—that is, on par with African Americans" (p. 77). Racial assimilation and Black marginalization travelled beyond the formation of European positioning, even colorized groups bemoaned and trampled Blackness to gain acceptance under a pseudo-form of whiteness or *model minority* status. Maneuvering through racial construction is possible because "Whiteness, it turns out, is not only valuable, it is shifting and malleable" (Delgado & Stefancic, p. 77). Thus, the benefits of whiteness eventually opened to anyone who would work, conform, and cohere to its amalgamation and racial invention. Asians in America strategized how to join white Jews, Italians, and the Irish in distancing themselves from Blackness. About this racial positioning and coopting, Delgado and Stefancic said:

> In addition to pitting one minority group against
> another, binary thinking can cause exaggerated
> identification with whites at the expense of other
> groups. For example, early in one state's history,
> Asians sought to be declared white so that they could
> attend schools for whites and not have to go to ones
> with blacks. (p. 72)

Racial jockeying for American position and power continues today, but it is imperative to connect to the roots or racialized processing. It is the power structure and institution of race that promotes the convictions of an eerie silence in the face of injustice, marginalization, and subjugation. Space cannot be found where race does not have an influential grip. It was created to harness and commandeer power and privilege, and until it is interrupted and dismantled, its discriminatory purpose will remain across all systems. The classic blueprint of the beginning stages of upward racial mobility was the dehumanization of Blackness. Ibram Kendi points out some of this racialized psychological demonizing with the comparative trap between Asian and African Americans, through the destruction and blaze of the Los Angeles Watts riot that began on August 11, 1965 and lasted six days. In response he highlights:

> On January 9, 1966, the New York Times Magazine
> contrasted these rioting 'ghetto' Blacks with the
> 'model minority': Asians. Some Asian Americans
> consumed the racist 'model minority' title, which
> masked the widespread discrimination and poverty
> in Asian American communities and regarded
> Asian Americans as superior (in their assimilating
> prowess) to Latina/os, Native Americans, and
> African Americans. (Kendi, 2016, p. 395)

The creation of race offers a systematic distribution of power and privilege to white people that are unearned and unmerited. A white person does not have to ask for the benefits of whiteness; they are automatically assumed and applied. Because of such, as stated in *Beyond Black and White*, "The white mind has been able to look without seeing" (Comer, 1972, p. 166). Freire said, "Through critical discovery, both the oppressed and the oppressor manifest behaviors of dehumanization" (2017, p. 48). The true effects of Eurocentric oppressive denial and blindness have produced devastating lifelong results. In addition to the suffrage, Black folk of the African diaspora that occupy America because of the Trans-Atlantic Passage, continually search for racialized identity within Pan-African contexts. In addition to the search for racialized identity by Black and other non-white groups, there is also a psychological element of coalescing from the bludgeoned trauma inflicted through globalized Eurocentric hegemony. Moreover, relating to European Spaniard brutality toward Native Americans, Stannard (1992), in *The Conquest of the New World: American Holocaust* quoted the following from *Mexico,* capturing the depraved mind influenced by a dehumanized and genocidal racial epistemic:

> It was a general rule among Spaniards to be cruel; not just cruel, but extraordinarily cruel so that harsh and bitter treatment would prevent Indians from daring to think of themselves as human beings or having a minute to think at all. So they would cut an Indian's hands and leave them dangling by a shred of skin and they would send him on saying "Go now, spread the news to your chiefs." They would test their swords and their manly strength on captured Indians and place bets on the slicing off of heads or the cutting of bodies in half with one blow. They burned or hanged captured chiefs. (p. 70)

To justify enslavement and discourage African emancipation in America, the castigation and racial dehumanization of Black people required intense enforcement. About racial rhetoric toward those of the African diaspora in America, "Black people were 'indolent, improvident, averse to labor; when emancipated, they would either starve or plunder,' one congressman argued, defending the interests of southern planters who were dependent on slave labor. Blacks were 'an inferior race even to the Indians'" (Kendi, 2016, p. 121). The manufactured inferiority placed on Africans and non-white groups operate consciously and unconsciously with the power of an unstoppable machine. My daughter Najja was reading chapter books as she entered a private Pre-Kindergarten through eighth-grade school, but she was denied acknowledgement of that honor during the promotion ceremony because it overshadowed the white kindergarten and first-grade students who were being honored for just learning to read. Similarly, while in the fourth-grade of her public elementary school, as she finished her test before all the other students, two male Filipino classmates shockingly blurted out: "The Black girl finished first." While in the first-grade of the same private school my daughter Sadé informed me that her white and Asian friends said, "We would play with you more if your hair was like ours."

Racial Toxicity on Children

Racialized and racist encounters are not isolated to adults; once racial constructions were placed in motion, children became vulnerable targets of bigoted victimization and socialization on both ends of the spectrum. It is critical that children receive early-education in racial socialization and mentoring. Tatum (1997) said in, *Why are All the Black Kids Sitting Together in the Cafeteria? And Other Conversations About Race,* "...Whether it is racist, or sexist or classist, it is an important skill for children to develop. It is as important for my Black male children to recognize sexism and other forms of oppression as it is for them to spot racism" (p. 47). Tatum continued:

But not only do children need to be able to recognize distorted representations, they also need to know what can be done about them. Learning to recognize cultural and institutional racism and other forms of inequity without also learning strategies to respond to them is a prescription for despair. Yet even preschool children are not too young to begin to think about what can be done about unfairness. (p. 49)

Not only are Black and non-white children grossly impacted by race and racism, so are white children. As stated about children and racial and racist language in "Words that Wound: A Tort Action for Racial Insults, and Name Calling," an essay within the 1993 work, *Words That Wound: Critical Race Theory, Assaultive Speech, and the First Amendment:* "Because they constantly hear racist messages, minority children, not surprisingly, come to question their competence, intelligence, and worth" (Delgado, p. 95). He also said, "The effects of racial labeling are discernible early in life; at a young age, minority children exhibit self-hatred because of their skin color, and majority children learn to associate dark skin with undesirability and ugliness" (p. 92). Adults often minimize the effect of racism on children, as if they are too young to be wounded, but Delgado also said about racially defenseless children, "Minority children possess even fewer means for coping with racial insults than do adults. 'A child who finds himself rejected and attacked ... is not likely to develop dignity and poise.... On the contrary he develops defenses...'" (p. 95).

The Power Behind White Racial Insanity and Delusion

No one is immune from the vicious impact of racist and racial marginalization, and based on perceived inferiority, racism, and men operating as pseudo-scientists—white skin was declared a prized possession, while darkly pigmented skin was deemed an illness. As will be discussed in the next chapter, some deemed dark skin a curse from God. Championing the cause of whiteness, if a Black person suffered from vitiligo, it was considered a blessing. Henry Moss developed vitiligo, but some misunderstood his condition and contorted it into a racist premise, favoring white superiority. Ultimately his Black skin was declared the result of a disease and his white skin was viewed as transformative healing, since he was returning to whiteness. I call this white racial insanity and delusion. Some scoffed at the notion, but enough in the so-called intellectual community of that day, convincingly explained positions on American national levels. "... Moss was a freak to some, but to others, such as Benjamin Rush, he was the future of racial progress" (Kendi, 2016, p. 127). The reality of the medical condition did not matter, because in situations of race and racism, "Truth never stopped the concoctors of racist ideas" (Kendi, 2016, p. 216). To the American Philosophical Society Benjamin Rush opined:

> ...That all Africans were suffering from leprosy. This skin disease explained why they all had ugly Black skin, Rush told APS members. And the whiter their skins became, the healthier they became. This skin disease was brought on by poor diet, he theorized, along with "greater heat, more savage manners, and bilious fevers." (Kendi, 2016, p. 128)

Racial categorization established a stronghold with such intense force that the harboring or protection of the enslaved was declared criminal behavior in policy and law. "What Jefferson and every other holder of African people had long feared had come to pass. In response, Congress passed the Fugitive Slave Act of 1793, bestowing on slaveholders the right and legal apparatus to recover escaped Africans and criminalize those who harbored them" (Kendi, 2016, p. 123). In the end and where America currently stands with its malignant and unconfessed racism, the burden of healing, resolution, and dismantling is left to the powerful and yet chained hands of Black folk to reconcile. Despite minor accomplishments and parallel setbacks to the veneer of American racial progress, the constructions, formations, and role of race in America and beyond, continue to stifle and cripple pursuits toward racial equity and equality. The goal is not for Black people and people of color to persuade white people of the essence of Black worth, it is time for white people to break silence, come to terms with their racial fragility, and holistically join the struggle on the antiracists battlefield for social justice—across all continuums. The burden must be removed from Black shoulders:

> This strategy of what can be termed uplift suasion was based on the idea that White people could be persuaded away from their racist ideas if they saw Black people improving their behavior, uplifting themselves from their low station in American society. The burden of race relations was placed squarely on the shoulders of Black Americans. (Kendi, 2016, p. 124)

Concluding Premise and Inquiry

As the concept, plague, creation-of-race, and Eurocentric hegemony are investigated, not only must the impact on the oppressed be analyzed, the influence on white and European psychology requires heavy scrutiny. The creation of race and its devastating effects created a psyche within whiteness that is monstrous. I am not sure if the inventors of race intended for its murderous, divisive, and discriminatory results, but it was set in motion and requires attention. The question is posed, "Why was the white mind able to conclude with such consistency, silence, and general white-approval, that Black and of-color barbarism, murder, lynching, and rape, was justified? How and why was white brutality toward the *other* accepted across substantial educational, religious, economic, and cultural institutions? Additionally, considering the amount of Black blood spilled in American streets by the hands and guns of law enforcement, how does the historical trend of *white violence* impact current forms of violence and silence? In the book *Ida B. Wells: A Woman of Courage*, a vicious encounter is described that exposes a violent white psyche and thirst for hate. Regarding the lynching of Henry Smith on a "mock throne" and the ten-thousand white people that gathered in anticipation of viewing the brutality, Ida B. Wells said:

...He was placed on a scaffold and his clothes torn off. Then, for the next fifty minutes, Smith was tortured. Red-hot irons were placed against his skin. His eyes were burned out. As he moaned in pain, the crowd cheered. Finally a red-hot poker was thrust down his throat. When it appeared he was dead, kerosene was poured over him and he was set on fire. (p. 53)

The creation of race and the legacy of its ugliness and terror have impacted every layer of American society and continue to swirl globally. Not only are American educational institutions affected, but one of the most destructive, abused, and racially hegemonic systems that operated as an insidious force of white supremacy, was the construction of colonized Christianity and the church in America. To this exploration, we now shift our focus.

CHAPTER 5

THE DECEPTIVE INSTITUTIONAL DEVELOPMENT OF COLONIZED CHRISTIANITY AND DESTRUCTIVE AMERICAN CHATTEL SLAVERY JUSTIFICATIONS

> What was most disturbing about these scenes is the
> discovery that the perpetrators of the crimes were
> ordinary people, not so different from ourselves—
> merchants, farmers, laborers, machine operators,
> teachers, lawyers, doctors, policemen, students;
> they were family men and women, good, decent
> churchgoing folk who came to believe that keeping
> black people in their place was nothing less than
> pest control, a way of combatting an epidemic or
> virus that if not checked would be detrimental to
> the health of the community. (Litwack, 2000, p. 34)

Visiting *Elmina Castle* and the slave dungeon in Ghana was a
profound part of my racial identity development, *Maafa*, and spiritual
development. As we arrived at the site our tour-guide walked us
through the facility, but I immediately broke free—I did not want to
tour the compound with the group—initially I needed to process and

intuit on my own. At some point I did reconnect with the group and tour-guide, but only after doing my own personal work. I was in tears for most of the visit, something my Akwatia brothers did not initially understand. While on-site I had one of the most unforgettable meals of my life. It was not just that my fried chicken, fried rice, sautéed vegetables, and bottled Orange Crush soda were delicious; it was that I ate my meal in tears, realizing I was freely eating at the same site where my ancestors virtually starved. From the scenery of the restaurant I could see the Atlantic Ocean and the *gate of no return*, the last steps the Ghanaians trudged on African soil before boarding slave ships. As we walked through what would have been the dining hall of the castle, I was amazed at the voluminous amount of biblical passages written on the walls. Although long before *Manifest Destiny* and the Mexican American war, the slavers and operators of *Elmina Castle* believed their efforts were ordained and sanctioned by God.

The current form of Christianity in America requires critical analysis and critique. Whether professed or confessed or not, the legacy of American slavery currently impacts the modern church. The July, 2018 article by Bobby Ross Jr. and Hamil R. Harris in *The Christian Chronicle*, entitled "Fifty Years After Historic Meeting, Race Still Divides Churches of Christ," confronts the current and historical Christian racial divide. They highlighted the 1968 two-day national meeting in Atlanta between Black and White Church of Christ preachers that was designed to discuss and begin a process of resolving racial division. The meeting was held in Atlanta, shortly after Dr. Martin Luther King Jr. was assassinated. Prominent Church of Christ preacher, Eugene Lawton of Newark, New Jersey was one of the African American participants and forty years later still "…Calls racism the No. 1 issue in America, suggesting that 'a black person can't even go into a coffee shop and not be arrested'" (Ross Jr. & Harris, July, 2018). Raphael G. Warnock, in *The Divided Mind of the Black Church: Theology, Piety & Witness*, said about Black theology, ecclesiology, and its missional liberation, that there is "an identifiable and distinctive liberationist trajectory of African American faith formed in the crucible of American chattel slavery" (2014, p. 174). Although this is decisively true, we must also confess that the origin of the first-century church was radical in its liberation and restoration plea from inception. Black liberation theology is only possible because the principles already existed in the biblical text. As it propelled forward, "Liberation theology not only theorized alienation, capitalism, and colonialism, but also inspired a large and influential social mobilization nurtured by a solid religious and political agenda which developed intricate relations with popular insurgency and liberation movements" (Moraña, Dussel, & Jáuregui, 2008, pp. 14-15).

The God of the Bible always functioned as a *Redeemer* of the oppressed and anyone else willing to cohere to the biblical premise. Some people have spoken negatively of Black liberation theology because they presume it to be contrived and a scriptural add-on, failing to realize it forcefully highlights the depths of a Messianic God; a premise white slavers ignored entirely. Today, some of what is happening in America religiously and spiritually, from a conscious community perspective, is a reaction to the published message, imagery, and institution of colonized Christianity. Because of the religious misleading and co-opting of the biblical text, some darker colorized people are looking to anything other than Christianity for the development of an ethnic, racial, and spiritual identity.

As a result of the force, insurgence, influence, and manipulation— an Americanized slavers version of Christianity—some people cannot see or simply miss the colorized essence within the Old and New Testaments, another designed ploy and plot of white supremacy. The entire theme of the Bible, including the historicity of the first-century church falls within the range of a *God-of-the-oppressed* theology and pedagogy. Universally the Eastern biblical narrative, *Genesis* through *Revelation*, proclaims a message of deliverance for the poor, oppressed, enslaved, and marginalized. It was when the Christian message arrived in America, seized by whiteness, that it became a postmodern religion and spirituality embraced and hijacked by whiteness and imperialism, with all others being perceived as feeble and privileged guests at the Christian table of God. This utter distortion of comprehensive biblical messages and that of the gospel, has forced people to search for the God of liberation outside the bible, with no true critical critique or consideration. The appropriate thought of some is, "A God who supported or condoned the institution of American chattel slavery cannot be the Messiah of colorized people." The problem is that because of systematic deceit through Eurocentric hegemony, the actual expressed God of the Bible has been recklessly re-packaged as a deific entity that prefers the powerful and privileged, promotes white supremacy, and from the heavenly realm prophesies a victim-blame theology toward the oppressed.

The Eastern context of biblical Scripture reveals a message of spiritual, physical, and psychological deliverance, but that is not the religious ethos that landed in America with slave ships. Those forms of Bible thumping Christian circumlocutions were designed to control, manipulate, and justify enslavement and harsh treatment of the *other* and so-called *savage*. Many people have dismissed the biblical narrative and Christian *faith* because they fail to conceptualize the bible and its theology through the appropriate lens. The power and influence of white supremacy has gripped and superimposed itself over the church and Christian tenets. This chapter is not *apologetics* or about the conversion of persons into the Christian faith, but it is designed to help people put the Bible in its proper context, confronting the myth that Christianity is the religion of the white man, and in its origin was designed to justify barbaric treatment through American chattel slavery. The greed of Europe sought to commandeer the Christian ethos, impacting global and especially American epistemology, using it to manipulate, control, murder, rape, pillage, and dehumanize Black existence and more. Christianity in America is forced to deal with and manage its racist, imperialistic, distorted, and destructive European hegemonic roots. I call it colonized Christianity or a slavers version of Christianity. If a person only knows formations of a colonized Christianity, they should rightfully reject it and run because it is repressive, oppressive, racist, and steeped in white supremacy. Through this chapter, the way Christianity was used to manipulate and dehumanize the enslaved will be explored, as well as its undifferentiated lingering legacy that continues to impact race, religion, education, literature, art, knowledge, thought, metaphysics, and politics today.

In *Stamped from the Beginning*, Ibram Kendi makes it clear that to support racist policy, racist ideas had to be floated into the epistemic stratosphere. The justification for the barbarism of chattel slavery and the violence toward the enslaved in America first required development, followed by the promotion of racist ideas. The Bible and church were not immune to this kind of psychological conditioning. As a historical narrative, the Bible is a reliable source, but *slaver* abuse of the biblical text forces people to question its validity. From a New Testament perspective, C. L. Blomberg speaks of biblical soundness in *The Historical Reliability of the New Testament: Countering the Challenges to Evangelical Christian Beliefs* (2016), and in *The Historical Reliability of the Gospels* (2007). About the comprehensive essence of the Bible and canonization, the work of D. N. Freedman (1992), *The Anchor Yale Bible Dictionary, Volume 1, A-C*, is a productive start, but biblical research cannot be exhausted. *How Came the Bible: The Turbulent and Fascinating History of the World's Greatest Book* (1981), by Edgar J. Goodspeed is quick and insightful, along with, *The New Testament Documents: Are They Reliable?* (1981), by F. F. Bruce.

Although it is one of countless books exposing the life of Constantine, a close read of the 2001 work of Dean Dudley, *History of the First Council of Nice: A Life of Constantine (A World's Christian Convention A.D. 325)*, reveals the true tenet and purpose of the New Testament faith system and deity of Christ, despite the religiously disruptive and heretical actions of men in the second and third centuries A.D. Every brave Christian should also brace themselves and read the research of Walter Williams in *The Historical Origins of Christianity*. According to Williams the "Council of Nicea I (325 A.B.C.E), the Council of Constantinople I (381 A.B.C.E.), the Council of Ephesus (431 A.B.C.E), the Council of Chalcedon (451

A.B.C.E.) and the Council of Constantinople II (553 A.C.E)," based on the influence of the Melchite Coptic Egyptian priest society were all designed to deify the lifeless god-icon *Serapis*, who was said to later be substituted by Jesus the Christ (p. 13).

There are many books that seek to discount the Bible like *Who Wrote the Bible? (1987)*, by R. E. Fridman. He questions and challenges biblical authorship. A. B. Kuhn, in *Shadow of the Third Century: A Revaluation of Christianity* (2007), likens exclusive biblical belief as folly. Such books must be read with a critical eye. From a church-age perspective, many books that are critical of the Bible, fail to trace the roots of Christianity to their genesis or connected shadows and types of the Old Testament. As some preachers classically opine, the New Testament is the Old Testament revealed, and the Old Testament is the New Testament concealed. Marcus Garvey was a bold Pan-African giant and advocate for global African justice and maintained an unapologetic Christian theology. The message of the Bible itself has not been altered, it is the racist interpretive slant that was annexed through Eurocentrism that has proven to be divisive, destructive, and murderous.

The goal of this chapter is not to defend the Bible; it is designed to illustrate the intentional distortion of ancient biblical stories and images for the benefit of white supremacy. If we can unlock and delink from a racist epistemic where the Bible is used as the literal and subliminal source of deception, the hegemonic systems of racism, white privilege, and white supremacy can be disrupted and dismantled. American disruption of racism and white supremacy has been in motion since the days of David Walker and Nat Turner, but it requires a continued galvanizing of new courageous minds and social justice soldiers, theologically equipped and Spirit-filled to advance the struggle. It was in New York (1922), Easter Sunday, April 16th where Marcus Garvey preached a sermon entitled, "The Resurrection of the Negro." Through it, he compared the struggle for justice, freedom, and reformation to the mission and ministry of Christ. He said, "The one who attempts to bring about changes in the order of human society becomes a dangerous imposter upon society, and to those who control the systems of the day" (Jacques-Garvey, 2014, p. 87). Comparatively, he said about Jesus, "He came to change the spiritual attitude of man toward his brother. That was regarded in His day as irregularity, even as it is regarded to-day" (Jacques-Garvey, 2014, p. 87).

Supporting the depths of his Pan-African pursuits, Garvey was firm in his religious convictions and beliefs about his worth saying, God "never created an inferior man," but decades and centuries prior Europeans had to conceive of a plan and method to justify their discriminatory practices toward African people. The creation of race started the process, but phenotypic difference was not enough to condone or provide permission for the malicious economic system of American chattel slavery. Thus, to begin the development of a notion and idea of Black inferiority and abject African savagery, they turned to the Bible and the story of Noah and his son's Shem, Ham, and Japheth. The dangerous misinterpretation of this biblical story, to maintain the entrenchment of white supremacy, is a prime example of how colonized Christianity was able to advance and remain firmly positioned in many pockets of Christendom today. As depicted in the *New Living Translation* of the Bible, the story is shared in Genesis 9:20-27:

> Noah, a man of the soil, proceeded to plant a vineyard. [21]When he drank some of its wine, he became drunk and lay uncovered inside his tent. [22]Ham, the father of Canaan, saw his father naked and told his two brothers outside. [23]But Shem and Japheth took a garment and laid it across their shoulders; then they walked in backward and covered their father's naked body. Their faces were turned the other way so that they would not see their father naked.

[24]When Noah awoke from his wine and found out
what his youngest son had done to him, [25]he said,
"Cursed be Canaan!
The lowest of slaves
will he be to his brothers."
[26]He also said,
"Praise be to the LORD, the God of Shem!
May Canaan be the slave of Shem.
[27]May God extend Japheth's territory;
may Japheth live in the tents of Shem,
and may Canaan be the slave of Japheth."

From this biblical episode was contrived the racist belief that African people are cursed by God. If the world could be convinced that African people were divinely cursed by a celestial force, they could seek erroneous justification for their enslavement. It is possible that lynching became a demonic staple of white racism because of the intentional misinterpretation of the biblical quote, "...Cursed is every one that hangeth on a tree" (Galatians 3:13 KJV). Since Black people were perceived to be cursed, their plight was then to be ultimately lynched for revolt or non-compliance. To that end, lynching became part of God's divine plan and white slavers, and even non-white slavers internationally, were helping carry it out. Racism is a sly foe and moves under ethereal conditions, traversing generationally without any explicit verbal messaging. Racist behaviors and beliefs are transmitted across epochs without some people having any critical understanding as to why they think Black is dangerous, white is beautiful, or that the Jesus of the Bible was white. Those are but a few simplistic examples and the church, under a Christian brand, has been one of many unexamined conduits. A person does not have to be racially conscious to be adversely impacted by racialized and racist occurrences. Just as the hegemonic presence of male dominance, patriarchy, or genderism—elements of racism and the hand of whiteness often operate and occur without immediate detection.

Based on the lore of the Genesis 9:20-27 narrative, Ham, who was said to be the representation of African existence in the story, was cursed because he looked at the naked body of his father Noah. The exact specifications of the curse cannot be deciphered, and for whatever reason the curse was specifically directed at Canaan, the son of Ham. The curse is mysterious, but despite it being directed at Canaan and not Ham, it also indicates that Canaan would be a servant to his Hebrew or Semitic family. If the curse was followed based on its embellished story for racist purposes, Canaan and the people thereof would be servants or the employees of the Semitic or Hebrew people. According to the biblical record the people of Ham settled in Kemet or modern-day Egypt, but instead of the people of Ham being subservient to Semitic people, the reverse developed. There is a continual nexus in the Bible record where the Hebrew people ventured into Kemet repeatedly for food and resources because of famine and pestilence. According to the Biblical text (Genesis 12), it was Abraham that God called to leave his country and kindred, which he swiftly did. After he left he ventured to Bethel, near Jerusalem where the Bible records, "Now there was a famine in the land, and Abram went down to Egypt to live there for a while because the famine was severe" (Genesis 12:10 NLT). While in Kemet Abram/Abraham "...acquired sheep and cattle, male and female donkeys, male and female servants, and camels" (Genesis 12:10 NLT).

Being of Hebrew lineage it was Abraham that needed to gain from Hamitic resources and this became a continual theme and scriptural pattern. The Kemetic and Hebraic biblical nexus is unmistakable. With all the African and Eastern influences in the Bible, it is impossible to declare it the work or exclusive religion of the *white man*. In addition to the Abraham-Egypt connection, Joseph ended up in Egypt after being sold by his brothers and ultimately became *Chief Steward* or second in command to the Pharaoh—later meeting all the needs of his father, brothers, and family—as the famine was severe and they needed food and resources from Egypt. The Pharaoh said to Joseph, "You will be in charge of my court, and all my people will take orders from you. Only

I, sitting on my throne, will have a rank higher than yours. [41]Pharaoh said to Joseph, 'I hereby put you in charge of the entire land of Egypt'" (Genesis 41:40-41 NLT). From that point forward the family of Israel lived in Egypt and were enslaved by the Egyptians. Additionally, and across the biblical spectrum, Moses was raised and educated in Egypt (Exodus 2:1-10; Acts 7:22), baby Jesus and his parents fled to Egypt for safety and refuge (Matthew 2:13-14), and while being arrested in Jerusalem the Apostle Paul was mistaken for being an Egyptian (Acts 21:37-39).

If the story classically called the Hamitic Myth was true, the people of Ham would have never rescued or brought the biblical Hebrew or Semitic people into servitude. Despite the truth of the biblical story of Noah, his three sons, and their historical lineage; it did not stop some people from promoting the racist idea of the Hamitic Myth and the inferiority of Black and African people. Even J. A. Rogers said in *Nature Knows no Color Line*, "Before proceeding to the fifth stage in the growth of color prejudice let us endeavor to see why the rabbis made the 'curse' of Ham a black skin" (p. 11). He went on to say, "...Hebrew writings, (called Christians 'The Old Testament '), says nothing whatever of Ham or Canaan's color. It merely says that a curse was placed on Canaan. So, too, does the Old Testament. (Genesis 10:25). That the 'black' skin was a later addition is indisputable" (p. 12). This is introduced to emphasize the continual epistemic influences toward the creation of a postulated inferior Black race. Since misinterpretations of the Bible were used in the creation of Black racial inferiority, the church must be part of the dismantling and undoing of the impact of white supremacy.

Hughes and Allen (1988) in, *Illusions of Innocence: Protestant Primitivism in America, 1630-1875*, discuss Christian theology of the antebellum South, which positioned Noah as a "primal patriarch." They said, "...Southerners viewed Noah as a prototype for the patriarchal structure of plantation life" (p. 198). They continued, "That narrative—the story of Noah and his three sons, Ham, Shem, and Japheth—became the soul of the civic theology of the south" (p.

198). Based on Noah being erroneously theologized as a plantation owner or at least justification for the system, based on the assumption that God divided the races through Noah and cursed the offspring of Ham, Hughes and Allen continued by saying, if "...Southerners could show that the primordial man/patriarch had pronounced the doom of perpetual bondage on the black race, they felt they possessed an invincible case for black slavery, a case rooted in the primordium itself" (p. 199). On a more postmodern scale, Tony Martin in *The Jewish Onslaught: Dispatches from thee Wellesley Battlefront*, describes the proliferation of the Hamitic Myth in America by Harold D. Brackman in his work, *The Ebb and Flow of Conflict: The History of Black-Jewish Relations Through 1900*. Martin provides two critical quotes below to assist in tracking the development and spread of the Hamitic Myth:

> The association of Ham with the African race made this myth a major rationalization for the European enslavement of Africans. For if God himself had ordained that Africans should forever be hewers of wood and drawers of water for the children of Europe and Asia, then the moral dilemma of slavery was resolved. The slavemaster was simply doing God's will.... Christians have customarily borne the brunt of the blame for the Hamitic Myth, and they certainly are not without sin in this regard. Yet, the Hamitic Myth (that is, the association of the African with the supposed curse of Noah), was invented by Jewish Talmudic scholars over a thousand years before the transatlantic slave trade began. (p. 33)

The demonization and dehumanization of *Africanness* are presented in a systematic package. Many people are completely oblivious to the depths and destruction of racist constructions. For some, they uncritically normalize racial patterns, images, and institutions, despite their embedded reality in European supremacy. The Bible as an ancient text that existed during a time before racial and racist constructions, was soon used to develop a theology, sociology, and psychology of race. As presented by many scholars, theologians, and clergy, Tony Martin captured from the racist dissertation of Harold D. Brackman, about the Hamitic Myth, the perpetuation of Black racial inferiority, inclusive of racial elements like physiognomy, phrenology, and pigmentocracy:

> Ham is told by his outraged father that, because you have abused me in the darkness of the night, your children shall be born black and ugly; because you have twisted your head to cause me embarrassment, they shall have kinky hair and red eyes; because your lips jested at my exposure, theirs shall swell; and because you neglected my nakedness, they shall go naked with their shamefully elongated male members exposed for all to see. (1993, p. 35)

According to the Hamitic Myth and a gross miscalculation of the Genesis story, a direct assault was launched against Black ontology. African skin was deemed ugly, kinky hair inferior, full lips undesired, and male genitalia fetishized. Such systematic schemes of inferiority were also promoted through the church. It would be one thing for an atheist or non-believing Biblical community to manipulate Bible messages for the promotion of elitism and white supremacy, but it is a completely different monster for the church to promote or act under such influences.

Biblical manipulation plays a large role in the creation of racial inferiority structures. The seductive plot has been to erase color from the biblical narrative, followed by a campaign to denounce the significance and value of melanin across the globe. The postulated notion is that if people with melanin cannot be found in the narratives of ancient holy writings, then they must not be of any value. Therefore, still today, biblical films are created, casting every character as European in appearance, aside from those depicted in positions of abject servitude. It most often goes without question, with eerie silence looming. J. A. Rogers discusses the Egyptian-Hebraic colorized nexus by explaining, "It could be that some of the Jews before they left Egypt imbibed some of the color prejudice mentioned by Massey but it could not have been strong because they were dark or even black" (p. 12). He went on to say, "There is no doubt that after four centuries in Egypt the Jews mixed much with Egyptians and Ethiopians, whom their legends describe as 'black' and wooly-haired" (p. 12). Old Testament differences were not rooted in formations of colorism and pigmentocracy, they were about culture and religion. Both the people of Ham and Shem were darkly pigmented, so color was not the source of contention. In Numbers chapter twelve, both Miriam and Aaron complained to their brother Moses because he married an Ethiopian woman, but they were not upset because of her color. J. A. Rogers said, "Thus the main difference between Hebrew and Egyptian was not racial but religious…. Miriam's objection to the Ethiopian wife of Moses, Zipporah, was not on color but on religion and more likely on culture" (p. 12). Although it started long before the American institution and invention of chattel slavery, the promotion of the Hamitic Myth allowed people in the name of God and religion to act out in the most inhumane of ways. And this was just the beginning of the deceptive institutional development of American Christianity and its destructive chattel slavery justifications.

Christian Abolitionist David Walker and Slaver Reverend Charles Colcock Jones Sr.

While exploring the intersections between race, racism, American slavery, and the Christian religion, two men must be introduced. David Walker was born in Cape Fear, North Carolina in 1796 and buried in Boston on August 6, 1830. David Walker was an activist, abolitionist, and one of the first African men to challenge the institution of slavery using the Bible. Charles Colcock Jones Sr. was born in Liberty County, Georgia on December 20, 1804, and died March 16, 1863, in the same city. In addition to being a *slaver* and plantation owner, Charles Colcock Jones Sr. was also trained at the Andover Theological Seminary and Princeton Theological Seminary. David Walker wrote *David Walker's Appeal in Four Articles* (1829), and Charles Colcock Jones Sr. wrote *The Religious Instruction of the Negroes in the United States* (1843).

I am not sure if David Walker and Charles Colcock Jones Sr. ever crossed paths or if their works collided, but I would not be surprised if the urgency of the Colcock Jones Sr. narrative was not in some regard motivated by the four essays in *David Walker's Appeal* and the Virginia 1831 slave revolt led by Nat Turner. David Walker provides a glimpse into the theological mind of a Black man using the Bible to refute chattel slavery, and Charles Colcock Jones Sr. used his pen and power to draft a biblical blueprint, instructing slave-owners in how to use the Bible to subdue, control, and educate the enslaved. The abolitionist content of David Walker is liberating and salvific, while the efforts of Charles Colcock Jones Sr., under the guise of Christianity, are viciously brutal classic American white supremacy, imperialism, denial, and religious terror. As I shared some of the information with my congregation during our nine-week course, I still remember the somber mood that overcame the room. In the name of Christianity, how could anyone publish such grisly instruction?

Because of the promoted biblical hypocrisy, it was David Walker who said, "How can the preachers and people of America believe the Bible" (p. 41). About David Walker and his influence, James Taylor said in *Black Nationalism in the United States: From Malcom X to Barack Obama*, "Walker's Appeal, as an early expression of what would become a traditional mode of prophetic discourse in black protest thought, anticipates a body of criticisms that would span the nineteenth and twentieth centuries" (2015, p. 160). David Walker was clear that the Christian rhetoric spewed from the mouths of slavers was a mythical façade. He said, "But pure and undefiled religion, such as was preached by Jesus Christ and his apostles, is hard to be found in all the earth" (p. 35). For Walker there was a resolute contradiction between the words and motif of biblical Scripture, compared to their treatment of the enslaved. They preached and pontificated as if *slave* and *master* served the same God, but God had more regard for the whiteness of humanity, over the enslaved, allegedly cursed by the Hamitic Myth. Walker knew that the abuse, torture, and terror inflicted on the enslaved were ungodly. He wrote:

> He then, by his apostles, handed a dispensation of his, together with the will of Jesus Christ, to the Europeans in Europe, who, in open violation of which, have made *merchandise* of us, and it does appear as though they take this very dispensation to aid them in their *infernal* depredations upon us. (p. 35)

Walker knew slavers were violating the very book they professed to love and obey. Walker spoke of the American Christian brutality even in prayer: "But Christian Americans, not only hinder their fellow creatures, the Africans, but thousands of them will absolutely beat a coloured person nearly to death, if they catch him on his knees, supplicating the throne of grace" (p. 37). Walker also expresses his bewilderment with the Christian hypocrisy advanced by so-called Christian planters and slave-owners:

> Indeed, the way in which religion was and is conducted by the Europeans and their descendants, one might believe it was a plan fabricated by themselves and the *devils* to oppress us. But hark! My master has taught me better than to believe it—he has taught me that his gospel as it was preached by himself and his apostles remains the same, notwithstanding Europe has tried to mingle blood and oppression with it. (p. 35)

The 1829 writings of Walker uncover and expose the true spirit and ethos of Christianity during the days of chattel slavery in America. Christianity was not used to deliver salvation to humanity, because of dehumanizing theories like the Hamitic Myth; enslaved Africans were rarely seen as human, let alone religious brothers or sisters *in-Christ*. Enslaved Africans who converted to the Christian faith were still treated like an under-class sub-culture. The duplicity of Eurocentric hegemony was extremely influential, and its toxic malignancy spread and still has remnant effects today. The literary work of Walker seems unreal, an overreach, or embellished, but as a man who wrote while being free, he captured the ugliness of American slavery and the hypocritical essence of colonized Christianity. He said:

> I have known tyrants or usurpers of human liberty in different parts of this country to take their fellow creatures, the coloured people, and beat them until they would scarcely leave life in them; what for? Why they say "The black devils had the audacity to be found *making prayers and supplications to the God who made them!!!!*" Yes, I have known small collections of coloured people to have convened together, for no other purpose than to worship God Almighty, in spirit and in truth, to the best of their knowledge; when tyrants, calling themselves *patrols*, would also convene and wait almost in breathless silence for the poor coloured people to commence singing and praying to the Lord our God, as soon as they had commenced, the wretches would burst in upon them and drag them out and commence beating them as they would rattle-snakes—many of whom, they would beat so unmercifully, that they would hardly be able to crawl for weeks and sometimes for months. (p. 37)

Through "The Hands of Ethiopia" essay in *Darkwater: Voices from Within the Veil,* Du Bois wrote: "…It was through Africa that Christianity became the religion of the world" (p. 32). The influence of Africa on Christianity cannot be downplayed but that is exactly how Christianity was, and in many ways still is, treated within American Christendom. Despite the rich African contributions to Christianity, centuries before its manipulative introduction into American chattel slavery, by the time it arrived and was funneled through US constructs, the biblical presence of Blackness was erased and explicitly ignored by European slavers. Charles Colcock Jones Sr. documented his approach to abusing the biblical text and using it to control the enslaved. About the African enslaved reverend Jones said, "They lie, steal, blaspheme: are slothful, envious, malicious, inventors of evil things, deceivers, covenant breakers, implacable, unmerciful. They are greatly wanting in natural affection, improvident, without understanding and grossly immoral" (p. 34). He took the first-century biblical text of Romans 1:29-31 and attempted to apply it to the essence of African existence—similar to the Grecian conceptual development of the *savage.*

The Charles Colcock Jones Sr. excerpts are extracted from the 2006 book by Kamau Makesi-Tehuti, *How to Make a Negro Christian: A Reprinting of the Religious Instruction of the Negroes and Other Works by Dr. Reverend Charles Colcock Jones.* In 1832 Charles Colcock Jones Sr. twice preached a sermon in two Georgia counties to the Association of Southern Planters. The sermon was published as *The Religious Instruction of the Negroes.* In 1847 he published an appendix entitled, *Suggestions on the Religious Instruction of the Negroes in the Southern States.* Quotes from both narratives are captured from their reprinting in the Makesi-Tehuti book, *How to Make A Negro Christian.* The content of Charles Colcock Jones Sr. is sobering and difficult to digest, but necessary to understand the depths and pervasiveness of the racialized and racist historical American landscape.

This slaver published, distributed, and encouraged the use of his slavery business model, sending it to slave-owners, instructing them in how to use Christianity to control the enslaved. He viewed the enslaved through a degenerate lens and said, "Generally speaking, they appear to us to be without Hope and without God in the world. A nation of Heathen in our very midst" (p. 34). He also said, "They are an ignorant and wicked people, from the oldest to the youngest" (p. 44). Reverend Colcock Jones Sr. twisted biblical theology and hermeneutics for his own gain. The privilege of white superiority and imperialism allowed European slavers to lift the biblical narrative out of properly applied context, using the Scriptures selfishly and recklessly. Colcock Jones intentionally misapplied first-century contextual messages and transformed them into a blueprint to justify and condone slavery. Whether during Old Testament or New Testament epochs, the vicious treatment of chattel slavery was never biblically condoned. At best the biblical language elucidated an employer-employee relationship, or at worst an indentured servant paradigm.

Remember, it was James Cone that stated in *The Cross and the Lynching Tree*, "What I studied in graduate school ignored white supremacy and black resistance against it, as if they had nothing to do with the Christian gospel and discipline of theology." Emotionally he also said, "Silence on both white supremacy and black struggle against racial segregation made me angry with a fiery rage that had to find expression." Lastly, he asked the question, "How could any theologian explain the meaning of Christian identity in America and fail to engage white supremacy, its primary negation?" (pp. xvi-xvii). Although these Cone quotes were shared in chapter two, I am reintroducing them here to confront the theology of Colcock Jones Sr., who received his religious training from two prominent institutions: Andover Theological Seminary (1827-1829) and Princeton Theological Seminary (1829-1830). The crime is that he was able to leave both institutions with a backwards theology and biblical lens. When James Cone entered Union Theological Seminary in 1969 he was frustrated with the biblical silence toward injustice and the lynching of Black people. This illustrates the normalization and complicit legacy of biblical American theology toward the institution of chattel slavery. Andover Theological Seminary was established in 1778 and is said to be the oldest in America. The theological training of Colcock Jones Sr. did not challenge his racist ideas, it refined and reinforced them. This kind of racial conditioning, using God as its base, is what contributes to eerie silence.

As described in Acts chapter two, the church discussed and chronicled in the New Testament was established in Jerusalem around 33 A.D. Both the Old and New Testaments speak to a culturally Eastern world and audience, with a Western nexus later developed. When investigating or applying interpretive hermeneutics to the biblical narrative, context, culture, and custom are essential. The bible is a book of principles, but the applied applications must first be considered against their original intent. Grave mistakes are made when people fail to utilize proper biblical *exegesis,* but instead foment a literary *eisegesis.* The bible is an ancient book originally written in Hebrew, Aramaic, and Greek; thus, making modern-day sense of it requires assistance with textual criticism, systematic theology, and management of the three biblical covenant systems and their timeframes. For a seminary trained bible student, this would be considered basic information and learning. The racist biblical *eisegesis* of Colcock Jones Sr. illuminates the pervasive, explicit, and intentional racism entrenched in American formations of knowledge and higher learning. As an example, Jones took advantage of the biblical texts that used the terminology of *slave* and *master* and developed his version of colonized, not biblical Christianity. For example, he took multiple passages that were over fifteen-hundred-years-old (Ephesians 6:5-6, Colossians 3:22, 1 Tim 6:1, Titus 2:9) and twisted them into a slavers theology. He said:

> Servants be obedient to them that are your masters according to the flesh, not with eye-service as men pleasers, but as the Servants of Christ, doing the will of God from the heart. Servants obey in all things

your Masters according to the flesh; and whatsoever
ye do, do it heartily as to the Lord, and not unto men.
Let as many Servants as are under the yoke count
their Masters worthy of all honor. And the Apostle
Paul commands Ministers to Exhort Servants to be
obedient unto their own Masters and to please them
well in all things. (p. 53)

I will not exegete each manipulated passage above, but the
provided biblical Scriptures do not offer justifications for lynching,
whippings, murder, starvation, forced free labor, brutal mistreatment,
family separation, kidnapping, or any form of *chattel* slavery.
American slavery was developed out of vicious greed and the Bible
was deceitfully used to promulgate national and international
justifications. The mistreatment and reckless use of the Bible was
executed with blatant disregard for the sanctity of the Scriptures.
To refute a slavers narrative the Bible says, "...Thou shalt not muzzle
the ox that treadeth out the corn. And, the labourer is worthy of his
reward" (1 Timothy 5:18 KJV). In addition to chattel slavery being a
forbidden practice, it is a biblical violation and an un-Christian spirit
to force someone to work for free. The reverse is biblically stated;
instead of being brutalized for labor, hard work is to be rewarded. Paul
told the Thessalonian church, "For even when we were with you, this
we commanded you, that if any would not work, neither should he eat"
(2 Thessalonians 3:10 KJV).

Another Jones Sr. manipulated biblical narrative is the Philemon
epistle, a story that depicts an employer/employee relationship, but
Colcock Jones Sr. weaved the episode into a *master* and *slave* saga
with no contextual truth. Philemon is a short but powerful New
Testament story and if it was a *slave-master* and *slave* tale, under
Christian constructs it would flip the institution of chattel slavery on
its head. The story has three main characters, Philemon the business
owner, Onesimus, the on-the-run employee or servant, and the story
author and actor, Paul the Apostle. The story provides some clues

but Colcock Jones Sr., disturbingly distorts the primary essence. The narrative is about radical *agape* love and liberation, but Jones irresponsibly contorts it into an encounter of *slave-master* power, privilege, and control. Colcock said in summation of the story: "...And other passages of like import which any one may see for himself by consulting the New Testament; particularly the Epistle to Philemon, where it appears that the Apostle Paul sends back Onesimus, a runaway slave to his Master" (p. 53).

In the biblical epistle referenced by Colcock Jones Sr., the Apostle Paul wrote a letter to his friend and fellow-Christian Philemon. In the letter he described Philemon with glowing and affectionate terms. Paul acknowledged that Philemon was faithful, beloved, generous, and operated a church out of his home; which meant he must have been financially wealthy. After the commendations, Paul suddenly informed Philemon that he met Onesimus while in jail, and wanted to share the good news of their friendship. I am sure it was a shocking revelation to Philemon because he did not expect for his mentor, Paul, to meet his servant or employee Onesimus. The exact nature of the Philemon/Onesimus relationship is not biblically specified, but clearly it was conflicted and Onesimus rapidly departed. Paul said about his encounter and meeting of Onesimus, "I became his father in the faith while here in prison. ¹¹Onesimus hasn't been of much use to you in the past, but now he is very useful to both of us" (Philemon 1:10-11 NLT).

It is possible that Onesimus stole something from Philemon because Paul also said, "If he has wronged you in any way or owes you anything, charge it to me" (Philemon 1:18 NLT). While Onesimus was away from Philemon he met Paul, who taught and baptized him, making him more than just an employee or servant of Philemon, but his spiritual brother. Paul made a profound statement to Philemon and indicated that Onesimus was soon returning, but "Not now as a servant, but above a servant, a brother beloved, specially to me, but how much more unto thee, both in the flesh, and in the Lord?" (Philemon 1:16 KJV). The theology of Colcock Jones Sr. completely missed the compassion and persuasion of Paul. His view of biblical Scripture was through the schematic lens of a slaver and white supremacist.

The ultimate story of the Philemon letter is that of divine and radical reconciliation. It typifies a broken and violated relationship, rescued and restored by another, indicating whatever was stolen or misused would be completely repaid by the Apostle Paul. Paul basically said to Philemon, "I love you, you love me, and now ironically I have befriended and preached the gospel to your servant and he has embraced the faith." Since Philemon loved and was indebted to Paul, he was expected to adhere to Paul's guidance. Because of Onesimus' embrace of the gospel, Paul emphasized that he did not expect Philemon to just accept Onesimus back to their former employer-employee relationship, but as a spiritual brother and family member. Thus, according to the logic of Colcock Jones Sr., if this was a *slave* and *slave-master* narrative it would mean that once a person became a Christian, they could no longer be enslaved by a Christian *slave-master* because they would then be of the same spiritual family. Based on the research of Katharine Gerbner in *Christian Slavery: Conversion and Race in the Protestant Atlantic World,* the seventeenth-century slavers in Barbados understood the Christian slave-owner/Christian-slave problem. Some of them refused to baptize the enslaved into the Christian faith because they knew physically, religiously, and spiritually it would equate to equality and freedom.

As reported by Gerbner (2018), referencing the Barbados encounter of Richard Ligon, it was against the "Lawes of England" for a Christian to be made a slave. During this time in Barbados a slave wanted to be a Christian, but the slave-owner said, "being once a Christian, he could no more account him a Slave, and so lose the hold they had of them as Slaves, by making them Christians..." (p. 13). The slavers of the *Atlantic* understood the twisted theology of a Christian slave-master owning Christian slaves, thus they denied conversion to victims of enslavement, another form of biblical violation and *eisegesis*. The biblical misapplication of Colcock Jones

Sr., as a slave narrative—viewing Onesimus as a Christian slave is deeply flawed—but he promoted the biblical story as a slaver having their human property returned. On transactional levels, slavers of the *Atlantic* denied Christian conversion, fearing reduction of the slave population, while some American plantation owners encouraged slaves to embrace the Christian faith for manipulative purposes and control. Colcock needed a distorted view of the Scriptures to support his demented belief about the African enslaved and what they deserved. He said:

> We are so accustomed to sin in the Negroes, which in them appears as a matter of course, that our sensibilities become blunted; we cease to abhor it, and then fall into sin ourselves. We also associate every thing that is mean and degrading with the Negroes, and almost necessarily so, from their mean and degraded characters. (Makesi-Tehuti p. 57)

Kamau Makesi-Tehuti, in *How to Make a Negro Christian: A Reprinting of the Religious Instruction of the Negroes and Other Works by Dr. Reverend Charles Colcock Jones*, critiques the colonized Christianity of Jones Sr., but does not critique his flawed biblical theology. Instead, Makesi-Tehuti treats the biblical hermeneutics and views of Jones Sr. as if they were contextually correct, thus using it to condemn and confront the Christian faith and biblical legitimacy. If Christianity, the church, and New Testament are to be evaluated, it must take place under first-century contextual analysis; but biblical critique that begins during European-American hegemonic epochs under sixteenth, seventeenth, or eighteenth centuries is too late. Even an investigation of Christianity during the third century, with influences of Constantine is too late for proper Christian and early church-age analysis. Some people view the Christian faith as mythical and a carbon-copy of ancient Kemetic religious systems and stories, but their assessment starts with latter formations of Christian construction. Similar to the sentiments of Kamau Makesi-Tehuti about Christianity, Alvin Boyd Kuhn (2007), said in *Shadow of the Third Century: A Revaluation of Christianity,* "In actual world life a religion based on faith is pretty nearly always confined to people of lower and median rank, the intelligentsia for the most part having 'risen above it'" (p. 275). Kuhn went on to say:

> An immense proportion of those who in childhood go through the customary mill of indoctrination in orthodox groups, leave that early faith as soon as they attain the power to think freely and study historical culture. Nearly all students cast off the puerile reverence for the churchly authority. (p. 275)

Theology reminiscent to Colcock Jones Sr. prompts a negative visceral and intellectual reaction, preventing some people from exploring the authenticity of biblical texts. Colonized Christianity and theology is so over the top, incendiary, and silent, it fills people with rage and fury. With that form of biblical manipulation, the true essence of a first-century ethos is missed, discarded, and not given a chance. The rhetoric and plantation prescriptions of Colcock Jones Sr. were inflammatory. In addition to some of the critical passages mentioned that were previously perverted, the preacher and plantation owner also abused the premise of 1 Corinthians 9:11. Jones Sr. created a slavers version of Christianity and it permeated across Christendom in America. In an admonition to other *slave-owners,* Colcock said, about their use of Christianity toward the enslaved, "Did you remember their neverdying souls?—While they communicated to you of temporal things, did you communicate to them of spiritual things" (p. 61). The actual King James version of the passage says, "If we have sown unto you spiritual things, is it a great thing if we shall reap your carnal things?" (1 Corinthians 9:11). Passages eleven and twelve in the *New Living Translation* reads as:

Since we have planted spiritual seed among you, aren't we entitled to a harvest of physical food and drink? [12]If you support others who preach to you, shouldn't we have an even greater right to be supported? But we have never used this right. We would rather put up with anything than be an obstacle to the Good News about Christ.

Slaver Colcock Jones Sr. flipped the original intent of the biblical passage and transformed it into a toxic message that benefited the enforcement of colonized Christianity on the enslaved. Even if a person does not believe in the Bible, it is only responsible and fair that it first be understood in its proper context before someone fosters and promotes an erroneous interpretation. Many people have not actually read the Bible, let alone studied it, thus they can be easy victims of biblical exploitation and embellishment. The Apostle Paul wrote the *First Corinthians* letter to the Christians in Corinth. Paul planted the church and years later they developed a conflicted relationship with him, despite him being their religious and spiritual guide and advocate. Paul refused to accept money from the Corinthian church because of their immaturity, but he emphasized that he did have a right to be paid for his ministerial services if he wanted to use the option. In many regards the people within the first-century church in Corinth could be described as a mess. The main premise of Paul in the passage is that if the preachers provide for the spiritual needs of the church, the church must reciprocate by meeting the monetary and resource needs of the preacher. Paul said "...The Lord ordained that they which preach the gospel should live of the gospel" (1 Corinthians 9:14 KJV). The New Living Translation phrases it this way, "...The Lord ordered that those who preach the Good News should be supported by those who benefit from it." About this same premise, Colcock Jones Sr. deviously switched it in his preaching and publication, but without biblical understanding it can go undetected. He said:

> They have worn out their lives to furnish us with the
> necessaries and luxuries of life. They have supported
> us in ease and fulness; and yet after they have thus
> communicated to us of temporal things, we have
> ungratefully failed to make them partakers of our
> spiritual things. Are they debtors to us? or are we
> debtors to them? (Makesi-Tehuti p. 43)

Can you see how this passage and principle was distorted to
further promote racism, greed, white supremacy, and chattel slavery
in America? Jones Sr. depicted the slaver as infallible and entitled
to the benefits provided by the enslaved, totally rejecting the true
message of the biblical motif. The original premise of the first-century
church, coupled with love, was voluntary collective sharing, ministry,
equity, generosity, evangelism, and expressed salvation. The preacher
preached and taught the Word and the congregation made sure he
had food, clothing, shelter, and covered travel expenses. This is still
the case today, but Colcock Jones Sr., in sly fashion, tried to guilt-trip
other *slave-owners* into using biblical religion as a means of control,
indicating that since the enslaved built a financial empire for the *slave-
master* (planting, picking, and plucking in the fields, cooking food,
cleaning houses, nursing babies, tending to livestock, etc.), it was their
pious and honorable responsibility to give them the Christian faith;
a truly narcissistic and self-absorbed disposition. I am not sure what
Colcock honestly believed about his theology, but what he published
emphasized the duty of every Christian *slaver* to use the Bible to
control, conform, educate, or manipulate the enslaved:

> Every owner of slaves has an account to render to God
> for his treatment of them. O, how fearful will be his
> account, who, knowingly and willfully, will permit
> them to go down from the fields, and from his very
> dwelling into the bottomless pit, without making a
> solitary effort to save them? (Makesi-Tehuti, p. 61)

Colcock Jones Sr. also developed a conniving theology to justify the capture, subjugation, and corporal punishment against the enslaved. In addition to influences of the Hamitic Myth, with shifty victim-blame logic, Colcock affixed the burden and solution of violence toward the enslaved to them. He blamed their resistance and lack of compliance for the punishment and violence slave-owners launched toward their ill-gained perceptual human property. Whether lynching, whippings, or other forms of torture, it was the fault of the enslaved African. The mind, blindness, and silence of the European slaver in America and all of whiteness that supported the institution of chattel slavery must be assessed and critiqued. The eerie silence of the American white community in this area is maddening. The audacious words and model of Colcock Sr. are being highlighted, simply to establish a baseline for the historic and scandalous essence of racial hatred in America and the investigation of its lingering legacy. It has not been resolved. In *100 Years of Lynchings* (1998), Ralph Ginzburg continues the work of Ida. B. Wells and chronicles the horrible essence of lynching in America. I believe he captures the essence of Colcock Sr. and every other racist by indicating, "...The race-hater is inwardly a man who hates himself. He finds it necessary to shift to others his own unconscious feelings of guilt.... To his victim he unconsciously shifts his own shortcomings and guilt-laden desires" (p. 5). Colcock Jones Sr. evidenced this shifting below:

> The consequence is, they do not seem worthy of our regard, they lose all our respect, and it is no marvel if our conduct towards them is dictated by our opinion of them. Planters will generally confess that the management of them is not only attended with trouble and vexation, but with provocations to sin. (Makesi-Tehuti, p. 57)

> It is certain that the salvation of one soul will more than outweigh all the pain and woe of their capture

and transportation, and subsequent residence amongst us. How slow have we been to second the designs of God! How astonishing is it that we have remained so long ignorant of our duty! May we not hope that at these times of ignorance God has winked; but now commands all men every where to repent? (Makesi-Tehuti, p. 59)

Slaver rage and violent outbursts, codified as sin, were blamed on the enslaved. Even the capture and kidnapping of the African family was sickly explained-away as the will or design of God. Every Christian today must be aware of how Christianity was manipulated and used in building the institutional empire of chattel slavery and vast white generational wealth. Are there signs of white supremacy in your church or educational system? Does your church, religious center, school, or community unconsciously promote white imperialism or elitism? Do you or those you love practice eerie silence in the face of racial injustice, the root of every other form of American hate and subjugation? "Large slaveholders like the Rev. Charles Colcock Jones worked to comprise a Christian primer for slaves to instill teachings that were designed as a response to the portents of revolution, and to serve as preventive measures to any insurrection" (Makesi-Tehuti, p. 15). The Christian embrace of Jones Sr. was not about a genuine Messianic salvation and liberation, but that of control, greed, and a cloaked and uncloaked white supremacy. When you investigate biblical theology, are you unconsciously superimposing a colonized Christianity or are you applying the proper hermeneutics with adequately aligned cultural context, social studies, linguistics, and authorial intent? Or have you arrogantly or blindly forced the biblical context to fit within white American manacles?

Charles Colcock Jones Sr. believed it was his duty to give the enslaved the Gospel, but his motive and heart was malignant. For the enslaved he believed the Gospel was "entirely above their comprehension, both as to language and thought.... It is customary amongst us to entertain very low opinions of the intellectual capacity of the Negroes" (Makesi-Tehuti, pp. 39-40). It is common to read about dehumanizing and unintellectual characteristics related to people of the African diaspora, but when whiteness is dehumanized and de-colorized it is viewed as wholly offensive and cruel. It was the late Ishakamusa Barashango in *Afrikan People and European Holidays: A Mental Genocide* (2001), that said of Queen Victoria (1837-1901), she "...won for herself the critical acclaim of having been the cleanest woman in all of Europe because she took a bath twice in one year. Furthermore it is reported that the stench of Queen Elizabeth's court was unbearable to those visitors generally unaccustomed to it" (p. 5). Will Durant (1957) said in *The Reformation: The Story of Civilization, Part VI,* "Personal cleanliness was not a fetish; even the King of England bathed only once a week, and sometimes skipped... The same article of clothing was worn for months, or years, or generations" (p. 244). Through *The Historical Origin of Christianity* Williams said before the Greeks and Romans entered Egypt they did not have an alphabet, God, goddess, or gods and "were instead an agnostic, physical, psychopathic, illiterate, uncivilized European race of people who were not in-tune with the spiritual rhythm of the universe" (p. 73).

Colcock could critique the sensibilities of Blackness, but he refused to critique whiteness. Insult to Black ontological existence is normalized, but the critique of whiteness and the institution of white supremacy has always resulted in physical, psychological, and career assassination. As a free man, it is presumed that David Walker was poisoned and killed because of his push for the enslaved to rebel and fight for their freedom.

According to Jones Sr. and his slaveholding fraternity, Christianity was said to be the healing agent to reducing plantation crime and marital stability. Hoping to develop more efficient plantations for economic growth, he preached to his fellow slave-owners, "There never will be a better state of things until Negroes are better instructed in religion" (Makesi-Tehuti, p. 56). He felt that white presence amid

Black fellowship and communing would assist in control and proper behavior. He promoted specific principles and tenets that continue to eerily hover above churches and worship styles today. In the March 2018 edition of *The Christian Chronicle,* related to Church of Christ identity, Brad Schrum said "We have trained ourselves to convert people to our brand of religion, not Jesus" (p. 17). I am asking, which brand of Jesus and Christianity is that; that of the authentic biblical text or an unknowingly slavers version of Christianity? This is critical because as Doug Foster said in the same edition, "Churches of Christ have been self-assured, mostly white and often exclusive" (p. 15). Thus, while arguing and debating formations of Christian expression and elegy, perhaps most believers in America can only trace their religious roots back to the time of chattel slavery, while blindly claiming to live, preach, and teach the authenticity of the Scriptures—ignoring their theological, psychological, and sociological socialization. Charles Colcock Jones Sr. devised a cunning plan and model to religiously socialize and control the enslaved and they are still present even in racially and culturally conscious postmodern Christians and churches today (for emphasis in the narrative below I have italicized some words):

> (*f*) For permanent impression and for the promotion of intelligence and piety, the *public worship* of God should be conducted with reverence and *stillness* on the part of the congregation; nor should the minister—whatever may have been the previous habits and training of the people—encourage demonstrations of *approbation* or *disapprobation,* or *exclamations,* or *responses,* or *noises,* or *outcries* of any kind during the progress of divine worship; nor *boisterous singing* immediately at its close. These practices prevail over large portions of the Southern country, and are not confined to one denomination but appear to some extent in all. The extent to which

they are carried, depends upon the encouragement given by ministers and denominations. I cannot think them beneficial. *Ignorant people* may be *easily excited, and they soon fall into the error of confounding things that differ essentially. The appearance is put for the reality; the sound for the substance; feeling in religious worship, for religion itself.* (Makesi-Tehuti, p. 83)

As stated in previous chapters, the Bible was written as an ideal and until that ideal is reached there must be continual struggle for righteousness, justice, and equity—despite race, culture, ethnicity, and tribe. But what Colcock Sr. described in his message above is the essence of European hegemony in the formation of a dominating white church. He castigated emotion and passion in the process of praise and worship. Emotion and passion are clear embedded elements of expression toward God in the Old and New Testaments. Colcock was afraid of Black emotion so he created a worship style that reflected his culture and one that he felt would keep the slaves in check. I am hesitant to list encounters of emotional and loud praise in the biblical narrative because the list is long, but King David danced before God with all his might (2 Samuel 6:14); the cripple man healed by the Apostle Peter at the Temple gate called *Beautiful* walked into the Temple leaping and praising God (Acts 3:7-9); as commanded by God the delivered Hebrew people marched around Jericho seven times and at the appropriate moment the priests blew the trumpets and the people shouted, watching the walls of Jericho fall without a physical fight (Joshua 6:15-17); it was even God who said to Cain after he killed his own brother Abel, "What have you done? Listen! Your brother's blood cries out to me from the ground! (Genesis 4:10 NLT). Despite the promotion of emotion and feelings in the Bible, some theologians and lay-persons alike, have created a silent, still, and solemn worship experience as most sacred, when it is simply *white.* Colcock Sr. even used the construction of *Sunday School* to educationally and religiously control the enslaved (for emphasis I have italicized some words):

> When well conducted, these plantation-schools, in the course of a few years, produce most decided and beneficial changes over the whole plantation. Civilization, intelligence, manners, habits, conversation, are all improved. The scholars *learn lessons of respect and obedience.to their superiors;* they make more pleasant and *profitable servants;* better children; and when grown, better husbands and wives. The wild, half-clothed, boisterous, lawless rabble of children, are *tamed* and *reduced to decency and order.* If an owner looked no further than his own comfort and interest as an owner, *he would establish a school* for the children and youth on his plantation. Such a school assists the *discipline* of a plantation in a wonderful manner. (Makesi-Tehuti, pp. 99-100)

Much more could be said about Charles Colcock Jones Sr., and his influence on American Christianity, but I encourage every Christian and Bible student to thoroughly investigate his writings, comparing them to religious cultural customs and church-practices today. Religious control was sought as an act to prevent slave revolt and rebellion, but intellectually systemic racialized rebellion is exactly what is still needed today to disrupt and dismantle the destructive force of white supremacy—which is not an assault on white people— but a confronting of the discriminatory, unjust, and racist patterns it produces, especially toward colorized people. The fight must continue, and advocacy must be engaged as Taylor points out related to David Walker and his push for freedom: "But the black jeremiad as expressed in Walker's thinking imagined blacks would act as God's vicegerents in executing justice because of the impact of slavery on them. Justice here is understood as total liberation" (2015, p. 165).

Just like education, politics, and economics—religion (especially Christianity) has always been a complex component of American tapestry and fabric in the fight for racial justice and liberation. As seen in the radical 1831 Virginia rebellion of Nat Turner, some were caught off guard by the thirst for an any-means-necessary zeal for emancipation and freedom. James Taylor speaks of the passion that David Walker understood but Thomas Jefferson and many others misunderstood:

> Walker argues that Jefferson (and other whites) did not understand that in blacks' oppressed state 'there is an unconquerable disposition in the breast of blacks...they want us for their slaves, and think nothing of murdering us in order to subject us to the wretched condition—therefore if there is an attempt made by us, kill or be killed.' (2015, p. 162)

Slavers and plantation owners had no genuine regard for the welfare of the enslaved—they were merely property. Lynching became more common in the days of Jim Crow than during the epoch of chattel slavery because the slave-owner did not want to kill his human property. "The financial investment each slave represented had operated to some degree as a protective shield for blacks accused of crimes..." (Litwack, 2014, p. 13). After the abolishment of chattel slavery, white fury erupted, pushing evil men into savage acts. Illustrating the animal-like rage, "What was strikingly new and different in the nineteenth and early twentieth century was the sadism and exhibitionism that characterized white violence" (Litwack, 2014, p. 13). The feverish sadism of whiteness was captured perfectly in the 2018 Spike Lee film *BlacKkKlansman*, while the white men feverishly watched the 1915 film *Birth of a Nation*.

Invited by Booker T. Washington to speak at the Metropolitan Church in Washington D.C., Ida B. Wells said, "Lynching is nothing more than an excuse to get rid of Negroes who are acquiring wealth and property. In this way, they try to keep us terrorized" (Rouff, p. 52). It was important for Ida B. Wells to ensure people did not promote the racist idea of Black-lynching-justification, thus of the 728 mob slayings reported from 1882 to 1891, "no one had been accused of rape in nearly two-thirds of the cases. Most lynching's, she pointed out, were committed against blacks who had competed against whites or were simply "too sassy" (p. 46). Colonized Christianity was never concerned with racial liberation; it was about dominance, control, and economic greed. The gospel message was used as a manipulative force to subdue the emotions and actions of the enslaved. Even after slavery and through the days of abolition, white people felt safer if African people were also Christian. They perpetrated as if evangelism was an act of piety, converting free Black people into the fraternity of Christianity, but in reality, it was about white comfort and safety in the presence of physically free Black people. They believed that a connection to the church and Christianity would improve Black marriages, education, and conduct. Kendi captured the same sentiments of Colcock Jr., but decades earlier:

> The American Convention delegates believed that
> the future advance of abolitionism depended on how
> Black people used their freedom. Periodically, the
> convention published and circulated advice tracts for
> free Blacks. Abolitionists urged free Blacks to attend
> church regularly, acquire English literacy, learn math,
> adopt trades, avoid vice, legally marry and maintain
> marriages, evade lawsuits, avoid expensive delights,
> abstain from noisy and disorderly conduct, always
> act in a civil and respectable manner, and develop
> habits of industry, sobriety, and frugality. If Black
> people behaved admirably, abolitionists reasoned,
> they would be undermining justifications for slavery
> and proving the notions of their inferiority were
> wrong. (2016, p. 124)

Summary

In closing this chapter, there is an attempt to motivate people beyond eerie silence and the role of passive spectator. The grip of white supremacy places educators, clergy, parents, children, students, medical professionals, lawyers, celebrities, first-responders, presidents, politicians, athletes, and people of all races, in a clutch as if we are locked in a block of cement. The ability to challenge elaborate systems of oppression, as chronicled by Charles Colcock Jones Sr., can be crippling. The tasks of advocacy and resistance are exhausting and feel insurmountable. It is often assumed that the work cannot begin until comfort enters the building or more people join the fight. David Walker was one brave man who walked in faith, but his work and sacrifice continue to inspire and influence today. He decided to write and advocate despite the cost. Colcock Jones Sr. was a tyrant, but his single actions resulted in the continued devastation of countless slaves, even impacting present-day American Christianity.

Be inspired to work for justice and do not separate it from your religious and educational philosophy; justice is an integrated premise within the work of God and spirituality. In the *New Jim Crow: Mass Incarceration in the Age of Colorblindness* Michelle Alexander said, "Du Bois got it right a century ago: the burden belongs to the nation, and the hands of none of us are clean if we bend not our energies to righting these great wrongs" (p. 217). The complexity, weight, and burden of the racial problem is consuming to the point where "The people who have the *ability* to eliminate Racism, do not have the *will* to do so, and the people who have the *will* to do so, do not have the *ability*" (Fuller Jr., p. ix). Ida B. Wells, in a groundbreaking speech of 1892, with tears streaming down her face at Manhattan's Lyric Hall, modeled what it means to push through fears when it feels like you are standing alone, illustrating that it only takes one person to spark or transform a movement:

> Ida began to read her speech, and panic seized her. So much had happened in the past few months. The

lynching of Tommie Moss and the others, the threats
on her life, the loss of her business and home...all of
these made her feel lonely and afraid. Yet she knew
she must speak out for all those who had been denied
justice. Even as she struggled to gain control of her
emotions, tears began flowing down her cheeks.
Still, she continued to read what she had written.
(Rouff, 2010, pp. 48-49)

Like Ida. B. Wells, break your eerie silence and continue to read
aloud and share what is in your heart; even the vulnerable and risky
parts. Just as Christianity was corrupted or distorted, not in the
biblical text but within the pontification thereof, so does education
in America have a troubling legacy that we have yet to overcome. To
that, we now briefly turn our attention.

CHAPTER 6
AMERICAN EDUCATION AND RACIALLY DESTRUCTIVE EERIE SILENCE

> Ultimately, a school's culture has far more influence
> on life and learning in the schoolhouse than the state
> department of education, the superintendent, the
> school board, or even the principal can ever have.
> (Barth, 2007, p. 159)

Before moving into the depths of racial eerie silence in American education, it is fitting to evoke the spirit and potent educational critique of Carter G. Woodson, who originally wrote *The Mis-Education of the Negro* in 1933. Related to race relations, America, and education—Woodson was not a pessimist but a realist. He spoke and wrote with formidable force, providing didactic critique of twentieth-century white and Black America. Analysis of his American appraisal is vitally important to assess twenty-first century educational and racial progress since Woodson launched his 1933 indictment. Woodson said, "Real education means to inspire people to live more abundantly, to learn to begin with life as they find it and make it better, but the instruction so far given to Negroes in colleges and universities has worked to the contrary" (p. 29).

Woodson was deeply concerned about the Black mind in America and how it was educationally conditioned through enslaved modalities. He said, "This is slightly dangerous ground here, however, for the Negro's mind has been all but perfectly enslaved in that he has been trained to think what is desired of him" (p. 24). Related to twentieth-century educational constructions Woodson said, "The present system under the control of the whites trains the Negro to be white and at the same time convinces him of the impropriety or the impossibility of his becoming white" (p. 23). About "Negro education" Woodson said it "…Is a failure, and disastrously so, because in its present predicament the race is especially in need of vision and invention to give humanity something new" (p. 138). Much more could be shared about the premise of *The Mis-Education of the Negro*, but sadly he also said as a result of an enslaved mentality, "Here in America, however, we are ashamed of being black" (p. 203). The 1933 epistemology and scholarship is timeless. How far have we come?

The words of Woodson unapologetically keep race and Eurocentric hegemony at the forefront of the dialogue so solutions, healing, and transformation can commence. To an extent, but not fully, race is a myth and Harlon Dalton said in *Racial Healing: Confronting the Fear Between Blacks & Whites*, "America has a race problem" (p. 117). This problem is the continual and perpetual ill that has plagued American education since its inception. This racial problem often strangles efforts of forthright racial dialogue, and consequently, America has yet to resolve its racial and racist enigma. The failure to boldly confront and articulate race, its construction, and place in American interpersonal relations, suppress real attempts at authentic progress. Because America is built on white supremacist ideology—racism, and racist ideas—when people of color are successful it is because they have strategically navigated or sadly assimilated into the ideals of whiteness. As of yet, nothing has been powerful enough—with any real sustainability—to break the spirit, *will*, and institutionality of white imperialism. Within the American educational system, whiteness and white supremacy edicts are consciously and unconsciously taught as the norm, while antiracist forms of education are tolerated in pockets, but generate levels of reactionary scorn. Seeking to instill a comprehensive social justice and antiracist paradigm within a school building or district is like swimming against the ocean current. Present-day white supremacy is a formidable force; anything that boldly negates white superiority, especially in public educational settings, is treated with caution and is only allowed to shine temporarily. Additionally, if an antiracism curriculum or course does exist on the TK-12 continuum, it is an exception and not the norm. We can find some charter or even private schools that maintain or attempt to maintain an antiracist frame within their practices and curriculum, but public education cannot make the same claim.

Nestled within structures of power and privilege is where we find engrained manifestations of race and racism in American schooling. Although the colorized population is the majority in America, the largest single racial group is white and without effort or merit whiteness is granted the benefits of being in the phenotypic class of power and privilege. Based on the American populace and its relationship to educational design, most educators, superintendents, administrators, teachers, counselors, school psychologists, and myriad support staff are white. The racial composition of America highlights the problem and exposes the ease of maintaining an eerie silence. On multiple levels and in numerous educational settings, faculty and staff are predominantly white; thus, we are asking for white people to have bold and vulnerable conversations around race, moving into sustained antiracist action and praxis with other white people.

In my experience of working with white friends, peers, session participants, and colleagues, there is an overwhelming fear connected to approaching antiracist work. One of the scariest scenarios in public education is for white superintendents, administrators, and educational leaders to facilitate discussions with predominantly white staff. It is difficult regardless of race, but many white educators, possessing racial power and privilege, have yet to figure out how to comprehensively negotiate, balance, process, and confront that power as an educational leader. Many white educators find ways to avoid this grave responsibility of twenty-first century educational leadership. Until more white educators break their eerie silence and boldly enter the educational battlefield of equity, social justice, and antiracism—disparate gaps, rates, and racial under-service will remain. The literature, textbooks, and historical referents in public education reinforce the structure of Eurocentric hegemony and whiteness. In "Teachers' Critical Reflections on Cross-cultural Understanding Through Participatory Research" (1991), Bayless said: "The textbooks used in American classrooms need to be written that give complete, accurate information" (pp. 165-166). Similarly, Robin DiAngelo (2018) said in *White Fragility: Why It's So Hard for White People to Talk About Racism:*

> Although white racial insulation is somewhat mediated by social class (with poor and working-class urban whites being generally less racially insulated than suburban or rural whites), the larger social environment protects whites as a group through institutions, cultural representations, media, school textbooks, movies, advertising, dominant discourses, and the like. (pp. 99-100)

As stated by DiAngelo, the design, honesty, and institution of textbooks are critical and in addition to the influence of whiteness and Eurocentric hegemony, John Robert Browne II in *Walking the Equity Talk: A Guide for Culturally Courageous Leadership in School Communities* (2012), discusses the concept of *Cultural Hegemony*. He said, "Cultural hegemony, the opposite of cultural democracy, includes societal conditions where particular racial, cultural, or socioeconomic classes have inordinate influence and dominance over others" (p. 3). Related to scope and pervasiveness of the entrenched reality Browne II went on to say, "There are culturally hegemonic practices throughout the educational enterprise from preschool through advanced graduate school degree programs" (p. 3). "Cultural democracy should help facilitate equitable educational opportunities and outcomes by all disaggregated student groups" (Browne II, 2012, p. 28). Antiracist advocates who provide professional development to transform educationally racist and unjust spaces, do so while being exhaustingly pushed against the spirit and tone of vociferous institutional white resistance. Education was never established in America for Black, Brown, and other students of color to be successful. Just like the Bible was used to control the enslaved, most forms of education in America are insidiously designed to indoctrinate and control students. The holistic educational goal has never been about liberating the minds of all students, especially the underserved. There is still a dreadfully painful eerie silence in the face of educational curricula in America. The silence, whiteness, and sanitization of didactic instruction and literature are so pervasive, even some students and families of color are not aware of how they are impacted by and carry unconscious ideals that support white superiority and unconscious Black inferiority.

Many books have been written about the history of education in America and the struggle for educational and racial integration. One of the essential elements of slavers was to forbid the enslaved from learning to read. They were aware that a literate and educated slave would be a dangerous person indeed, because not only could they physically fight for freedom, but they could intellectually struggle for justice. Through my twenty years of working in the trenches of public education, I witness this fear and denial daily. There is a fear for America's educational institution to be honest about its racist and shackling history and arming students with the tools, texts, and knowledge to become radically and critically conscious. There is educator trepidation over what Black students will do when they learn about the depths of an America that has denied racial liberation, but graciously applauds and feels comfortable when witnessing assimilation. According to many race is a myth, but exposing the truth of racial function and its mystical construction is frightening across average American classrooms. For the most part, educators are ill-equipped to discuss race and its stimuli. To state it bluntly, American public education systems and educational institutions in general, are petrified to inform Black students about their African heritage and history, so there is a fixation on the slave narrative. And the obsession on the slave story is a brilliant plan of white supremacy because it has pushed many African students in America away from embracing or wanting to know about the depths of their identity. Because of that they settle for an eclectic racialized identity, formulated in America without any African or ancient American understanding.

If the basis of the creation of race is a myth, America and the world is forced to deal with the raw essence of humanity and the origin thereof. Because America was established on racist principles and practices, it is not built for or prepared to highlight Africa as the birthplace of humanity or to codify the resources. Instead, Africa is depicted as a place of undesired, backward, unintellectual savages. Unless some special teaching and consciousness has happened within the home, community, church, religious center, or from a radical teacher who unapologetically teaches from a critically Pan-African frame, most students, regardless of color, view Africa as irrelevant, dusty, and inferior. The plan of white supremacy to erase African ontology and existence has been supremely successful in public education. I walked into a fifth-grade class to participate in a restorative circle and I saw a large poster; the students were creating maps of the globe. I immediately noticed the depiction of the poster-size map on the top of the pile and Europe was double or triple the size of Africa. This is how white supremacy and dehumanization works; it does not have to be explicitly taught—over time, even with children—it is intuited. I wanted to take a picture of the map, but I did not want to make a scene in the class. Whoever the fifth-grade student was had already unconsciously bought into the socialized script that Europe is more important than Africa.

The necessity for racialized conversation and action within public education is not one of rhetoric; it is supported by annual predictable data. The same groups historically oppressed on American soil are the same ones underserved in public education. Howard said in *Why Race and Culture Matter in Schools: Closing the Achievement Gap in America's Classrooms,* "What is imperative about the groups who have been excluded from educational opportunities over the past several centuries is that by and large they are the very groups who continue to be at or near the bottom of the achievement hierarchy today" (2010, p. 11). About the concept and label of student underservice, Lindsey, Graham, Westphal, and Jew said in *Culturally Proficient Inquiry: A Lens for Identifying and Examining Educational Gaps* (2008): "Culturally Proficient educators understand that underperforming students have been *underserved* by our educational system. These educators know that conversations must shift from how students are *underperforming* to how all adult stakeholders are underserving students and families" (pp. 17-18). They went on to say, "This shift in perspective is the first step in developing a pedagogy for closing the gap, which above all must be pedagogy of caring" (p. 18). *"Historically underserved students,"* according to Browne II "...Refers to those of diverse racial/ ethnic backgrounds who have throughout the history of the United States been victimized by prejudice and discrimination in educational policy and practice" (p. 3). The business and profession of public education is predominantly white and radical change will only happen if people break eerie silence and develop antiracist and social justice actions.

When searching public education databases across the United States, specifically related to academic achievement, discipline, and attendance, patterns are crisply discovered to be historical, predictable, and pervasive. It is not fully a money issue either, it is about mindset, practice, and antiracist approaches. New educational systems, policies, and practices are implemented annually but, "More and more historically underserved students of color have become alienated despite new reform efforts, partnerships, funding, and legislation" (Browne II, 2012, p. 2). In chapter five we briefly investigated the impact of slavery on the Christian religion and church; we must do the same for the influence, nexus, and intersectionality of white supremacy on education. Despite the amount of colorized people in American Christian churches today, most of them still function or have features of white supremacy, and the same is true for American schools. Aside from the rare exceptions, even our schools that are predominantly Black, Brown, Native American, and Pacific Islander, have a dominant cultural theme of adult whiteness. It does not mean that the students are *acting white,* as the late John Ogbu discovered in his research, it means the cultural and compliance standards are rooted in whiteness. It is when students veer outside the code of whiteness that the power structure of the school squeezes them and their families, resulting in the predictable negative outcomes, inclusive of the school-to-prison-pipeline trap. From an adult-educator perspective, if people of color, especially those of the African diaspora, do not professionally assimilate into white cultural customs or navigate *whiteness* with wisdom and precision, we will not survive the profession.

Referencing educational, racial data predictability, marginalized and dehumanized groups impacted by *Manifest Destiny,* the *Mexican American War,* or ravished by genocide on American soil, are the same groups on the wrong side of educational data today. There has not been a recovery. The push for desegregation and the ability for Black children to sit next to white children in school did not cure the impact of racism in America or its schools. The allurement of whiteness and an insidious Black desire for acceptance by the dominant power structure created an unhealthy and unrealistic integration expectation. "As indicated by Adair (1984) Black people must be aware of the illusion of progress…. At the inception of desegregation, many Blacks believed it to be an ostentatious opportunity and resolution to ending racism and equalizing access to wholesome education" (Saheli, 2003, pp. 13-14). Ta-Nehisi Coates said in *We Were Eight Years in Power: An American Tragedy,* "For now the country holds to the common theory that emancipation and civil rights were redemptive, a fraught and still-incomplete resolution of the accidental hypocrisy of a nation founded by slaveholders extolling a gospel of freedom" (p. 64). The mechanics of integration and desegregation have been implemented, but many Black and non-white students remain negatively impacted.

When we investigate the negative categories and student-racial-rates for discipline out-of-class referrals, suspensions, expulsion referrals, expulsions, truancy and chronic-absenteeism, probation, arrests, or Individualized Education Plan (IEP) referrals and qualifications—African American students are almost always at the top. Typically, Latino/Latina students are second to the top, and Native American students are either the same as African American students or worse, but the population is often so small it is overlooked. That reflects the continued legacy of white supremacy in how Native American or *Indian* people were decimated. Concerning the positive school categories of graduation rates, A-G course fulfillment, Advanced Placement course enrollment, and honor roll, the same trend continues, but with Black students now at the bottom, along with Latino/Latina, and Native American students. It is predictable each year which racialized student groups will be at the top in every negative category, and at the bottom in every positive category. Contrastingly and still with precise predictability, white and Asian students fair at the top in positive categories and the bottom in negative categories. Despite the pervasiveness of the predictable data, an *eerie silence* prevails as if it is unseen, expected, or normal. Although the data captured by Tyrone C. Howard in *Why Race and Culture Matter in Schools: Closing the Achievement Gap in America's Classrooms,* is almost twenty-years-old, not much has changed in 2018:

> Racial disparities are more puzzling. Research has shown that even when social class is held constant, sizable gaps are still present between different racial groups (Jencks & Phillips, 1998). In other words, African American and Latino students in affluent school settings still lag behind their White and Asian counterparts; even more disturbing, some research has suggested that Black and Latino students from

affluent homes perform *worse* than poor White students on some academic measures. (p. 10)

The real purpose of education must connect to the struggle for liberation, which necessitates a classroom dialectic that delinks from the constraints of an epistemic rooted in Eurocentric hegemony—boldly fostering an antiracist blueprint. Can the unadulterated truth of America be shared, discussed, and critiqued in public education school buildings? One night I randomly looked through my daughters Advanced Placement English Literature textbook, and I was appalled. Every prominent white figure was sanitized and deified; this is how the institution of white supremacy remains unchecked and status quo. When will our American educational systems comprehensively begin to help underserved students identify the oppressor? Under common constructions, to do such is considered divisive. What some inside and many outside are oblivious to is that public education school systems are academically assessed on state and federal levels, inclusive of race, gender, English Language Development (ELD), disability, Foster Youth, homelessness, socioeconomic status, and more. Data related to Lesbian, Gay, Bisexual, Transgender, Questioning/Queer, and Intersex (LGBTQI) status is also starting to be tracked in various ways.

Schools and school districts are not just informed of how they are performing as an aggregate; disaggregated data is also assessed. Within that reality, the most troubling data is that which is racially disaggregated. After sifting through and controlling for every other factor, race continually magnifies academic and opportunity gaps. For example, if schools assess the educational performance of socioeconomically disadvantaged students as an aggregate, within that category African American students are often still at or close to the bottom. Having explicit conversations about all the other areas of concern are not easy, but they are easier than the *race* conversation. Race remains as the elephant in the room regarding authentic educational reform and equity driven approaches. Why does the racially predictable trend remain consistent year after year? I believe it goes back to what Dalton said at the beginning of the chapter, *America has a race problem.* Not only do we struggle to help students find out the oppressor, but we also fail to admit one exists.

Using California as an example and under the national Common Core frame, the California Department of Education now tracks every school and school district through the publicly accessible *California School Dashboard.* This monitoring and tracking tool observes the domains: Suspension Rate, English Learner Progress, English Language Arts, Mathematics, Graduation Rate, under the categories of All Students, English Learners, Foster Youth, Homeless, Socioeconomically Disadvantaged, Students with Disabilities, African American, American Indian, Asian, Filipino, Hispanic, Pacific Islander, Two or More Races, and White. Again, some people may question why there is a need to be racially aware and culturally competent instructionally, but those people are often unaware of the public education statewide and federal accountability systems.

Bountiful work is done around racial educational equity, but the same racist force that propelled America to its current status of empire, still acts as an undertow, firmly repressing efforts of justice. The problems and disparities have been crisply identified and codified, but denial and oblivion continue. The report by Wood, Harris III, and Howard, *Get Out! Black Male Suspensions in California Public Schools* (2018), chronicles the suspension trends of African American male students across California for the 2016-2017 school year. Although the data is specific to California, the trends are nationwide. The disproportionality in the discipline of African American male students is even more staggering when viewed through the lens of missed instructional minutes. We also cannot overlook the staggering discipline data related to African American female students. Using 2011-2012 Department of Education data, Kimberlé Williams Crenshaw revealed in her report, *Black Girls Matter: Pushed Out, Overpoliced, and Underprotected,* that Black boys are three times more likely to be suspended or expelled than their white counterparts, but

Black girls were six times more likely, and in Boston and New York they were ten times more likely to be suspended or expelled compared to white girls. "…The relative risk for suspension is higher for Black girls when compared to white girls than it is for Black boys when compared to white boys. As such, these data reveal that in some cases, race may be a more significant factor for females than it is for males" (Crenshaw, p. 19). Additionally, with the 2011-2012 data, "Only 2 percent of white females were subjected to exclusionary suspensions in comparison to 12 percent of Black girls" (p. 18). Using the same data, "In Boston, Black girls comprised 61 percent of all girls disciplined, compared to white girls, who represented only five percent of such girls" (p. 21). Related to California and 2016-2017 data, "…Black girls and young women have the highest suspension rates among all their female peers, accounting for 6.6% of all unduplicated suspensions. In comparison, White girls and young women account for only 1.5% of all individual suspensions" (Wood, Harris III, & Howard, p. 5). Staggeringly and related to New York student expulsion rates Crenshaw highlighted the following:

> In New York City during the 2011–2012 year, ninety percent of all the girls subjected to expulsion were Black. No white girls were expelled, and thus, no ratio can be calculated; but the magnitude of the disparity can be captured by simply imagining that one white girl had been expelled. Were that the case, the ratio would be 53:1. (p. 23)

Even though the data above is from the 2011-2012 school year, even as overall suspension and expulsion incidents decline, the racial gap and rates are remaining static with some variation up or down. Related to *Get Out! Black Male Suspensions in California Public Schools* and 2016-2017 academic year data, "While African Americans account for only 5.8% of the state's public-school enrollment, they represent 17.8% of students who are suspended in the state and 14.1%

of those who are expelled" (Wood, Harris III, & Howard, p. 1). Across California during the 2016-2017 academic year, 7.1% of students with disabilities were suspended, but 17.5% of African American students with disabilities were suspended. America still has not come to terms with its implicit bias toward Black America. Restorative Practices is designed to be a responsive tool and *way-of-being* that will minimize harsh and biased forms of school discipline that are disguised acts of punishment and humiliation, but even the use of restorative methods has a discriminatory racial component.

Allison Ann Payne and Kelly Welch (*Youth & Society*, 2015), reported in *Restorative Justice in Schools: The Influence of Race on Restorative Discipline*, "Just as schools with more Black students use harsher preventive and punishment tactics in response to student misbehavior, schools with more Black students may be less likely to use restorative justice techniques, such as student conferences and restitution (p. 543). This insight requires more exploration because in my own experience in public education, the more Black and Brown students exist in a school or district, the more the school implements practices and policies designed to control and restrict student action and opportunity. The whiter the school, the less control and restrictive measures are discussed and emphasized. Related to Restorative Practices and African American students in urban school settings, because the practice is misunderstood, it is viewed as not being harsh or punitive enough for Black student misbehavior. Reminiscent of the Colcock Jones model, the educator reaction is more about a desire for control than implementing discipline that restores.

In *Get Out! Black Male Suspensions in California Public Schools,* Wood, Harris III, and Howard offer eleven "research-informed recommendations" (pp. 27-33). I support all of the recommendations, and of them, I strongly suggest: Intensive, On-Going Professional Development; Analysis of School and School District Data; Assessment of District Existing Policies and Procedures; Provide Avenues for Student Voice; Prepare District Personnel to Understand, Identify, and Respond to Trauma; and Recognize that Cultural

Differences are Not Cultural Deficits. There are many scholars, educators, and consultants working in the field of racialized equity, antiracism, social justice, culturally responsive teaching, culturally relevant pedagogy, culturally and linguistically responsive pedagogy and more, to attempt to shift public education into an institution that provides liberating and transformative instruction for all students.

On a state level I do what I can through Saheli7 Educational Consulting and there are more prominent people that have personally impacted my life and educational advocacy like my father John Jeffrey, the late Laura Head, Dr. Stephanie Graham, Dr. James L. Taylor, Chris Lim, Glenn Singleton, Dr. Patricia (Patty) Bayless, Gene Barresi, Dr. Sharrokie Hollie, Dr. Noma Lemoine, Dr. Mildred Browne, Bev Hansen, Dr. Alan Young, and Dr. Eddie Fergus; also social justice warriors. Also scholars from a distance like Dr. Pedro Noguera, Dr. Brené Brown, Dr. Gloria Ladson-Billings, Dr. bell hooks, Dr. Cornell West, and so many more.

Despite the powerful work of these warriors and countless others, there is still just a small dent in the white supremacy portals of public education. From a private and charter school perspective, there is much more room to be exclusive toward a liberating pedagogy, but the grip of supremacy and hegemony on public education is suffocating. The struggle and fight continue. The same force and power that told Dr. Martin Luther King Jr. that he needed to become a gradualist and slow his approach and assertiveness for Black voting rights is the same sentiment toward those who tirelessly work to embed an anti-bias framework across the expanse of public and private education.

To compound the issue, not only is it a racial and discipline problem, but it is also an instructional malady. In *Teaching to Transgress: Education as the Practice of Freedom,* bell hooks described her education before entering desegregated schools as "counter-hegemonic, profoundly anticolonial, a sheer joy, and the place of ecstasy-pleasure and danger" (pp. 2-3). But upon entering desegregated education hooks said, "Gone was the messianic zeal to transform our minds and beings that had characterized teachers

and their pedagogical practices in our all-black schools." She said, "...
we soon learned that obedience, and not a zealous will to learn, was
what was expected of us. Too much eagerness to learn could easily
be seen as a threat to white authority" (p. 3). The quotes from bell
hooks serve as a blueprint and challenge to current public education
pedagogical practices. Educationally, bell hooks was raised in the
small town of Hopkinsville, Kentucky. The contrast between the
segregated and desegregated schooling of hooks is jolting and not
much has changed today. For all K-12 public education students today,
education should be counter-hegemonic, profoundly anticolonial,
a sheer joy, and a place of ecstasy-pleasure, and danger. Although
desegregation had its benefits, it sharply removed the Black radical
instructional love between the teacher-student paradigm. Although
segregated American schools were inferior in physical buildings,
materials, resources, and the number of school days, they were rich
in love, life, and critical consciousness. Carol Anderson in *White Rage:
The Unspoken Truth of Our Racial Divide* said:

> In one county in Mississippi, 350 black children had
> only three teachers among them. The low priority the
> government placed on schools for African American
> children was reflected not only in the paucity of
> resources but in the truncated school year as well.
> The academic term for black children in Dawson
> County, Georgia, was six weeks. (p. 45)

Related to the premise and public education of bell hooks in
Kentucky, we must ask ourselves, what is the educational experience
today, especially among African American students and others of
color? Counter-hegemonic and anticolonial instruction is not just
liberating for students of color, but also for the scholarship and racial
identity development of white students. Based on the schooling
experience of hooks she said, "Gone was the messianic zeal to
transform our minds and beings." The educational practices of

transforming and liberating Black students requires touching and stirring the soul and spirit. In addition to emancipatory contextual content, rhythm, cadence, movement, ethos, pathos, and logos are critical to the instructional milieu. About the spirit Marimba Ani said in *Let the Circle Be Unbroken: The Implications of African Spirituality in the Diaspora,* "The idea of 'spirit' is especially important for an appreciation of the African American experience" (p. 3). What bell hooks described about her desegregated educational experience was stale, cold, rote, and mechanical. For Palou Freire and as captured in *Paulo Freire: Pedagogue of Liberation,* wholesome education must force students to "...*confront the social, cultural, and political reality* in which they live. For Freire the words have to suggest and mean something important for the people; they must stimulate both mind and emotions of the participants" (p. 19). Additionally, Freire did not refer to his pedagogical structure as a classroom but a "culture circle" (Elias, 1994, p. 19).

Because of the ugly history of modern-America, beginning in August of 1619 with "twenty Afrikans aboard an English ship," arriving in Jamestown, Virginia, there has been a painful struggle to speak and receive the truth about the land (Barashango, 2001, p. 8). The denial and refusal of the American story surfaces in schooling. America has perfected the art of disconnecting traditional instruction from paideia. Second Timothy 3:16 KJV says, "All scripture is given by inspiration of God, and is profitable for doctrine, for reproof, for correction, for instruction in righteousness." The Greek word for instruction in the passage is paideia/παιδεία. According to Moulton and Milligan (1930) in *Vocabulary of the Greek Testament,* paideia refers to training, education, both on intellectual and moral sides (p. 474). Our schools are missing paideia, not religious instruction, but teaching that integrates with real-life experiences, guiding students through local, national, and international landmines. Paul instructed his mentee Timothy to offer paideia, and the same is valid for American educational systems. It is ironic that most American educators are not familiar with the concept of paideia. What hooks received in her segregated Kentucky school(s) was paideia, but that drastically shifted with desegregation.

Not only is paideia necessary, it is vitally important that students receive a praxis of liberation, by way of the development of critical consciousness. Freire said, "For without an increasingly critical consciousness men [and women] are not able to integrate themselves into a transitional society, marked by intense change and contradictions" (1973, pp. 15-16). Reflexively Paulo Freire frames the essentiality of critical consciousness and his "...central message is that one can know only to the extent that on 'problematizes' the natural, cultural and historical reality in which s/he is immersed" (Freire, 1973, p. ix). Critical consciousness is operationalized by Kieffer (1981) and Freire. "For Freire 'critical consciousness' is as a process through which Men develop their power to perceive critically *the way they exist* in the world *with which* and *in which* they find themselves" (Freire, 2017, p. 83; Kieffer, 1981, p. 7). I also conceptually framed it as "the mental turning point where African American men, women, boys, and girls begin to critically recognize oppressive elements in society and fight against them for social change and justice" (Saheli, 2003, p. 15). Additionally, critical consciousness is the crux of knowing who you are on the deepest level (self-identity) and acutely understanding how you are perceived. The pedagogical principles of Gloria Ladson-Billings, regarding students gaining the mastery of both home and mainstream culture, coincide with the explicated conceptions of critical consciousness. An example of a student assignment and project could be to have middle school and high school level students analyze, compare, contrast, and critique the 1921 Pan-African views of Marcus Garvey in his "Address to the Second Universal Negro Improvement Association (UNIA) Convention," the 1963 non-violent social justice approach of Martin Luther King Jr. in, "Letter From Birmingham Jail," (using as a guide, *Gospel of Freedom* by Jonathan Rieder), and the 1964 Black Nationalist views of Malcolm X in the "Ballot or the Bullet." This multi-level project would be an excellent entry into the world of paideia and social justice, also juxtaposing it with the fight and American resistance launched against the British Empire, as boldly proclaimed in the *Declaration of Independence*, ratified on July 4, 1776.

Transformative education, praxis of liberation, or *paideia* is instructionally vital and a civil right; it is the intellectual medicinal balm that can set students on the proper path to freedom. Due to the engulfing levels of racial and racist conditioning in America, schooling is a primary place where the delink from Eurocentric hegemony must occur. Melissa Weiner, in her potent book *Power, Protest and the Public Schools: Jewish and African American Struggles in New York City*, noted the distinction between segregated and desegregated education stating: "Though poor, these schools fostered a strong sense of community. Teachers nurtured African American children and provided them with safe spaces to learn, express their ideas, and develop the tools necessary to survive and succeed in a white world" (p. 15). As stated by Du Bois about American education, Weiner also points out "Negroes are admitted and tolerated, but they are not educated; they are crucified" (p. 16).

Too often Black children and teenagers survive public education as opposed to being inspired by the pedagogical experience. As a solution and frame, Geneva Gay provides a foundational structure for instruction that unshackles the mind and soul in *Culturally Responsive Teaching: Theory Research, and Practice*. By definition, Dr. Gay says, "Culturally responsive pedagogy is liberating in that it releases the intellect of students of color from the constraining manacles of mainstream canons of knowledge and ways of knowing" (p. 37). Culturally responsive pedagogy is the type of anti-hegemonic education bell hooks received in her Kentucky segregated schools. If you ask students today to explain their classroom experience, would they use the radical and inspirational terms bell hooks referenced, describing her all-Black school experience, or would they use the shackling terminology and sentiments she shared about her integrated experience? Gay also said:

...If education is to empower marginalized groups, it must be transformative. Being transformative involves helping students develop the knowledge, skills, and values needed to become social critics who can make reflective decisions and implement their decisions in effective, personal, social, political, and economic action. (pp. 36-37)

As hooks said, because "Too much eagerness to learn could easily be seen as a threat to white authority," some teachers retreat from gritty counter-cultural instruction that promotes social critique of racialized, political, economic, and militaristic agendas (Epperson, 1995). In his essay, "Culture in Question" Roland Barth defines an at-risk student as, "any student who leaves school before or after graduation with little possibility of continuing learning" (2007, p. 165). Both bell hooks and Geneva Gay speak to the pedagogical experience as the instructional spark that ignites a desire for continued learning beyond the classroom; it is this type of learning that transforms and transfixes life. However, because we have not resolved the racial and racist cosmology in America, our school systems unconsciously replicate the climate of the slavers plantation, peddling control and punishment. American education rarely liberates because we have a fear of telling the truth about the murderous and violent American narrative and the truth about Black global contribution and existence. Failing to be authentic with teaching and instruction that liberates, forces students to view school as a means-to-an-end, as opposed to a conduit of lifelong learning. The excerpt is lengthy, but the story shared by Roland Barth perfectly captures the sentiment and student perspective toward American schooling today. He said:

I remember visiting a high school just after the last spring exams and before graduation. As I approached the school grounds, I saw a group of students standing around a roaring fire, to which they were heartily contributing. I went over and asked, "What's up?" "We're burning our notes and our books," replied one. "We're outta here!"

On further conversation, I learned that these students were not occupants of the bottom ability group, but rather A and B and C students, many headed for college. That little incident continues to trouble me. I wonder how many students not so labeled are in fact at risk, with little possibility of continuing learning? How many graduate from our schools and exult in the belief that they have learned all they need or intend to know?

One reason why those youngsters burning those books, literally, and why so many other youngsters burn their books, figuratively, at the conclusion of our treatment of them in schools is that, lurking beneath the culture of most schools (and universities) is a deadening message. It goes something like this: Learn or we will hurt you. We educators have taken learning, a wonderful, God-given, spontaneous capacity of all human beings, and coupled it with punitive measures. We have developed an arsenal of sanctions and punishments that we inextricably link with learning experiences. "Johnny, if you don't improve your multiplication tables, you're going to have to repeat fourth grade. Mary, if you don't improve your compositions, I'm not going to write a favorable recommendation for college." "Sam, if you don't pass this next test, I'm calling your parents in." "Tom, if your state administered standardized test scores don't improve, you don't graduate." And so it goes. What the students burning their books are really saying is, "You can't hurt me anymore." But so closely have we coupled learning and punishment that the students throw one into the fire with the other. School cultures in which students submit to learning, and to the threats of punishment for not learning generate students who want to be finished with learning when they graduate from school. (2007 pp. 165-166)

"Learn or we will hurt you" is often the perceived young-person sentiment toward school and church, and it has been unintentionally set up this way by adults. Cornell West said, "An intelligentsia without institutionalized critical consciousness is blind, and critical consciousness severed from collective insurgency is empty" (1999, p. 13). The panacea for educating the youth of America through an antiracist frame is obvious, but fighting through the forces of white supremacy makes it a daunting task. As Weiner points out, "…Public education has historically been, and remains, a homogenizing, Americanizing, and assimilatory force that conscientiously sorts different groups according to their initial position in the racial and class hierarchies and replicates existing stratification" (p. 154). As an example of the power of white supremacy and its resistance to a socially just and antiracist educational system, Weiner also stated the response, through two different American epochs where Jews and Blacks pushed for educational equality: "In doing so, they critiqued America's system of racial nationalism and capitalism. But these longstanding racial ideologies and the racial ascription machine proved too resilient to allow for change" (p. 158). The racial ascription machine is still entrenched across American educational systems.

Referencing Geneva Gay, Culturally Responsive Teaching calls for instruction that validates, affirms, builds, and bridges—while also empowering, liberating, and emancipating the minds of students. Culturally Responsive Teaching "Is very explicit about respecting the cultures and experiences of African American, Native American,

Latino, and Asian American students, and it uses these as worthwhile resources for teaching and learning" (Gay, 2010, p. 36). Any teacher today that ignores the place and role of race and racism in our postmodern world should not be in the classroom. Students cannot be appropriately prepared to navigate the rigors of America or the world without a schematic understanding of the structural systems of white supremacy racism. Failing to do so is educational negligence. "Knowledge or education for Freire takes place when individuals recognize a cognizable object in a dialogical and problem posing process. The task of education is to get students beyond *doxa* (mere opinion) to *logos* (true knowledge)" (Elias, 1994, p. 64).

In addition to the work of Geneva Gay, it is imperative also to promote the Culturally Relevant Pedagogy approach of Gloria Ladson-Billings. As reported in *The Dream Keepers: Successful Teachers of African American Children,* she says this form of relational engagement and instruction is "A pedagogy that empowers students intellectually, socially, emotionally, and politically by using cultural and historical referents to convey knowledge, to impart skills, and change students" (p. 13). Similar to Gay, this style of instruction poses a challenge to teachers and educators across America, but it is essential. How often can we say the education students receive stimulates or inspires them in all the stated domains deemed vital by Ladson-Billings? In addition to the utilization of cultural and historical references to develop and enhance a student epistemic, she also suggests, as a best practice, that teachers do this through Academic Achievement or Student Learning, the development of student Cultural Competence, and Socio-Political Consciousness. For Ladson-Billings, this also includes the mastering of home-culture and mainstream culture.

In *Culturally and Linguistically Responsive Teaching and Learning: Classroom Practices for Student Success,* Sharroky Hollie introduces CLR saying, "Culturally and Linguistically Responsive Pedagogy is the validation and affirmation of the home (indigenous) culture and home language for the purpose of building and bridging the student to success in the culture of academia and mainstream society" (p.

23). Whether looking at the instructional strategy process of Paulo Freire, Geneva Gay, Gloria Ladson-Billings, bell hooks, Sharroky Hollie, or others, the link to exposing the ugliness of American truth is inescapable. Again, this is not instruction designed solely for students of color, although mind-altering, white students need this form of liberating instruction also, helping them break the *eerie silence*, understanding their privilege, while adopting and moving forward with antiracist advocacy.

The Black Educator Experience

Not only is it difficult for students of color, chiefly African American, to navigate educational institutions of all sorts, this is also true for adult educators. The racist landmine of American education does not only impact students, it also touches Black teachers, administrators, those in certificated or classified roles. I am aware that the profession of education is demanding for all, but I am compelled to call out the unique struggle of Black administrators and educators. I have witnessed countless Black educational colleagues and friends be inappropriately labeled, targeted, and pushed out because of their push for social justice or willingness to be a bold advocate for racial equality and instruction that is antiracist. Each time I am made aware of these occurrences, it forces me to ask the question: If this is the treatment adults receive in the profession, do students have a realistic chance? In my limited experience, Black educators are pushed out of positions and districts or demoted at a rate much faster than any other group. Similarly, the same way African American students are marginalized and disproportionately represented negatively in the data, Black educators have a similar, yet undetected trajectory.

White educators get away with behaviors and incidents that result in termination for Black educators and administrators. Although it is unspoken, Black educators are also required to have more education, degrees, credentials, and experience than white counterparts. Black educators and administrators develop informal groups to provide and receive counsel about how to navigate the racist institution of education when being evaluated unfairly or blamed for results that previous white educators could not accomplish. Most profoundly, I have seen the destructive and unprofessional actions of white men ignored or swept under the rug by Human Resource Departments. Black educational adult success requires wise and strategic navigation. It is unfortunate that we must do more because sometimes, in the end, it still is not enough. In the field of education, Black adult voice is frequently marginalized, discounted, disbelieved. Racialized encounters, laced with micro-aggressions, fueled by implicit-bias occur repeatedly. When Black administrators, teachers, or support staff voice concerns, especially related to race, they are viewed as divisive, racially fixated, or neurotic; this is the result of pervasive White Fragility.

Although I will not go into specifics, while white and non-Black educators discuss their affliction of adult compassion-fatigue and vicarious trauma, Black educators are suffering daily psychological and psycho-social injuries on the job. I am not suggesting that Black educators are not respected and valued; indeed we are, but we also experience more resistance, discrimination, barriers, and professional assaults than any other racial, cultural, or ethnic group. Additionally, Black women face deeper levels of discrimination because of the *intersectionality* of race, sexuality, and gender in the workplace. Kimberlé Williams Crenshaw coined the concept of *Intersectionality* and through her essay "Beyond Racism and Misogyny: Black Feminism and 2 Live Crew," in *Words that Wound,* she said, "Intersectionality is thus in my view a transitional concept that links current concepts with their political consequences, and real-world politics with postmodern insights. It can be replaced as our understanding of each category becomes more multidimensional" (1993, p. 114). Recently I concluded a keynote speech for an educational conference and afterword an African American woman educator approached me, acknowledging her termination at the end of the year because of her advocacy for underserved students. Black educators are not asking for special treatment, just fair treatment.

Navigating the institution of education is challenging and exhausting. The mentioning of safety is brought up with Black educators and administrators frequently. If a Black person speaks too loudly, exhibits too much emotion, or operates with confident passion, it is not uncustomary for someone to accuse them of being angry or suggesting they do not feel safe. Such environments place African American educators and administrators in a predicament where they must walk on school and district eggshells because they are not sure who will be offended. Related to White Fragility, DiAngelo says, "Whites often confuse comfort with safety and state that we don't feel safe when what we really mean is that we don't feel comfortable. This trivializes our history of brutality towards people of color and perverts the reality of that history" (2011, p. 61). The comfort-versus-safety paradigm is essential because the mislabeling frequently happens in the educational workplace. Related to the fragility of whiteness not being able to handle frank talk from Black people and people of color, DiAngelo continued by saying, "Thus, they confuse not understanding with not agreeing. This racial arrogance, coupled with the need for racial comfort, also has whites insisting that people of color explain white racism in the 'right' way" (p. 61). If adult Black educators face disparaging treatment, sincerely our Black boys and girls have massive mountains of duress to climb educationally.

Capacity v. Competency

Before ending this chapter, it is critical to address what I call the *capacity-competency paradigm*. The American institution of education suffers from deficit thinking. Deficit thinking is a continuing result of the racist foundation of America. Racism and implicit bias lead to harmful student assessment and aptitude misjudgments. Unconsciously, elements like phenotype, zip-code, linguistics, speech patterns, family structure, race, socioeconomic status, etc., are used to determine student ability. Attempting to assess student ability based on outward appearance or circumstance is a futile expedition. Within educational circles, it is common to brand professional developments as *capacity-building*; this is a misleading concept because although capacity can be built into a system or organization, it is impossible to grow capacity within an individual. This analysis of capacity may seem strange and counterintuitive initially, but the misnomer has created a problematic pattern while also contributing to the deficit-thinking enigma. Deficit thinking is the attempt to look at outward appearance and circumstance, thus assigning pity or blame to the person, followed by offering a depreciated level of school-work or a solution out of misguided sympathy. Capacity is a limitless ability within people, but deficit thinking and the genesis of racism in America and across the globe, established a system of human superiority and inferiority. We have yet to recover from this condition and educational platforms are continually plagued. Paulo Freire, historically one of the world's greatest educators, was impacted by teacher-deficit-thinking and is a salient example of capacity assessment failure. About the early years of Freire, Elias said:

> In the early years of his life, Freire experienced firsthand a struggle against poverty and hunger when the depression of 1929 struck his middle class family. The family moved in 1931 to Jatatao, where his father soon died. As a result of this situation, Freire fell two years behind in his schoolwork, and some of his teachers diagnosed his condition as mental retardation. He barely qualified for secondary school. Freire was deeply affected by this experience of poverty and vowed because of it to work among the poor of the Northeast to try to improve their lot. (p. 2)

The teachers of Paulo Freire misread his grief and affixed it to his learning capacity. The teacher of Paulo Freire had no idea he would one day become a trainer of teachers, but neither did they work with him from a place of resilience and rigor. Instead, they went into deficit thinking and labeled him with an intellectual disability. Despite Freire experiencing school outside America, the scenario and pattern are replete within Western schooling systems, especially where racial diversity is present. Too many children, especially Black children, are negatively labeled, cast aside, or placed in remedial instruction because of their energy, disposition, zeal, relentless exploration, questioning, and relational style—not to mention their attempt to cope with neighborhood violence, grief, family disruption, or other external factors that make life difficult. *Capacity* is not the issue for individual students, it is *competency*. Education is not about growing *capacity* in students, the goal of instruction is to help them grow in their competency, thus manifesting the depths of their inherent capacity treasure. Grief, poverty, hunger, and the death of his father profoundly impacted the childhood of Paulo Freire, but it did not diminish his capacity for greatness, resilience, and resolve. Along the way, whether his mother, additional family members, the community, future teachers, and probably a combination thereof, helped Freire grow in competency to overcome his setbacks and life-trials. He did not need help with capacity growth; like all children, teenagers, and adults, he needed help and guidance with competency to access his already-embedded ability and capacity to be great, resilient, and inspirational. This perspective is sorely missing and genuinely required in public educational systems, so educators, community, and family members can stop stifling the growth of young people because of what we believe to be irrecoverable life-limiting circumstances.

Asa Hilliard III in *Young Gifted and Black: Promoting Achievement Among African American Students,* said: "Language and cultural diversity, poverty, crime and drug-ridden neighborhoods, single-parent, mostly female-headed households may determine *opportunity* to learn, not *capacity* to learn" (pp. 133-134). This insight is revolutionary in the scheme of working through the barriers of white supremacy, racism and how they surface in schools. Many students in urban educational settings are forced to work through difficult life and educational challenges, but it does not mean they cannot or will not excel exponentially, based on their grittiness, resolve, dedication, and the love that surrounds them. Hilliard III also said, "Popular explanations for low performance of African students help to frame approaches to service that will ultimately limit the *capacities* of students" (p. 147). Students arrive at school with an insatiable desire for learning and success and adults in the school building must ensure that they do not allow personal bias, misguided compassion, or a need to save, to block student success, resilience, and capacity. Refusing to motivate a student beyond their believed capabilities can also be a racist and biased stance. Educators cannot wait for students to acquiesce to traditional schooling systems and approaches; Hilliard III said:

> Will we say that we have to wait until students change their attitudes, fears, and perceptions on their own before they can be taught? Will we call for therapy and counseling to resolve their problems of low academic self-esteem? The great teachers do not see it that way at all. (pp. 146-147)

Culturally responsive teaching and critical pedagogy are required in the process of helping every student access, illuminate, and ignite the latent brilliance within their capacity. Type of school, family, peers, or neighborhood are not the deciding factors in student success; in addition to social-emotional learning platforms, love, support, and relationships are the crucial aspects that shape student accomplishment, when receiving high-quality, culturally relevant, student-relevant instruction. Good teaching makes a difference, and eerie silence cripples educational achievement. Students who have fallen multiple grade levels behind can access the power of their capacity as solid, prophetic, and authentic instruction helps them harness their capacity. Hilliard said:

They were able to show that by providing three good teachers in a row to students as they took third, fourth, and fifth grade mathematics, and comparing them with students who had three weaker teachers in a row, the students with the good teachers showed achievement fifty percentile ranks higher than those whose opportunities to learn were obviously impeded by poor teaching! (p. 144)

Moving Forward

I recall Superintendent Gary McHenry sharing a compelling story about the first day of kindergarten for his granddaughter. He informed the school teacher or principal that he was entrusting his granddaughter into the gracious hands of the school and she was smiling. He said upon his return to pick her up from school he wanted her to still be smiling. That is a majestic benchmark for all educators. As the students arrive with a bright and inquisitive smile in pre-kindergarten, transitional-kindergarten, or kindergarten, by the time they walk across the twelfth-grade graduation stage, are they or will they still have a bright smile? The question is not are they smiling because they are exiting an institution in which some of them hope to never return, but are they gleaming with joy because of the love, support, guidance, and antiracist education they received, that will help them become and remain inspirational life-long learners? American public education, discipline, attendance, and instructional data are institutionally predictable, and time for systemic change is overdue. What needs to be done is evident, and the only thing standing in the way are the hearts of the American people and our willingness to confidently disrupt and dismantle racist and oppressive systems, replacing them with those that are full of love, socially just, and honest.

CHAPTER 7

IN SEARCH OF RACIAL IDENTITY AND THE ORIGIN OF BLACK PRESENCE IN AMERICA AND THE BIBLE: EXPLORATION OF THREE RACIAL AND GEOGRAPHICAL THEORIES

Black-Worth & Cultural Annihilation

The debilitating assault against Black civilization has been devastating; this is true on multiple levels, and one of the more significant and lingering results is the continual search for racial, ethnic, and cultural identity in America. Americans of the African diaspora, out of all other racial and ethnic groups in America, are the most dehumanized—stripped of culture, language, and religion. Many groups have suffered collective tragedy, trauma, and genocide, but most can presently identify and practice family, cultural, linguistic, and religious customs. Because of the assault and erasure of African contribution and ontology, many people in Black America are seeking the specifics of ethnic or tribal identity. This chapter will explore Black presence in the Bible and three theories related to Black existence in America. Although three theories will be examined, the ultimate question is how did people with significant levels of melanin and darker skin populate America? Who were the first people to set foot on American soil? The attempt to exterminate Black presence from global contributions and conceptions like the development of mathematics, literacy, science, architecture, biblical imagery, hermeneutics, textual criticism, systematic theology, the general essence of epistemology, and intellectualism, has forced some colorized people to distance themselves from African ontology completely—while others relentlessly search for racialized, ethnic, and cultural identity.

I recall a situation where an elementary-age Black student was denied access to school transportation because he was deemed dangerous. There was no other way for the child to get to school so I drove him to and from school until the district transportation department could be convinced to allow the student to return to the bus. Driving him home one day from school, I spoke with the student about his African roots; I was going to use it conceptually to engender pride, self-esteem, a positive racial identity-attitude, ancestral, and educational accountability. Within seconds of the introduction of Africa into the conversation, he immediately repudiated any connection to Africa. For this beloved student, Africa was to be despised; I know he was young, but he had come to know Africa through the lore of Eurocentric hegemony as America intended. About Black racial castigation Du Bois said in *Darkwater: Voices from Within the Veil*, "Everything great, good, efficient, fair, and honorable is 'white'; everything mean, bad, blundering, cheating, and dishonorable is 'yellow'; a bad taste is 'brown'; and the devil is 'black.'" He went on to say, "The changes of this theme are continually rung in picture and story, in newspaper heading and moving-picture, in sermon and school book" (p. 25).

In this chapter, I will discuss and explore some of the racial possibilities of ancient Black American existence, but also due to forms of unconscious self-hate, some Black people, typically described as African American, of the African diaspora, or as John Ogbu said, involuntary immigrants—some purport to be anything but Black. Based on research, some Black people claim to be of original Native

American heritage, while others make such claims, like the elementary-age student, that they are anything but African, being taught Africa is terrible, ugly, unsophisticated, and backward. I am suggesting that most of the negative within-race (colorism) reactions to Black racial identity by people of the African diaspora, are unconscious. Because of colorism, self-hate, and phenotype aversion, some Black people marry a spouse in reaction to features they hope to have depicted in their children. This is not to suggest that Black people are the only racial group that connects with a spouse, partner, or significant other because of perceived racialized genetics, but it does occur. Some people have married or had children with a significant other because they have lighter skin, straight or wavy hair, or eyes that are not black or brown. I remember sitting in my Black Psychology class at San Francisco State, when a white female student and mother of a biracial child randomly shouted, "I do not know what it is, we just want color." Because of racist socialization, some people have been conditioned to despise and fear African essence; they do not want children with kinky or tightly-coiled hair or dark skin. Colorism, within-racial group discrimination based on skin complexion, is a reaction to the institution of pigmentocracy, the global phenomenon and structural system of measuring human beauty and value, based on skin complexion—with white being the most desired. Engaging in this type of racial genetic attraction, partnering, and birthing are rooted in European standards of beauty and the vilification of African existence. Marriages and romantic relationships should be based on love and attraction and not an unconscious fascination with European and Grecian standards of beauty. Malcom X captures the superlative essence of maintaining a critical consciousness toward Black life and beauty:

> But the enduring appeal of Malcom's message, the portion that reaches out from the Audubon Ballroom to the South Lawn, asserts the right of a people to protect and improve themselves by their

own hand. In Malcom's time, that message rejected the surrender of the right to secure your own body. But it also rejected black criminals' preying on black innocents. And, perhaps most significantly, it rejected the beauty standard of others and erected a new one. (Coates, 2017, pp. 100-101)

The N-Word

The disparagement of African presence and beauty also contribute to the protection and silence of the illicit use of both forms of the N-word. Referencing America, both terms are toxic and highly incendiary in the English language. Some in the Black community support its sole use within the African American milieu, and others believe it should not be used under any circumstance. Although divided on the usage of the terms, the Black community is united in the position that white people cannot use the word in any fashion. African American usage of the racial slur has created grave levels of confusion that benefit the white power structure. Unique forms of African expression like rap, Hip-Hop, and comedy are riddled with the N-word and it has confounded many people. Even though most white people know they cannot use the term in demeaning or endearing ways, other groups of color use the term ad nauseam. When I walk on a school campus with teenagers of all races, the slang version of the N-word is one of the most common terms overheard. Whether a person is pronounces the N-word with "a" or "er" at the end, they are still racial slurs given to the African enslaved by white oppressors. The clumsy usage of the term has also resulted in white educators not knowing what to do or how to take a stand against the use of the word in classrooms or school buildings. Thus, the n-word is often tolerated.

Although inexcusable and also confusing, the repetitive use of the n-word in Hip-Hop is partially what led the white female repeating the N-word, after being pulled on stage by Kendrick Lamar, reciting the lyrics of one of his songs during his concert. He eventually removed her from the stage and the complexity and confusion of the situational etiquette must be considered. Either the eager white Kendrick Lamar fan was overtaken by excitement and uttered the word several times on-queue with the song, or she thought it was acceptable since she was being asked to rap along. The main problem with the continued use of the racial slur, regardless of how it is pronounced, is that Black people in America of the African diaspora are the only ethnic group branded with a racial slur that is currently used as a term of endearment, pervasively used by countless groups today. No other group in America has this unique situation and history. The racial enigma is the result of the lingering assault and conditioning of Eurocentric hegemony.

While debates about the usage of the N-word within and outside the Black community continue, it is essential to recall the message of Na'im Akbar, as presented in August of 1979 at the 13th Annual Convention of the Association of Black Psychologists in Atlanta. In his conference paper entitled, "Mental Disorder Among African Americans," he said Black "normative" usage of the N-word, "is a form of 'anti-self-personality disorder' (a manifestation of self-rejection and self-hatred), and it is in the best psychological interest of our future generations to eliminate its colloquial use altogether" (Akbar, 1979, p. 82). Although this statement was powerfully made over thirty-five years ago, it is more relevant today than ever before.

During or after some of my presentations regarding race, advocacy, social justice, critical pedagogy, and how to work with Black students, I am often asked by white educators how they should address the usage of the N-word in their classrooms and schools. The inquiry is frequent, and I recall a time, during one of my full-day seminars, a white or Latina elementary school teacher unabashedly opined her justification and allowance of the n-word by Black students in her classroom, because of its use in Hip-Hop, cinema, and various forms of Black pop-culture. When I asked her if students were allowed to use profanity in her classroom she was angered and appalled. She responded with a resounding "No"! Sadly, and destructively, profanity was unacceptable, but the n-word was approved because she deemed it culturally appropriate. Although most non-Black educators are not as reckless in their position regarding the term and usage, many white educators have voiced that they do not feel equipped or possess the authority to educate or encourage students to not use the term. The logical problem with the assertion is that homophobic, anti-Semitic, Asian, or European slurs evoke immediate discipline and even punishment. But the pervasive use of the N-word is excused and ignored. Educator silence toward student use of the n-word is negligent, toxic, and destructive. The eerie, sophisticated, and collective silence is the result of the global depreciation of what I have coined as *Black-Worth*, and because of it, groups have surfaced like Black Lives Matter to remind the world that Black lives matter too! The depreciation of *Black-Worth* has driven some darkly colorized people to distance themselves from an African ontology, while others are trying to critically discern the accuracy of their ethnic and continental origin, especially on American soil.

Africa, the Bible, and Blackness

The depreciation of *Black-Worth,* Eurocentric manipulation and the distortion of biblical imagery have forced many people to view the Bible as white Christian supremacy. According to the biblical text God said through prophet Hosea, "My people are destroyed for lack of knowledge: because thou hast rejected knowledge" (Hosea 4:6a KJV). Without critical biblical analysis, many Black people in America begin searching for non-biblical or un-Christian sacred texts that appear Eastern or African, because of the perceived whiteness of Christianity. It is not uncommon for Black people to be raised in a Christian church setting, but in most cases, the congregation was not prophetic, did not advance a Black liberation theology, and was silent regarding issues of injustice, oppression, economic depravity, and racism. That kind of stale, static, or impotent Christian influence established a cognitive dissonance that exemplified external compliance, but internal detachment—igniting a thirst for authentic spiritual relationship and knowledge. That longing was for a deeper connection with a God that does not ignore pain, emotion, or injustice, but responds with power and justice.

Because radical power was often missing and ignored in predominantly Black churches and every other church in America and abroad (unconsciously impacted by white Christian supremacy) as soon as young people could separate from forced church attendance, they did. Countless Kemetic, Pan-African, and Black-Nationalist scholars began their journey under Christian influences, but because of its silence toward Africa, Black people, and a movement of liberation—they ultimately searched for a spirituality that touched the psyche and soul. The blame for an eerie silence, lack of soul, and a tired prophetic Black experience in sterile colonized African American churches is charged to the Black community, but it was contrived through the support and influence of white Christian Supremacy. Just like American educators must awaken to social justice scholastics in the classroom and school building, biblical scholars and church leaders must place Africa back into the centrality of the cross and biblical text before another generation forfeits their opportunity of an honest look at the Christian faith. If you read the Bible or are connected to the Christian faith in any capacity, which version of Christianity is influencing you? Is it that of coloniality or that of an authentic first-century biblical ethos?

One of the fatal assaults of white Christian supremacy deception is that of biblical imagery. Through European imagery, Jesus Christ, an Eastern man that spent time in Africa and the region of Jerusalem, is depicted as white. Additionally, most movies about Biblical times reveal prominent characters as white. This reality immediately sends a message that whiteness is supreme. Without any explicit teaching and no pastoral challenge to the images, over time it becomes normalized, believed, and sadly promoted. At this point unconscious self-hate surfaces, creating the conditions for people wanting to be anything other than Black or African. The reality is, the Bible is rich in

African culture, custom, theology, epistemology, and intellectualism; however, because of the grip of white imperialism and the way Christianity was introduced and abused in America, the truth was rarely taught. Chancellor Williams said in *The Destruction of Black Civilization: Great Issues of Race from 4500B.C. to 2000 A.D.,* "Africa was naturally among the first areas to which Christianity spread. It was next door to Palestine, and from the earliest times there had been the closest relations between the Jews and the Blacks, both friendly and hostile" (p. 135). To get you started on your culturally responsive critical journey, we will now share some of those truths overlooked in churches of Christ across America, and the colonial, modern, and postmodern world.

The biblical student, baptized *convert*, or purveyor of the Scriptures must trace their Christian explorations beyond and before a slavers version of Christianity. One must trek back to a first-century ethos and spirituality; especially if you are Black or colorized. As a reference, it is important to note that Egypt did not turn lighter phenotypically until after 600 AD. Because of the slavers version, barbarism, and coloring of everyone biblically white, the popular schema of Christianity is that it is not about colorized people indigenously. It is critical to mention this because Eurocentric hegemony has hijacked Christian conceptions and images to dominate and dehumanize nations. The fallacy and distortion of the Christian faith is detected when religious fixation surfaces regarding biblically absent concepts and images like the Madonna of the Catholic church or Koranic emphasis on Catholicism.

Andrew Finlay Walls is a respected scholar and profoundly speaks of African influences on biblical scripture and Christianity. At the Dallas Theological Seminary Lectureship in 2012, Dr. Walls uttered powerful and chilling words that can delink a person from viewing the Bible through the lens of a Eurocentric hegemon. His lecture was entitled, "Two Thousand Years in African Christian History." Based on his lecture and shared research he said: "Africa may have a special place in the plan of salvation." About the firm place and contribution of

Africa and the Bible, he said, "The first reminder is that we are dealing with 2000 years and that some features that we see in the earliest African Christianity continue and recur over that time." With his British accent and hypnotic cadence, Dr. Walls said, "So we can claim that Christianity is indigenous to Africa. That there is a story which shows Africa historically Christian, primordially Christian; Christian not only before the white man came, but before Islam came." Walls is clear in expressing that Western Christian theology was birthed and influenced by an African theology, along with the disciplines of textual criticism, systematic theology, and the process of biblical commentary development. He spoke of a pre-Arabic Egypt, that was first of Nubian or Kushite people. He addressed the silence of the Western world regarding African biblical influences, but also said the Christian religion and faith "...Is indigenous to Africa, it did not come with a white man. Africa has a long Christian history and a story that will join up with a westward story and all the others in the kingdom of God." The tragic plunder and failure of American Christendom is that this information was not readily shared in predominantly white or non-white religious spaces and seminaries; thus, Black people in particular have felt like feeble guests at the Christian table.

Growing up as a child in the 1970s at the Uptown Church of Christ in San Francisco, under Minister James Milton Butler Sr., we had an active ministry in Addis Ababa, Ethiopia. Then-Assistant Minister, Billy Curl, now Bishop at the Crenshaw Church of Christ in Los Angeles, spent multiple years in Addis Ababa planting churches, establishing schools, building medical facilities, and more. After almost fifty years the ministerial relationship is still established and thriving. Around the age of eight or nine I recall J. M. Butler Sr. telling the church that the oldest Bible found in Christendom was discovered in Ethiopia. Information like that has remained in my consciousness and soul, spiritually, racially, culturally, and ethnically. It helped my schematic theological development, knowing the Bible and Christianity predate American formations of white supremacy and the institution of chattel slavery. There is more discussion today regarding the African-biblical-nexus and there is still tremendous ground to cover. Despite an authentic understanding of Eastern biblical theology, the Eurocentric commandeering of scriptural imagery eroded Black contextual presence, culture, and historicity.

How Africa Shaped the Christian Mind: Rediscovering the African Seedbed of Western Christianity, by Thomas C. Oden powerfully places Africa at the center of the biblical text and Christian thought. Removing the contributions and role of Africa from the biblical narrative and record vastly distorts the Christian message. Every Christian, theologian, and historian should wrestle with the question of who benefits from African biblical silence and what is the motivating purpose? Resulting from racism and formations of contrived epistemological hegemony, "Modern intellectual historians have become too accustomed to the easy premise that whatever Africa learned, it learned from Europe" (Oden, 2007, p. 56). Oden also said, "Cut Africa out of the Bible and Christian memory, and you have misplaced many pivotal scenes of salvation history." He went on to say about the African-biblical-nexus, "It is the story of the children of Abraham in Africa; Joseph in Africa, Moses in Africa, Mary, Joseph and Jesus in Africa; and shortly thereafter Mark and Perpetua and Athanasius and Augustine in Africa" (p. 14). In a 2014 Inter-Varsity Press interview, Oden said about the flow of African biblical influence, it was "A flow of intellectual energy from south to north, that is from Africa to Europe finally, and to America finally." Many have attempted to completely erase African biblical and Christian scholarship, but it is reemerging. Northern Africa, by way of Libya, Egypt (Kemet), and Alexandria were epicenter to not just Christian development, but textual and hermeneutical enhancement. As stated by Oden in the 2014 interview by Dr. Jerry Pattengale of The Green Scholars Initiative, "The African Christian tradition emerged right there in Alexandria and right in the middle of just a marvelous tradition of literary, philosophical, intellectualism."

Under the guise of eerie silence, the purpose and intent of African intellectual denial must be questioned. Forms of African self-hate and systemic Black-student failure is persistent, but what would be the comprehensive result if applicable students were routinely instructed and encouraged by the legacy of their ancestors? In the American conscious or *woke* community, Pan-Africanist Marcus Garvey is touted as a model leader for Black people and ideals, but how often is his Christian philosophy and belief system promoted? Not transplanted, but indigenous African minds are responsible for the birth of the European *university* system, Scriptural *exegesis*, *ecumenicism*, and much more. Through a forcefully concerted effort of whiteness and Europeanism, "There is, however, a kind of amnesia among historians about these matters. For various reasons they have lost track of the African underpinning these legacies" (Oden, 2007, p. 43).

Black ecclesia and clergy can be excused from not emphasizing theologically Black and African contributions out of ignorance, but once informed, it must be exclaimed. The pressure of white supremacy is a burden, but despite the lack of support, accurate historical biblical preaching is required. The Black church cannot remain silent about African presence in the Scriptures or geographical influences. Over the past seven-hundred years, African epistemology was slowly removed from the conversation of biblical axiology—over time developing into the notion that anything of critical influence or importance is from Europe. The historical erasure became true of most every ancient African contribution, whether scientific, linguistic, artistic, mathematical, Kemetic-pyramidal, architectural, anthropological, metaphysical, cultural, musical, or theological. Involving the African early church dialectic and theology, "The deliberative process that led to consensual Christian orthodoxy were worked out largely in North Africa. Yet the literature on the history of ecumenicism hardly mentions this" (Oden, 2007, p. 50).

In *The Cross and the Lynching Tree*, James Cone brilliantly and passionately confronted the silence of Reinhold Niebuhr and Thomas C. Oden exposes G. W. F Hegel. About Hegel and a "liberal bias" toward Africa it was "...the prejudice of Heglian idealism to assume that everything of intellectual importance that happened near the Mediterranean is really at heart European and therefore hardly could be imagined to have had African origin" (2007, p. 58). Some people start their American dialogues at the place of Constantine, but the primary patterns and styles of textual criticism and biblical hermeneutics toward "the apostolic writings were those hewn and refined in Africa before they found a home in Europe or the Near East. This is the sweet kernel of the grain that fed Christian intellectual history before Constantine" (Oden, 2007, p. 14). The Gospel of Jesus Christ according to Mark was written by John Mark; he was born in Libya, died in Alexandria, and may have also planted the first Christian church in Alexandria.

African Christian influence and custom is pervasive through the biblical text, but in America, it is referred to as the religion of the white man because of its manipulative use in chattel slavery and the refusal of whiteness to give credit to scholars in Africa for Christian contributions. It must also be noted that denial, rejection, and silence did not exist during the first few hundred years of the early church. African councils engaged in a dialectic process as early as 45 A.D., debating and solving thorny theological issues. The practice continues today, but often without understanding the roots of such discourse or ancestral and religious linkage. Starting American Christian discussions with the 325 A.D. Council of Nice is too late. "A century prior to the First Council of Nicea (325), these African churches were firmly established, courageously led, actively growing and vital worshipping communities.... They debated disruptive issues through rigorous scriptural inquiry" (Oden, 2007, p. 49). However, just to point out clear first-century church episodes in the Bible, notice the words of Luke the Physician:

> And a certain Jew named Apollos, born at Alexandria,
> an eloquent man, and mighty in the scriptures, came
> to Ephesus. [25]This man was instructed in the way of
> the Lord; and being fervent in the spirit, he spake

and taught diligently the things of the Lord, knowing
only the baptism of John. (Acts 18:24-25 KJV)

Additionally, it was Luke that penned the words concerning
the African and *Kemetic* training, education, and wisdom received
by Moses. In a biblically divine story, for the first forty years of his
life, as a concealed Hebrew, "Moses was learned in all the wisdom
of the Egyptians, and was mighty in words and in deeds" (Acts 7:22
KJV). Out of all the lands and cultural groups, God selected Egypt
as the educational training ground for His to-be-leader of Hebrew
emancipation and liberation. Egypt was instrumental and influential
in the Biblical Old Testament and continues in the New Testament.
At the birth of Jesus "...The angel of the Lord appeareth to Joseph in
a dream, saying, Arise, and take the young child and his mother, and
flee into Egypt, and be thou there until I bring thee word" (Matthew
2:13 KJV). The Bible continued by saying when Joseph "...Arose,
he took the young child and his mother by night, and departed into
Egypt" (Matthew 2:14 KJV). As recorded by Matthew, after Jesus
was beaten, mocked, and stripped of His robe He could barely walk,
thus they found a man of Africa to carry His cross: "As they came out,
they found a man of Cyrene, Simon by name: him they compelled
to bear his cross" (Matthew 27:32 KJV). Paul was confused as being
Egyptian; Luke recorded:

And as Paul was to be led into the castle, he said
unto the chief captain, May I speak unto thee? Who
said, Canst thou speak Greek? [38]Art not thou that
Egyptian, which before these days madest an uproar,
and leddest out into the wilderness four thousand
men that were murderers? [39]But Paul said, I am a man
which am a Jew of Tarsus, a city in Cilicia, a citizen of
no mean city: and, I beseech thee, suffer me to speak
unto the people. (Acts 21:37-39 KJV)

Long before the barbaric invention of the slave-master and chattel slavery, Africa was a valued part of the biblical text and history. Unfortunately, this discussion is rare in Christian churches, theological seminaries, within the Black community, or in Christian homes. Eerie silence remains and it is as if white society has not granted permission for the dialectic to comprehensively begin. Because the depths of biblical African influence launched in North Africa, looking toward the Mediterranean—but back toward continental Africa— some have declared the region white. Biblical imagery and cinema help to promote this fallacy. Historical Kemet/Egypt was the land of deeply pigmented people, but through invasion and racial-mixing phenotype, culture, custom, and ethnicity changed. Some people might be unaware, but concerning the racial landscape of Egypt, Robin Walker (2014) said in *Blacks and Religion*, "...The ancient peoples of Sudan and Egypt were in fact indigenous Black Africans. North Africa is today dominated by a people whose ancestors came from Arabia. They conquered North Africa in waves of invasion beginning in December of 639 AD" (p. 12). Because of the hypocritical racial constructions in America, if a person does not share the radical truth about history, one is then complicit in the promotion of white supremacy ideology. Kendi said about how this worked in America, "When Black revisionists chose not to revise, then they seemingly allowed racist studies excluding or denigrating Blacks to stand for truth" (2016, p. 267).

Robin Walker declares that everything before 639 A.D. in Egypt is considered African history. In his 2016 lecture, "Quick Overview of Religion in African History," for the Center for Pan African Thought, Walker said: "There is also an indigenous African history that is Christian. There were civilizations in North Africa such as Carthage and Numidia. They were Black civilizations, pre-Arab civilizations. One of the first Black Christian martyrs was a Black woman named Felicitas." We cannot separate Africa from first-century Christian origin, but many people that bemoan or reject Christianity rarely trace or affix their resistance to first-century Eastern and African

Christian conceptions. As an example, I participated on a panel concerning the positive and destructive elements of religion. After I shared my introduction, the panelist to my left began her discourse. I cannot recall all that the woman of color said, but two comments resonated. She said she was not sure if Jesus "actually existed" and then she admitted that she had never read the Bible. Particularly not true for all, but it is not uncommon for some dissenters to despise the Bible or Christian faith, without having read or studied its tenets. Christianity existed before chattel slavery. Before a Black person is ridiculed in America for being a Christian, the accuser needs to be aware of the African presence in first-century religious formations, and Black people who are Christians need to be mindful of the type of Christianity they are following. Are you following or critiquing colonized Christianity or that which is indigenous to ancient formations of the authentic Christian spirit and messianic God of love, liberation, and justice?

Hebraic Roots and the African Nexus

The pressure and dominance of Eurocentric hegemony makes this brief section challenging to write and question. One of the most curious aspects of modern biblical imagery is the depiction of most biblical characters as white, including the Hebrew people. Despite the fact that Moses and Jesus found refuge in Egypt, a land of dark complexioned people, Hebrew or Jewish people today are represented as white. The question becomes, when did the Hebrew people of the Bible become phenotypically white? When the phenotypic landscape of Europe is viewed, most of the people are white. How does this mesh with the Eastern and African geography and anthropology of biblical times? Because of pervasive forms of anti-Semitism, just surfacing the issue can be considered offensive. However, because race is a concept created under institutional dominance, dismantling oppressive and misrepresented systems requires stiff analysis. The ignored topic plays a destructive racial and spiritual role in the ethnic identity search and development of many Black people in America. When Black people consistently see images of biblical figures and white Jewish people today, the message is toxic, especially when there is no conversation about how the Hebrew people of the Old Testament vacillated into whiteness. Controversially, Rabbi Harry Rozenberg said in a lecture about white Jews potentially being converts to Judaism:

> Most likely there is something there. And most likely, maybe, that they were the original Israelites; and maybe that the Jewish people today, who are white-Caucasian people, came in a little bit later on. We know that some of the greatest sages of the transmission of the Torah were converts from Rome.

The cultural and racial annihilation of Black people is profoundly significant. Outside of Blackness, cultural customs are valued and celebrated, but Americans of the African diaspora are expected to assimilate. The American dominant white structure is more comfortable with mainstream Black assimilation than it is with uncompromised Black expression. While my wife was in college, a group of Black women started wearing their hair natural; the white female students were startled asking, "Is there a revolution?" When operating outside of mainstream American culture, Black-expression is frequently questioned. The impact is pervasive, and some Black people are unaware of its daily influence, and at the same time, it is hard for some non-Black people to conceptualize and emotionally feel the depths of the erasure and annihilation problem. Some people have referred to white people as *devils*, this literary work does not subscribe to such labeling and is concerned with biblical Jews transitioning into whiteness without explanation. Is the assertion made that the Hebrew people held in Egyptian captivity for over four-hundred years were white (Exodus 12:40-41)? Because the message of the gospel transcends race, culture, and ethnicity, what would be the purpose of appropriating the colorized premise of the original people of the Scriptures?

Black African people of Egypt built the pyramids, but some scholars sought to claim Egypt as populated and governed by Europeans. To work through a divine scheme of redemption for all of humanity, God selected Hebrew people as His chosen. He did not elect Hebrew people because they were unique or superior, God pre-destined them as the seed through which His ultimate blessings would flow, benefitting the entire world. However, as with Egypt, the elect of God is now subliminally illustrated as white. Addressing the issue and posing the questions is not about slighting white Hebrew or Jewish people; it is about promoting dialogue regarding a topic that has resulted in psychological, racial, and ethnic harm amongst Black people because of the messages that exude from images and pseudo-science. White supremacy refuses to allow linkages of dark complexioned people to the divine scheme of God because such a message negates the institution of white supremacy. Regardless of how the Jewish or Hebrew diaspora formulated over time and across Africa, Western-Asia, and Europe through a diversified colorized spectrum, the fact that mostly phenotypically white Jewish people are personified benefits and bolster the institution of white supremacy, marginalizing and dehumanizing Blackness.

Eerie silence prevents necessary conversations from occurring that quietly impact people racially and psychologically, starting with children. The erasure and silence toward Black contribution and creation have resulted in the depreciation of *Black-Worth*. Through precise and calculated imaging, Black people are depicted negatively, sending a destructive message to the world about the dispensability of Black people, aside from the few tokens that are viewed as exceptions and not an expected standard. The effort to annihilate, discredit, and erase Blackness is inconceivably powerful and systematic. Remy Ilona wrote the book (2014), *The Igbos, and Israel: An Inter-Cultural Study of the Largest Jewish Diaspora*. Through his research he explains the alignment of Igbo religion, culture, and custom with that found in the

Old Testament. He said, "Is it believable that there are forty million persons of possible Jewish descent in Nigeria?" (p. 15). About *The Igbos, and Israel,* Daniel Lis said Ilona "...Rightly points out that the modern day Igbo are not Rabbinical Jews (although there's a growing number of them) but that their customs rather resemble Israelite culture as described in the Five Books of Moses" (p. 10).

Addressing the complexity and malleability of the white Jewish nexus, Emma Green, in her 2016 *The Atlantic* article— "Are Jews White?"—quoted Emory University history professor Eric Goldstein who said, "Jewish identity in American is inherently paradoxical and contradictory." About this Hitler-persecuted group in America, "In the space of two generations, they've become one of the most successful, integrated groups in American society—by many accounts, part of the establishment. And there's a lot of dissonance between those two positions." Green said, "Over time, Jews have become more integrated into American society—a process scholars sometimes refer to as 'becoming white.' It wasn't the skin color of Ashkenazi Jews of European descent that changed, though; it was their status." In the December 2015 HuffPost article by Taryn Finley, she explores the YouTube video of Franchesa Ramsey, that exposed the process and whitewashed imagery of Jesus. Through it all, she surmised, "Ramsey's point isn't that Christianity is bad because it's been misused to oppress. But rather that white power structures excluded images of Jesus with a darker complexion to spread racial bias." Cognitive dissonance, racial avoidance, and erasure of this sort continue to haunt America, fostering a destructive eerie silence.

Whether Rabbi Harry Rozenberg was correct or not, postulating that he and other white Jews may have been later converts to the Hebrew faith of the Old Testament, the dialectic goal is not to omit or shame anyone, but to elicit and usher to the forefront, the method in which race and phenotype are used to discard and discredit segments of humanity—with a bold laser, aimed to destroy, distort, and confuse positive Black existence and worth. When investigating the domains and concepts of theology, religion, spirituality, education, race, culture, and ethnicity—honesty is required. The institution and idea of white supremacy have attempted to globally transform human technological, scientific, mathematical, archeological, linguistic, cultural, and anthropological advancements and evolutions to the creation and ingenuity of white people. Pulling off this feat of international Eurocentric hegemony has been incredible and one of the greatest deceptions of the world. Challenging the myth of white superiority has led many Black people in America of the African diaspora to search for racial and ethnic identity, relentlessly seeking the answer of how Black people populated America, even before the Trans-Atlantic Passages. To this brief investigation, we now turn.

How and When did Black People Populate Ancient America?

> Race does not exist! Is it to say that nothing allows me to distinguish myself from a Swede, and that a Zulu can prove to Botha (Prime Minister of the White Minority government of South Africa) that they both are of the same genetic stock, and that consequently, at the genotypical level, they are almost twins, even if accidentally their phenotypes, meaning their physical appearances are different? (Diop, 1991, p. 17)

Even though race has mythical implications (Carl Linnaeus even included *American* as a racial category, along with Asiatic, European, and African), it also serves as a scientific conundrum. In *Civilization or Barbarism: An Authentic Anthropology,* Cheikh Anta Diop in the statement above, challenges the notion that race is merely mythical. For Diop, there is more to it. Fully explaining away the idea of race leaves gaps regarding racially inherent hereditary medical trends and patterns. Diop said, "...When dealing with the transmission of hereditary defects as in the case of sickle-cell anemia, the notion of race reappears: sickle-cell anemia, genetically speaking, strikes only Black people, says the same science that denies race" (pp. 16-17). Comparatively, he went on to say, "In the case of thalassemia, another hereditary defect that afflicts the alpine race, or the White Mediterraneans, physical anthropology asserts that this disease attacks only the inhabitants of the Mediterranean periphery" (p. 17). After leaving a Kaiser Hospital medical appointment I noticed the following statement on one of my discharge documents: "Federal law requires that your Kaiser Permanente medical record identify your race because this information could improve your health care. If your record incorrectly identifies your race, please correct the error by informing a staff member or by contacting member services."

The fictitious creation of white racial superiority overshadows science and medical elements of race; thus, what we can say is that race has some scientific relevance, but it is the Eurocentric hegemony connected to it that is mythical. In addition to the scientific and medical sinews of race, there is also more to the foundational genesis of race. The April 2018 *National Geographic* issue, "Black and White," a special issue about race and in the Elizabeth Kolbert essay, "Skin Deep," she said, "Everyone has the same collection of genes, but with the exception of identical twins, everyone has slightly different versions of some of them." About the discovery of this genetic diversity, Kolbert also said, "That has revealed the second deep truth: In a very real sense, all people alive today are Africans" (p. 34). Not everyone is willing to make this claim, and many scholars have postulated a sharply opposing view. The power of white supremacy is designed to stamp out Black existence and worth.

Reacting to racial constructs, throughout this project I have used the terms Black, African American, *colorized*, of the African diaspora, and melanated to refer to people of the darkest complexion and those who have descended from them. Some people readily described as African American, do not agree with the African or African American label. By this point in this book, I have shared enough to make this potentially controversial statement. I consider my indigenous ethnic and racial roots as originating with the continent of Africa, but I am still investigating the depths of my identity and how people who look like me first inhabited America. For people with deep melanin, comprehensively impacted by Eurocentric hegemony, there is a search for authentic ethnic and racial identity. I am aware that some Black people believe they arrived in America through the Trans-Atlantic Passage, original inhabitants of West Africa, while others have concluded they too arrived in America through the Trans-Atlantic Passage and enslavement trade, but from the Hebraic diaspora that scattered into West Africa, escaping persecution. There are others who believe they are of Kemetic lineage and independently traveled to the Americas, influencing Ancient American people. Lastly there is another group that believes the Trans-Atlantic enslavement trade occurred in reverse and that the Kemetic and Hebrew story originates in America. Through the remainder of this chapter, I will briefly explore the three theories, related to the ethnic and racial identity of darker melanated people and how they populated North America. The three theories of exploration are:

1. Common West African Diaspora Theory: African natives were kidnapped from West Africa and brought to America, through the Trans-Atlantic Passage and enslavement trade.

2. West African and Ancient Egypt Theory: Natives of West Africa and Kemet (Ancient Egypt), with their invented sailing technology, navigated the seas to America on African-built ships. Once in America, they influenced the indigenousness ancient Mexican/Olmec people.

3. Indigenous Ancient American Theory: Deeply melanated people were the first inhabitants Ancient America.

Common West African Diaspora Theory

Most people typically classified as Black or African American believe they ended up in America through the Trans-Atlantic Passage and enslavement-trade, beginning in West Africa. This is the traditional and most common view of African American involuntary existence in America. Through this perspective, many exclaim a deep connection to Ghana as their West African motherland and nation. This is also the frequent theory taught in most American schools. There are countless books written on the West African-to-American enslavement experience, and it is often unquestioned or critically critiqued. Because of the commonality of this view and theory, I will not spend much time extrapolating it. Although it is thoroughly taught in schools, still with a biased slant, it is also where Black history in America is stuck. The African enslavement narrative in America overshadows the history of Black people across the continent of Africa, thousands of years before the Middle-Passage.

Beginning in the fifteenth-century, African people were captured and sold into a system of slavery and forced migration across the world. From African coasts Black people were shackled and boarded on ships, sailing to the Americas, Caribbean, India, Europe, and more. For the European, African enslavement was a business with brutal and barbaric outcomes. Millions of Africans were sold and born into slavery over hundreds of years and many people believe this is the primary way African people ended up on American soil. Not everyone believes this position; some postulate African people sailed to America hundreds of years before Columbus and the Trans-Atlantic enslavement voyages.

Said by Asa Hilliard, "There was a brutal destruction of African civilizations, even in the name of Christ, and savage murder and enslavement of approximately 200 million people. This barbarism was unequaled in written world history" (1995, p. 52). Browder (1992) said, "For more than 350 years, tens of millions of Africans were torn away from their homeland, enslaved and systematically stripped of their name, culture, and historical memory" (pp. 13-14). He went on to say, "Today, thousands of African Americans are awakening from a state of cultural amnesia and are discovering that Africans possessed a mighty history prior to their enslavement and colonization" (1992,

p. 14). The Kanye West comments during his May 1, 2018, TMZ interview were reckless and unwise, as he postulated that 400 years of slavery was a choice made by Black people. As captured by Mahita Gajanan of *Time*, Kanye West said, "When you hear about slavery for 400 years — for 400 years? That sounds like a choice. Like, you was there for 400 years and it's all of y'all? It's like we're mentally in prison." African enslavement, subjugation, rape, murder, and family separation on American soil was not a choice.

Despite the horror, evidence, and scholarship, there is a faction of people postulating that chattel slavery never occurred in America, or transpired in reverse, with indigenous Africans in America being captured and relocated around the globe, subjugated as slaves. To help demystify such a belief it is necessary to understand that established on December 19, 2003, was the *National Museum of African American History and Culture*, which opened in Washington D.C. on the National Mall, September 24, 2016. This breathtaking museum captures the spirit, climate, brutality, murder, and European terrorism inflicted on Black people in America. Additionally, in Montgomery, Alabama *The National Memorial for Peace and Justice* opened on April 26, 2018 and is "dedicated to the victims of American white supremacy. And it demands a reckoning with one of the nation's least recognized atrocities: the lynching of thousands of black people in a decades-long campaign of racist terror" (Robertson, 2018). About the visual experience, Beth Harpaz of *The Washington Post* said, "... Markers begin at eye level, then gradually move overhead, evoking the specter of hanging bodies. Some of the killings are described in detail: Victims were lynched for asking for a glass of water, for voting, for testifying against a white man." Chattel slavery in America was real and all its deadly Jim Crow, civil rights, and mass-incarceration lingering exploits.

West African and Ancient Egypt Theory

> The people who were host to these Negro-African
> figures are known as the Olmecs. At the sacred center
> of the Olmec culture—La Venta—about eighteen
> miles inland from the Gulf of Mexico, which flows
> into the Atlantic, there stood four colossal Negroid
> heads, six to nine feet high, weighing up to forty tons
> each. (Van Sertima, 2003, p. 32)

Without nullifying the Trans-Atlantic Passage enslavement trade, some scholars have concluded that Black people entered America long before slavery. *They Came Before Columbus: The African Presence in Ancient America,* written by Ivan Van Sertima makes the documented claim that African voyagers sailed to the Americas and influenced the rich ancient American culture already in existence. Van Sertima does not conclude that Africans were the first to populate America, but that upon arrival they heavily influenced it. This does not negate the African Middle-Passage, it asserts the influential presence of Blackness in America before slavery. Van Sertima said, "...Some of the Negroid stone heads found among the Olmecs and in other parts of Mexico and Central America are from as early as 800 to 700 B.C. Clearly American history has to be reconstructed to account for this irrefutable piece of archaeological data" (p. 26). Van Sertima also said of his research:

> When in 1862 a colossal granite head of a Negro
> was found in the Canton of Tuxtla, near the place
> where the most ancient of pre-Columbian statuettes
> were discovered, the historian Orozco y Berra
> declared in his *History of the Conquest of Mexico* that
> there was bound to be an important and intimate
> relationship between Mexicans and Africans in the
> pre-Columbian past. (p. 26)

Because this information does not typically traverse mainstream channels of American education, some people of the African diaspora in America search for racial identity outside of African inspiration. Kemetic, West African, and Malian influences, voyages, and global contributions are ignored. Intense, overindulged, and often inaccurate information is shared in classrooms about Columbus, even an American holiday exists in his honor, but it would be rare to walk into a classroom or turn on the television and hear honest discussion about ancient African maritime, seafaring, and ship and boat building. All scholars do not agree that the Olmec stones possess African facial features, but the research of Van Sertima is convincing. He said, "A head from the post-Classic period stares at us across five centuries with a lifelike power and directness," and went on to say, "This is clearly the type of African who came here in 1310 in the expeditionary fleet of Abubakari the Second of Mali" (p. 27). Such research findings force America and the world to confront the eerie silence toward African existence and ontology. The traditional view is that Black people in America (involuntary immigrants according to John Ogbu) are descendants of the enslaved, however, if the research of Van Sertima is correct, not all Black people in America are descendants of those captured and born into chattel slavery. Continued research is required in this area and may never be fully understood, but what are the nuanced patterns, trends, and trajectories of African people who voyaged to America freely, compared with those who endured the traumatic Middle-Passage?

Many of the African navigators that sailed from the West African empire through the Atlantic Ocean never returned to Mali. Destined and committed to voyage to America, Abubakari the Second, in 1311, "conferred the power of the regency on his brother, Kankan Musa" (Van Sertima, p. 49). This was done to ensure the kingdom would be secure in case King Abubakari the Second never returned. Van Sertima said, "Then one day, dressed in a flowing white robe and a jeweled turban, he took leave of Mali and set out with his fleet down the Senegal, heading west across the Atlantic, never to return" (p.

50). Also according to Van Sertima and others, there is evidence that some Mali voyagers accidentally landed in Mexico and this could explain the Negroid heads, "which represent Africans appearing on the plateau of Mexico and other parts of Mesoamerica just before and after Christ" (p. 28). "In all, eleven colossal Negroid heads appear in the Olmec heartland—four at La Vent, five at San Lorenzo and two at Tres Zapotes in southern Vera Cruz" (p. 33). The number of stone-images is not refuted, what is debated is whether the discovered images are African or Mexican. In the next section this will compel us to investigate and integrate the work of David Imhotep, *The First Americans Were Africans Revisited*.

Van Sertima does not claim Africans were the first to populate America, which included Mexico before Manifest Destiny and the Mexican American war, but he does acknowledge that it only took a few Africans to influence Mexican culture and custom upon arrival. Collective Black influence of this nature remains true today. Anytime Black people exist in society and occupy space, our cultural rhythm, cadence, and swag is coveted and adopted. Van Sertima links the timing of ancient Egyptian art, architecture, and cultural custom in Mexico to the influence and creation of the Negroid stone heads. He said, "Is it not strange that it is in this very period when the Negro-African begins to appear in Mexico and to affect significantly the Olmec culture that the first pyramids, mummies, trepanned skulls, stelae and hieroglyphs begin to appear in America?" (p. 34). Not only did West African culture impact Mexico and the Americas, but so did the ways of ancient Egypt. Van Sertima said "But what impact could a boatload or even a fleet of Negro-Egyptians have had on the Gulf of Mexico? These men would have been, in numerical terms, a drop of water in the human ocean of Mexico" (p. 35). Van Sertima recognizes that some question the possibility of a small number of Africans having the ability to impact a vast Mexican culture. However, he noted that "Cabello de Balboa cites a group of seventeen Negroes shipwrecked in Ecuador in the early sixteenth century who in short order became governors of an entire province of American Indians"

(p. 35). Ivan Van Sertima died completely convinced that Olmec culture was influenced by a minority of Africans and the Olmec people influenced all future Mesoamerican civilizations. As will be discussed later, as claimed by Horace Butler in *Rocks Cry Out*, the Olmecs arrived in America originally from Africa. Before moving to that section additional information will be shared regarding Van Sertima and ancient Egypt sailing.

Ancient African Sailing Technology

Because of eerie silence and the continued attempt to erase global African history and scholarship, some have contrived a notion that "Africa had no knowledge of the sea, never had mariners, never made boats, nurtured a landlocked race; that her empires ended at the edge of the desert, unwashed by the world's seas. Africans were navigating the Atlantic before Christ" (p. 57). Van Sertima went on to say, "The shipping of the ancient Egyptians is well-documented. Archeology is rich in its evidence of these ships (paintings, graffiti, sculpture, reliefs on temple walls, ancient texts, even shipyard accounts and most recently the wrecks themselves)" (p. 58). Some have reconstructed ancient African ships and replicated the navigational routes, making it to America from the Atlantic. Maritime sophistication was mastered in Africa long before Europe had the capability, thus to assume that African people could not make it to the Americas decades and hundreds of years before Columbus is inaccurate. Again, some Black people search for a realized identity outside an African nexus because they are unaware and duped by white supremacy and Eurocentric hegemony, categorizing Africa as a land of backward savages. Van Sertima discussed the attempt and force behind Black dehumanization, influenced by the conquests of Columbus and slavery. Because of this, African ingenuity and technology would be downplayed, distorted, and ignored. Since the days of Columbus "The image of the Negro-African as a backward, slow and uninventive being is still with us. Not only his manhood and his freedom but even the memory of his cultural and technological achievements before the day of his humiliation seem to have been erased from the consciousness of history" (Van Sertima, p. 29).

When I was a child, if we were lost or describing some unknown place, we would say things like, "I do not know where we were, we were in Timbuktu." At that time there was no conversation about the place, benefits, purpose, or actuality of Timbuktu. I do not believe we thought it was an actual place, let alone one of the prestigious intellectual centers the world has ever known. This is another example of how people ignorantly search for a racial identity outside of Africa, failing to know or understand the rich international benefits generated by African thought and intellect. According to Asa Hilliard, in *The Maroon Within Us*, the oldest university was in Kemet. This system of higher education was in the city of Waset and speculation places the age of this headquarters as far back as 3,000 B.C. (Hilliard, 1995, Saheli, 2003). Many famous Greek scholars studied and learned at Waset. Timbuktu was the prestigious eleventh-century university in Mali, named after a woman of the Sahelian Kingdom of the Sahel. During the reign of Abubakari the second (1307-1311) the Malian university, "Timbuktu had already become a seat of learning," and Abubakari had equipped and expeditionary fleet (p. 68). This knowledge came through the learnings of Timbuktu. Ancient Egyptian or Kemetic knowledge was fostered through the learning centers of Waset, and for the Malian empire and Kingdom, it was through Timbuktu. African intellectualism influenced European thinkers, scholars, and philosophers, despite the erroneous notion of savage Africa. The more Black people and those outside the Black African community investigate the history of African civilization and global contribution with integrity, the sooner dehumanization can be reversed, and African identity understood.

Africa, Aztecs, and the Olmecs

Before moving to the next conceptual view and theory, included is some of the Horace Butler research from *Rocks Cry Out*. When searching the resource-rich treasures of anthropological and archeological discoveries, one of the difficulties is harmonizing and synthesizing the evidence. Every scholar and investigator does not arrive at the same premise, and the researcher and lay-person alike must develop personal concluding positions after analyzing the data. Comparatively, Ivan Van Sertima and Horace Butler reveal similar sets of information, but their conclusions about how African people entered America are not identical. The same is true for the research of David Imhotep in *The First Americans Were Africans Revisited*. Despite the nuanced conclusions of researchers and scholars about global African influence and scholarship, one thing is abundantly clear: The eerie silence and attempts of Black contributory erasure are entirely unfounded and unjustified. The efforts to distort and ignore Black contribution has backfired; the silence highlights and reinforces the fact that there have been and remains concerted efforts to conceal Africa as the cradle of civilization. Continued exposure to this kind of information and critique can help Black people stop searching for identity outside of their true ontological existence. Both Van Sertima and Horace Butler conclude that African presence influenced Olmec culture, but Butler purports that Olmec and Aztec people voyaged across the Atlantic from Africa to ancient America, while Van Sertima indicates that African people impacted Olmec culture upon arrival to Mexico and the Americas. Butler said, "I had seen ancient records that unveiled the world's most explosive secret. 'Egypt' had crossed the Atlantic Sea, in ships, more than 10,000 years before the time of Christ." He went on to say, "They had built the world's largest cities, in South and Central America, and in Mexico they had united those city-states into a nation that stretched from Brazil in South America to Mexico, and into Africa" (p. 16). Butler believes he cracked the secret code of ancient American historicity and said, "Christopher Columbus knew these secrets. He wrote that South America's Orinoco River flowed out of 'Paradise,' where Adam and Eve had lived. I was stunned to see that Columbus had promised he would recapture Jerusalem when he reached the Americas" (p. 17). Both Van Sertima and Butler speak to the work and research contained in books entitled *History of the Conquest of Mexico*, written by two different authors, Orozco y Berra and Antonio de Solis. About his research and quest for truth Butler said, "I saw a centuries-old illustration that depicted black-skinned Aztecs meeting Cortes when he arrived at the Aztec capital. The illustration was published in 1724 on a front page of Antonio de Solis' *History of the Conquest of Mexico*" (p. 60). He said, "Beyond the Solis illustration, I had seen pre-Columbian images of the Aztecs, and the Aztecs had painted themselves as black-skinned Africans" (p. 54). He went on to say, "1 had seen the famed, ancient, Olmec stone heads from Mexico that showed African features on these original Mexicans who had followed Meci. I had seen the pre-Columbian images of the Aztec deities, with their Black African features" (p. 61). Butler strongly asserts that the pyramidal images in Mexico are influenced and built by ancient Egyptians and those of the Nile Valley. In *Mexico: From the Olmecs to the Aztecs*, Michael D. Coe and Rex Koontz appear silent regarding the African influence on the Olmec people that became the base of Aztec, Mayan, and Inca civilizations. The ancient African technology used to construct pyramids and large stone-heads originated in ancient Egypt or the Nile Valley. Many refuse to acknowledge the African essence in ancient America and such action results in unjustified Black inferiority and a search for racial, ethnic, and cultural identity outside of Africa. We rarely see the back of the Mexican Olmec heads, but some depict braided hair. Before moving to the next section, notice the words of Butler:

> Sahagun's *Forbidden Histories* provided the names of two men who came with the Olmec ships to Mexico. One of these men, "Meci" may be the reason the land

was called "Meci-co" and the people, "Meci-cans."
Three thousand years later we still call the land
"Mexico" and its people, "Mexicans." (p. 54)

Indigenous Ancient American Theory

Regarding the earliest arrival of Black people to America, two
positions have been advanced to grapple with: 1) Either Black
people arrived in America through the Trans-Atlantic Passage, or 2)
Hundreds of years before that, sailing from the West African Empire
and Ancient Egypt. To add a third premise, like Horace Butler, I am
classifying the Ancient American theory as the idea that melanated
or darkly pigmented people were the first inhabitants of Ancient
America. Under this notion these people were African. Because of
white supremacy this view is controversial because the world is taught
to devalue Blackness or that which springs from Africa. As the case
with the Olmecs, to suggest that Olmec people originated in Africa or
influenced Olmec people upon Arrival to Mexico and the Americas,
poses a significant challenge to people of Ancient America, which
would include Mexican and Native American people. Along with
other scholars, David Imhotep concludes that African people were the
first to populate ancient America. Without jumping into the debate
of how many millions or thousands of years the world is, it appears
without question that groups of African people had the technology
and navigational skill to sail the Atlantic to America. This information
is critical to the Black diaspora in America because many of us first
unconsciously embraced a racial identity of self-hate. Almost every
other ethnic or racial group in America can trace their familial roots
generationally.

The African in America, linked to involuntary lineage, struggles
to trace authentic and accurate ancestral roots. As stated before, other
groups can claim their historical language, religion, music, art, and
family practices; their culture has been preserved. The plight of my
people in America, typically referred to as African American, Black,

and formerly Negro and Colored, were viciously stripped of identity. Thus when scholars, researchers, and educators fail to honestly explore, research, and record the global African story—the machine of white supremacy remains entrenched. People do not have to be white to uphold white supremacy, and when other colorized groups attempt to maintain a narrative of African or Black servitude and inferiority, they have partnered with Eurocentric hegemony. This has occurred academically, religiously, theologically, economically, racially, and through all streams of mass-media, television, and cinema.

As stated by Asa Hilliard, "Long before Columbus and nearly one thousand years before Christ was born, Africans established contact with and influenced the cultures of the nation we now call Mexico through a people who are known as Olmecs. This was 145 generations ago" (2016, p. 51). He went on to say, "There have always been Africans or Black people in America who have been both physically and mentally free" (Hilliard, 2016, p. 52). The research of David Imhotep boldly purports African people as the first inhabitants of ancient America.

David Imhotep in his work, *The First Americans Were Africans Revisited*, distinguishes his ultimate research conclusions from many others. Although he agrees that African people influenced life and culture in ancient America, he believes Olmecs and Egyptians were not the first to arrive in America. For Olmecs, Egyptians, and other African groups he said they "entered the Americas thousands of years after the first Africans began arriving from Africa around 100,000 B.C." (p. 91). Regardless of debates related to timelines or the accuracy of how old planet earth is, David Imhotep conceptually reveals information that jolts the hypocrisy of white supremacy and Black African suppression. As stated previously in this project, the primary reason why this information is worth critical sharing and wrestling with is that the denial of African contribution and historicity has destructively contributed to the dehumanization of Black people. The Black elementary-age child who unconsciously devalues their African essence or the child of any race that draws a small Africa but a large

Europe on the map is often not aware of the genesis, richness, and value of Africa. The world has been taught to dismiss Blackness; thus, the work of David Imhotep may be hard for many people to conceive, process, or honestly investigate.

Under racial construction and discussion, related to African ontology, it is not customary to discuss Egyptian presence or influence in America. However, if one takes a closer look at American architecture across the US, ancient Egyptian influences are evident. Because of the premise of white supremacy, African influence is to remain in Africa, and the people of Africa are to be labeled savages. This attack on African humanity is designed to conceal and destroy a positive, royal, and noble image in the racial minds of society. Despite it all and connected to the "Mound Building Civilization," Imhotep said it was the "...Egyptians who had catacombs of caves off the Colorado River in Springville, Arizona. Then in Central America there were the Olmecs and the pyramid builders in Central America such as the Pyramids of the Sun and Moon complex" (p. 93). Van Sertima, Butler, Imhotep and countless others attribute the pyramidal buildings of ancient America to ancient Egyptian influences and people of Africa. Despite the silence, the effect is pervasive. In *Egypt on the Potomac: A Guide to Decoding Egyptian Architecture and Symbolism in Washington, D.C.* (2006), Anthony Browder highlights the architectural influence of Egypt in America. He said, "Learning to appreciate the architectural and symbolic relationship between Washington, D.C. and Ancient Egypt requires deeper knowledge of Ancient Egyptian history (p. 5). What if this information was taught in school? Could it impact the achievement, opportunity, and discipline gaps in American education today? Could this level of sustained and consistent knowledge about African presence and contribution curtail or eradicate African racialized self-hate, the use of the n-word, and unconscious feelings of inferiority? What would be the impact on white and non-Black children?

Although David Imhotep indicates there was an African presence in America that preceded the Olmecs who voyaged the Atlantic to the Americas, he reports, "Arguments continue until today saying, 'The Olmec civilization appears to have suddenly appeared in Mexico without any evidence of a preceding culture.' The Olmecs were... 'the Mother Civilization, copied and adopted by all others'" (p. 109). About the voyage he said, "The sun rises across the sea in the east. This means the Mayans and the Aztecs said the Olmecs came from across the Atlantic Ocean" (p. 110). Additionally he shared from his research, "To be precise, the Olmecs were supposedly a mixture of Manding and Amerinds. Do not forget that the Manding made up the base of the Olmecs. The Egyptians, the Manding, and the base of the Olmecs are related to each other" (pp. 110-111).

Summary

Although the thrust is shifting, there has been a vociferous revisionist-history effort to write Black people out of the narrative and it has resulted in unhealthy Black racial identity attitudes. Every person must arrive at their own conclusion and the goal of this brief chapter was to highlight a few possibilities of how darkly pigmented people originally populated ancient America. The goal is not to replace white supremacy with a formation of Black supremacy or superiority, it is designed to confront and challenge the eerie silence and suppressive powers of Eurocentric hegemony that have attempted to stamp out Blackness.

In addition to the Trans-Atlantic enslavement trade and Middle-Passage, we must also consider the ancient African technology that made it possible for African people to sail across the Atlantic, profoundly influencing the indigenous people in the Americas, or that African people were the first of humanity to populate ancient America. There is a fourth position that requires more research, but it postulates that Black Jews or Hebrews were persecuted in what is now labeled the Middle East, scattered into West Africa and then brought to America through the slave trade. People who claim this position believe involuntary immigrant African people in America are descendants of the Hebrew diaspora and people of the Bible, the lost tribe of Israel. Regardless of which theory or combination is correct, the subliminally espoused message of a Black underclass, cursed people, or an inherently subjugated population is false. The entrenchment of Black devaluation results in eerie silence in response to injustice, oppression, marginalization, and the unconscious promotion of white elitism and superiority within the Black community. As James Brown declared in his 1968 hit song, *Say it Loud – I'm Black and I'm Proud*, more Black people need to embrace this mantra psychologically and the world needs to support its reality. It was historian and scholar Anthony Browder that said in *Nile Valley Contributions to Civilization: Exploding the Myths Vol. 1*:

> Any culturally orphaned people would delight at the prospect of uncovering the smallest fragment of their historical past. Passion, enthusiasm and anger are just some of the emotions felt when people begin to come face to face with formerly hidden truths. (p. 13)

CHAPTER 8
A BLOODY MESS

This chapter wrestles with the eerie silence and castigation of the biblical narrative, stimulated by the pervasive grip and sleight-of-hand through white supremacy. Some people of the African diaspora and beyond have ignored comprehensive biblical conceptions because of its American link to whiteness, Christian supremacy, violence, silence, and its complicit stance on and support for chattel slavery. Global disdain for Blackness has been strong enough to cause people with indigenous African roots to reject their essence. We will briefly explore the nexus and *Intersectionality* between the notion of Christianity being a copycat religion of Kemetic or ancient Egyptian mythology, mysticism, and the presence of blood, coupled with analysis of the redemptive nature and blood of the biblical Messiah, Yeshua, or Jesus the Christ. Like and as stated in chapter five, the goal of this chapter is not to anxiously defend Christianity and the existence of Christ, but to clearly declare His biblical purpose; especially as compared to the gods of ancient Egypt. At no point is the revealed information intended to offend, dismiss, or disrespect the history of Kemetic deities, religious systems, or Ma'at, but I am posing this inquiry: If a person can believe in the ancient mythological stories of Asar, Aset, Set, Heru, Isis, Osiris, and Horus, and the blood of ancient rituals and sacrifices, why is the story of biblical deity deemed preposterous?

Before moving forward it is critical to introduce the concept of *Ma'at*, the ancient Egyptian system of balance, as described by

Walter Williams in *The Historical Origin of Christianity*. Williams said "Always remember, our ancestors, the Ancient Egyptians, never had or practiced religion." He went on to say, "They practiced what is called today the 'Maathian Creed,' a natural spiritual way of life that was in tune with the spiritual consciousness and rhythm of Maat (truth, justice, peace, wisdom, and love)" (p. 102). I am not sure if the principles of the Maathian Creed have a specific order, but I prefer the sequence of, love, truth, wisdom, peace, and justice, and I will share why later.

Christianity, the Copycat Religion?

The force, energy, and sentiment behind rejecting Christianity and labeling it a plagiarized or copycat religion is real and should not be under-estimated. The rejection of the Scriptures is not warranted or accurate, but the reaction some have, especially within the Black community, to colonized Christianity is an appropriate response— but only until a person can dive beneath the shallow depths of American Christianity. The Bible is not an ancient book devoid a justice motif. Edgar J. Goodspeed said in *How Came the Bible?* (1981):

> Long before the Old Testament was written, or even begun, men had felt its power. But it remained for the Hebrew prophets of the eighth century before Christ, to make their spiritual discoveries of the justice, the love, and the holiness of God and to set them forth in unforgettable terms. (p. 126)

Although salvation is global and not limited to any group of people, the roots of Christianity are Eastern in context, and later made their way into the Western world. American espoused Christianity, and the New Testament are presented like their genesis began in the benighted West, and every other nation, population, and people are backward and without sophistication. An eerie silence has allowed the false narrative and epistemic to flourish. Although it has existed for years, a nineteenth-century resurgence was sparked by the book, *Ancient Egypt: The Light of the World*, written by Gerald Massey, who was born in England on May 29, 1828, and died on October 29, 1907. Social-media, YouTube, and the *Woke* and *Conscious Community* have also contributed to the rebirth of this denial and challenge to the Christian faith.

Ancient Egyptian art is said to predate Christ by thousands of years, revealing a story of a virgin birth and the likes of a man that could be viewed as a *Christ,* who died and was resurrected. Some presume that the Bible, and especially the story of Christ, is a modified version of an original ancient Egyptian story. One of the problems is that many historians have no evidence of a Kemetic god system influencing first-century Christianity or early-church development. Influence surfaces in the second and third century A.D., making the alleged Kemetic-Christian parallels post-Christian as opposed to pre-Christian. According to Browder, reported in *Nile Valley Contributions to Civilization: Exploding the Myths Vol. 1*, it was Constantine in "333 A.C.E." that stamped Christianity the official religion of Rome and "... ordered the closing of all Egyptian temples, in an attempt to eradicate any and all competing religious systems. The *African Trinity* of Ausar, Aset and Heru (Osiris, Isis, and Horus), which existed for more than 4,000 years, was replaced with the Trinity, which consisted of the *Father, Son, and Holy Ghost*" (p. 68). Expressed by Browder and many other scholars of ancient Egyptian and Kemetic legend, archeology, anthropology, history, and mythology, Ausar was killed by his brother Set. Browder records:

> After a long search, Aset found all the parts of her husband's body except the phallus, which, as legend has it, was consumed by a catfish when it was discarded into the Nile. Aset recreated the missing member of Ausar in the form of a tekhen (obelisk), which later became a symbol representing the resurrection of Ausar. (Browder, 1992, p. 89)

As the story continues, Aset resurrected the body of her husband Ausar and "Shortly thereafter, Aset conceived of a child upon being immaculately impregnated by the spirit of her husband and gave birth to a son, Heru (Horus), who avenged the death of his father by slaying his uncle Set (1992, Browder, p. 89). Other versions of the story include how the evil brother Set plotted a scheme, bringing a beautiful chest to a party, offering a challenge to any person that could perfectly fit inside. The winner of the challenge would receive the sarcophagus or chest as a gift. Many guests tried, but no one fit perfectly. Unknowingly to him, it was customized for Ausar/Osiris, and when he jumped in the coffin, his brother slammed and sealed it shut. Based on the multiple versions of the story, Ausar either suffocated inside the sarcophagus or died after it was tossed into the river. Regardless, after Ausar was trapped inside, Set ordered his servants to toss the chest into the Nile River. Aset/Isis eventually recovered the body of her husband and when Set heard of it, he found the body and chopped it into fourteen pieces and scattered each part across Egypt.

There are various versions of this story, but upon piecing the body of Ausar back together Aset and her resurrected husband were able to have sex one last time, producing their son Heru (Finegan, 1989). It is supposed to be from this story and various writings and phrases from the ancient Egyptian Pyramid Texts, Coffin Texts, and Book of the Dead that Old and New Testament conception originated. The birth, life, sacrificial death, resurrection, and ascension of Jesus are supposed to be plagiarized from ancient Egyptian mythology. There are some who postulate and label the biblical narrative and Christian faith as a hoax and the goal of this project is not to discount or deem African, Egyptian, and Kemetic history and mythology as false, but to properly share the biblical and historical role and purpose of Yeshua, distinctly differentiated from the Ausar, Aset, and Horus account.

Responding to the Alleged Christian Hoax

Eerie silence about Africa, injustice, and the contagion of white religious supremacy set the stage for the bashing of the Christian faith. In chapter one the case was made, illustrating the first-century church as being both activated and radical in love and social justice, engaging in direct action confronting discrimination and oppression. The first-century church—strongly influenced by African and Hebraic conceptions—produced a cooperative spirit of sharing. The problem today is, the assault and pain of modern and postmodern church and Christian harm has forced people to view only its colonized formula and not its biblically indigenous roots. Truly, some people in the church are more American than they are Christian and are more patriotic toward the flag than they are the cross of Christ. Blind American patriotism results in Biblical castigation, but the biblical story is not a replica of ancient Egyptian mythology. The biblical story of the Old and New Testaments have a definitive influential nexus to ancient Egypt, but the redemptive theme of the Scriptures is not a contrived and fabricated source of amusing fiction or a tool explicitly developed to control the African enslaved.

Copan and Craig in *Come Let Us Reason: New Essays in Christian Apologetics,* have two essays, one by Mary Jo Sharp and another by Mark W. Foreman that attempt to conceptualize ancient Egyptian mysticism related to Ausar, Aset, and Heru with the biblical record. Ancient Egyptian mysticism has only influenced the veneer and sideline of Christianity. In his 2012 essay, "Challenging the Zeitgeist Movie: Paralellomania on Steroids," Foreman said: "One cannot deny the post-Constantinian Christianity [fourth and fifth centuries AD], both Eastern and Western, adopted not a few pagan rites and practices" (p. 174). He went on to say, "For example, mystery religions may well have influenced the selection of December 25 as the celebration of the birth of Christ, but this date was not widely observed until the fourth century" (p. 175). The ancient Egyptian deity Horus was said to have been born on December 25. Many people today believe Christ was born on December 25, celebrating the day labeled Christmas, failing to understand the date and observance is connected more to Kemetic mythology than responsible biblical interpretation and context. There is nothing in the Old or New Testament canon that provides a date Yeshua was born or authorization to celebrate His birthday, as is common today. Christians and non-Christians are often duped and ultimately frown on Christian ontology, developing aversions to the materialism and exploitation of Christmas.

"Zeitgeist: The Movie" seeks to discredit the deity of Christ, categorizing Him and the surrounding circumstances of His birth, life, death, and resurrection as symbolic astrological action with Jesus as the Sun god and not the Son of God. The film aligns prominent Old and New Testament figures and stories to zodiac and astrological signs. For example, because Jesus miraculously fed people with fish and bread, He is connected to the zodiac age of Pisces. Through this kind of biblical interpretation, stories are explained astrologically and not theologically. Mark W. Foreman refutes the film and advances several fallacies saying:

> One of the most blatant is the *terminology fallacy*. That is, events in the lives of the mythical gods, for example, are expressed using Christian terminology in order subtly to manipulate viewers into accepting that the same events in the life of Jesus also happened in the lives of mythical gods. We are told, for instance, that Horus, Krishna, Dionysius, and others were 'baptized,' 'born of a virgin,' 'crucified,' and 'resurrected'—just to mention a few. Examples of such locutions, however, involve assertions with no evidence, are ripped out of their Christian context, or obtained from post-first-century sources. (p. 177)

As will be discussed later, the biblical story of Jesus Christ is specific and prophetic, with prefigured types and shadows revealed hundreds and thousands of years before His birth, life, crucifixion, death, and resurrection. Biblically the Christ is depicted as a savior and redeemer of humanity. That is not the case with Ausar or Heru; the alleged comparisons are not aligned considering purpose and intent. Foreman discusses another misnomer that he labels, *nonbiblical fallacy* and one example is the birth of Jesus being declared as December 25. That is an extra-biblical claim affixed to the Bible, never stated in Scripture. Following copycat surmising forces a person to believe that Old and New Testament writers were aware of the ancient Egyptian deities and seductively modified names and characters, creating an elaborate scheme of biblical epochs, spanning multiple covenants and dispensations. The problem is, pre-first-century evidence of Kemetic mythology influence is missing and Foreman said "...There is no evidence that there was any pagan mystery influence in first-century Palestine. Second, the mystery religions evolved over time, and as they did, their beliefs and narratives changed. This results in several versions of the various pagan myths" (pp. 180-181). He went on to say: "Most of the evidence we have of their narratives comes from sources dated in the second and third centuries, a time when they were experiencing the peak of their influence in the Mediterranean world" (p. 181). Additionally Foreman said:

> Because these ancient religions evolved over time,
> often no one authoritative story exists to which
> one may appeal. For example, the story of Horus in
> *Zeitgeist* is pieced together from a number of sources,
> some of which conflict. It is like playing 'connect the
> dots,' but interpreting how to connect those dots is a
> slippery, unscholarly enterprise. These writers seem
> to use the life of Jesus as a guide for how to connect
> the dots for the life of Horus and then proclaim that
> the story of Jesus is based on Horus—when actually
> it is the other way around! (p. 182)

In the same book, *Come Let Us Reason: New Essays in Christian Apologetics,* Mary Jo Sharp addresses ancient mythologies in her essay, "Does the Story of Jesus Mimic Pagan Mystery Stories?" I am primarily focusing on an African ethos of mythology because it has a larger impact on identity development of those from the West African diaspora, arguably the most dehumanized group in the world, reinforced by colonized Christianity in America. Sharp makes the point that most researchers have moved away from the notion of antiquity that the Jesus story is a myth and that He is not a historical figure, but some presently exist. However in noting that the issue is dead at the level of higher academia, she said "...In surveying the most influential communication media—the Internet, television, and movies—the accusation of mythological origins is one of the most utilized arguments against beliefs in Jesus Christ. While not much scholarly work in the past 20 years has been focused on this argument, at the popular level it is alive and kicking" (p. 151). This is especially true within segments of the Black community where many people are searching for a noble, royal, and valued identity, separate from the one America has branded savage, uneducated, criminal, and inferior. Sharp explains the contention this way:

> Basically the argument is this: the biblical narratives of Christ's life and teachings are mythological in nature and origin rather than actual historical accounts. Many offshoots of this overarching theme have cropped up over the years: (1) Christian dependence on mystery religions to explain baptism and the Lord's Supper, or (2) the doctrine of salvation evolving from mystery religions, or (3) Christianity as just another Hellenistic mystery religion, or (4) Christian beliefs and practices dependent on similar beliefs and practices in the mysteries.

The biblical story is nestled in historical antiquities, cultures, and customs but ancient mythological gods are obscure in time and context. The goal is not to discredit ancient mysticism, it is to differentiate the Bible narrative, deity, and salvific nature of Christ specifically. The Bible story is public and open for scrutiny, but the same cannot be said for the secrecy of ancient mythological god-systems. "...Mystery religions were cults that were named 'mysteries' because of the vow of secrecy taken by followers concerning the cult's teachings and the wisdom the teachings imparted" (Sharp, p. 152). Sharp also said:

> Most people who are impressed by the mystery-cult-influence argument have not scrutinized the claims meticulously enough, probably not going any further than watching a television show, viewing a few YouTube clips, or glancing through an article or two on random blogs. The person who lacks a solid grounding in Christian doctrine and knowledge of history can easily fall prey to confusion and doubt induced by poor arguments left unchallenged. (p. 152)

The story of Jesus is not a fancied replica of Ausar, Aset, Horus, and Set mysticism, it is distinct and does not align in intent, purpose, or mythological symbolism. As concluded by Sharp, when sifting through the mythical stories of ancient gods, "(1) get the whole story, (2) take the parallels head to head, and (3) set everything in context" (p. 168). When this is done, it becomes emphatically clear that Jesus is not a myth.

Understanding the Old and New Testament Schematic

The Bible evokes many reactions. Some people believe the entire Bible and characters therein are fictional, others are convinced the Old Testament is accurate, but the New Testament a fraud, while others believe in the complete accuracy and historicity of the sixty-six books in the canon. The Bible is a complex ancient literary source, written over thousands of years by multiple authors confirming biblical stories through types, shadows, and physical events. Typical biblical misunderstandings occur because of a lack of knowledge in its schematic, covenant, and dispensational framework. The Bible spans three primary covenants or dispensations, and each one has a different authority or contractual system. Failing to apply and understand this biblical premise results in passage contortion, abuse, and manipulations for self-serving purposes. When used deceitfully and without proper hermeneutics and discipline, the Bible can be made to support any personally convenient claim or behavior. As an example, Christians are mocked because of their dietary customs that on the surface appear in violation of the Scriptures. People who lived during the biblical times of Mosaic, Ten Commandment, or Levitical priesthood law, were forbidden to eat certain foods. Moreover, instead of that system being understood in its proper biblical context, it is merely extracted out of the Mosaic Law system and applied to Christians universally. This is just one example. To clarify and expose the inappropriateness of this kind of biblical eisegesis, elements of Deuteronomy chapter five must be explored. It says:

> Moses summoned all Israel and said: Hear, Israel, the decrees and laws I declare in your hearing today. Learn them and be sure to follow them. ²The LORD our God made a covenant with us at Horeb. ³It was not with our ancestors that the LORD made this covenant, but with us, with all of us who are alive here today. (Deuteronomy 5:1-3 NIV)

As declared by Prophet Moses, the passage above indicates that ancient Hebrew people received a governing covenant system that was not enforced during the life of their ancestors. The three biblical covenant systems can be described as *Patriarchal* (Adam to the reception of Mosaic Law by Moses), *Mosaic* or *Ten Commandment* (Reception of the Law of Moses from God, through the Resurrection of Jesus), and the *New Testament, Church-age,* or *Christian* (From the resurrection of Christ and biblical establishment of the church until the end of time). As an example, Adam, Noah, and Abraham lived during the Patriarchal covenant, hundreds of years before the Ten Commandment Levitical precepts and laws were given to Moses. Abraham was not instructed to keep the Sabbath as Moses and the Nation of Israel. All three epochs are contained under differing covenants, divine agreements, and timelines—with the last one enacted, fulfilled, and prescribed during the church-age and Christian era. After receiving the Mosaic Law, the Hebrew people were not allowed to eat pork as a one of many dietary restrictions. God said to Moses and the ancient Israelites, "The pig has evenly split hooves but does not chew the cud, so it is unclean. ⁸You may not eat the meat of these animals or even touch their carcasses. They are ceremonially unclean for you" (Leviticus 11:7-8 NLT). However, just like this dietary law was not commanded during the days of Noah or Abraham, it does not transcend into the Christian covenant system today or that of the first-century, unless explicitly stated in the covenant. For example, notice the words of Paul below to the early-church Christians of first-century Rome:

> For this, Thou shalt not commit adultery, Thou shalt
> not kill, Thou shalt not steal, Thou shalt not bear
> false witness, Thou shalt not covet; and if there be
> any other commandment, it is briefly comprehended
> in this saying, namely, Thou shalt love thy neighbour
> as thyself. (Romans 13:9 KJV)

Commonly the Bible is discussed because of its Ten Commandments and they are viewed as rules that govern the totality of biblical Scripture. Now that covenants have been explained, Romans 13:9 can be used to illustrate how principles from one covenant can be carried into another, if explicitly stated. Although more actually existed, Exodus 20:1-19 provides the Ten Commandment list given to Moses. Although some of the elements are listed in the Romans 13:9 passage, it is not inclusive of all the Exodus elements because the covenant systems are not biblically identical or concurrently enforced. Biblical covenant system mismanagement is like a citizen of California trying to hold the legal system in New York to the laws of California. Understanding biblical law and covenant systems require careful analysis.

Old Testament circumcision provides one of the first prophetic shadows of the bloody mess that would turn divine through the work of Christ on the cross. Blood is a continuous theme throughout Scripture, beginning in *Genesis* and continuing through *Revelation*. More will be shared about this later, but according to Genesis 17:10-11 and under the Patriarchal dispensation, circumcision was enacted through an Abrahamic covenant and was also carried into the Mosaic dispensation (Leviticus 12:1-3). Without the explicit command in Mosaic Law, there would be no circumcision requirement for the Hebrew people delivered from Egyptian bondage. However, in the church-age of the New Testament, physical circumcision is not required, its real purpose, shadow, and type are revealed as a spiritual process. Circumcision moves from being a physical act and medical procedure to a cosmic operation of God in the hearts of anyone willing to come to Him by faith through grace (Ephesians 2:8). The Apostle Paul, a Hebrew man said:

> When you came to Christ, you were "circumcised,"
> but not by a physical procedure. Christ performed
> a spiritual circumcision—the cutting away of your
> sinful nature. 12For you were buried with Christ
> when you were baptized. And with him you were
> raised to new life because you trusted the mighty
> power of God, who raised Christ from the dead.
> (Colossians 2:11-12 NLT)

New Testament Scripture reveals the spiritual purpose of Old Testament physical laws. Relating to diet, there was nothing inherently sinful about eating pork, but to show His elected people as sanctified and differentiated, God gave the Hebrews distinctively different laws. Similarly, it was never about the restrictions; dietary boundaries were used as a prefiguring of church-age spiritual sanctification—just like it was never about physical circumcision, but spiritual baptism and rebirth (John 3:1-8). The religious physical elements of the Old Testament are revealed and explained in the New Testament. The Old Testament Tabernacle, Solomon's Temple, and the second Temple were physical shadows of the prophesied New Testament Church (Matthew 16:18). If a person is unaware of this type of biblical schematic, they will confuse and misapply Bible concepts.

Prophetic Old Testament Foreshadowing of the Crucifixion

If a person only believes in the Old Testament, there are strange biblical episodes they must wrest and rationalize theologically. The combined nature of the Old and New Testaments congeal as a comprehensive story of triumphant deliverance and liberation. Without the historical narrative of the Old Testament, liberation theology is incomplete. The emancipatory and momentous work of the cross, slowly builds in the Old Testament, climaxing in the New Testament. If the New Testament is excluded from the narrative, the sovereignty and love of God are missed and some stories and scenarios are abandoned as irrational and irregular. As previously stated, blood is a thread throughout biblical writ. Working through a bloody theological mess, the trajectory of two stories must be linked for their foreshadowing and prophetic import. First is the faith-testing story of Abraham in Genesis 22:1-13, followed by the suffering description contained in Psalm 22. Isaiah 53 will be reserved for later referencing.

I recall a conversation with a staunch believer in Old Testament historicity, but she loathed the New Testament, deeming it complete folly. If the New Testament is purely fiction, what would be the purpose of the faith-testing of Abraham? In Genesis 22:1-13 God instructed Abraham to take his only promised son Isaac to the land of Moriah and sacrifice him on a mountain. Who can understand the traumatic emotions that silently erupted in the mind and body of Abraham as he made his journey to the sacrificial location, knowing he was to kill his son? The story sounds bleak, depressive, unfair, and ungodly. What kind of God would ask a man to slay or sacrifice his child? There are many applications of faith and obedience in the story, but for revealing the Old and New Testament nexus, an emphasis is placed on how this Old Testament story prophetically foreshadows the life and work of a New Testament Messiah. Referencing the command God said to Abraham, "Take your son, your only son, whom you love—Isaac—and go to the region of Moriah. Sacrifice him there as a burnt offering on a mountain I will show you" (Genesis 22:2 NLT).

If the Old Testament and book of Genesis, contained within the Torah, is a private account without New Testament linkage, it is merely a crude Abrahamic test orchestrated by God. Why would God ask a man to kill his only son that he dearly loves? The story points to what God the Father and God the Son would do thousands of years later. Adequate interpretation and understanding of the story of Abraham being asked to sacrifice his son Isaac are impossible to understand without the fulfillment of its Christological conclusion.

Despite the request of God, Abraham somehow maintained his faith and believed after sacrificing his son, God would revive him back to life. As Abraham prepared to sacrifice his son, he said to the men that traveled with him, "...Stay here with the donkey while I and the boy go over there. We will worship and then we will come back to you" (Genesis 22:5 NLT). Abraham believed they both would return. I am sure it must have broken his heart, but as Abraham walked up the mountain in Moriah with knife and wood in hand, his son said:

> My father: and he said, Here am I, my son. And he
> said, Behold the fire and the wood: but where is the

lamb for a burnt offering? [8]And Abraham said, My son, God will provide himself a lamb for a burnt offering. (Genesis 22:7-8 KJV)

Unarguably, this encounter must have been terrifying for Abraham and either Isaac possessed as much or more faith than his father, or he was oblivious to the reality that he was the subject of the sacrifice. As Abraham and Isaac made it to the sacrifice site, he built the alter, arranged the wood for the burnt offering of his son, bound him, and placed him on the alter. Then Abraham "…Reached out his hand and took the knife to slay his son. [11]But the angel of the LORD called out to him from heaven, 'Abraham! Abraham!'" (GENESIS 22:11 NLT). Witnessing the faith of Abraham and his willingness to follow the command, God said, "'Do not lay a hand on the boy,' he said. "Do not do anything to him. Now I know that you fear God, because you have not withheld from me your son, your only son'" (Genesis 22:12 NIV).

The faith of Abraham was tested by God because he was asked to sacrifice his son. In the process, no human blood was spilled because God stopped him. However, "Abraham looked up and there in a thicket he saw a ram caught by its horns. He went over and took the ram and sacrificed it as a burnt offering instead of his son" (Genesis 22:13 NIV). Although it was not the blood of his son, it was the bloody mess of a ram, included in this climactic convening. In the New Testament, the spiritualized fulfillment of this story is revealed with God the Father not stopping the sacrifice of His Son. In New Testament fulfillment Jesus is not prefigured as a ram but a lamb (Revelation 5:12). The Apostle Peter said about the redemption of those who come to Jesus by faith, "…it was not with perishable things such as silver or gold that you were redeemed from the empty way of life handed down to you from your ancestors, [19]but with the precious blood of Christ, a lamb without blemish or defect" (1 Peter 1:18-19 NLT).

In addition to the prophetic link between the metaphoric imagery of the Christ in Genesis 22 and its New Testament fulfillment on the cross (John 19:30), Psalm 22 provides a similar prophecy. In Matthew

27:46 (KJV) and while hanging on the cross Jesus said, "...Eli, Eli, lama sabachthani? that is to say, My God, my God, why hast thou forsaken me?" If a person theologically operates on a binary, only investigating the Old or New Testament, they will miss the schematic premise, prophecy, and construction of the book. Reading the Bible requires proper contextualization and responsible exegesis necessitates astute management across biblical covenant and dispensational systems. The distressing words Christ uttered on the cross in Matthew 27:46, were first prophetically declared in Psalm 22:1 (KJV) where Jesus said, "My God, my God, why hast thou forsaken me? why art thou so far from helping me, and from the words of my roaring?" Before the Old or New Testaments are discounted, it must be understood that they are inextricably linked. The horror of what happened to Christ on the cross was prophesied centuries before. What distinguishes the Bible from any other book is its prophetic fulfillment nature, yet written by authors from different eras. The author of Psalm 22 was most likely King David, but miraculously he never met or knew Jesus. David was divinely inspired to poetically write about that which was to come.

Not every reader approaches the Scriptures with cross-biblical and prophetic-pattern understanding, thus continuing the psalmist said, "All they that see me laugh me to scorn: they shoot out the lip, they shake the head, saying, ⁸He trusted on the LORD that he would deliver him: let him deliver him, seeing he delighted in him" (Psalm 22:7-8 KJV). Centuries later Mark recorded the ridicule and mockery of the crucified Christ, "And they that passed by railed on him, wagging their heads, and saying, Ah, thou that destroyest the temple, and buildest it in three days, ³⁰Save thyself, and come down from the cross" (Mark 15:29-30 KJV); and centuries later Matthew declared, "And they crucified him, and parted his garments, casting lots: that it might be fulfilled which was spoken by the prophet, They parted my garments among them, and upon my vesture did they cast lots" (27:35 KJV). Before Matthew declared this treatment of Jesus, David had already written the song that included the words, "They part my garments among them, and cast lots upon my vesture" (Psalm 22:18 KJV). Related to the excruciating suffering of Christ, as declared in the Gospel accounts of Matthew, Mark, Luke, and John, King David prophesied of his trauma and pain:

> My life is poured out like water,
>   and all my bones are out of joint.
> My heart is like wax,
>   melting within me.
> 15My strength has dried up like sunbaked clay.
>   My tongue sticks to the roof of my mouth.
>   You have laid me in the dust and left me for dead.
>   (Psalm 22:14-15 NLT)

To understand the importance of the blood of Christ, a person must embrace the prophetic style of the Scriptures. There is a cross-biblical link to the Old Testament Garden of Eden, Ark of Noah, Tabernacle, and Temples, as connected to the New Testament church. The Old Testament shadows and types prophetically pointed to the sanctity and safety of the New Testament church. The various formations of blood and sacrifices in the Old Testament were a prefiguring of the blood and ultimate sacrifice of Christ. This will be discussed in more detail at the close of this chapter, but before discussing that we will explore the intended purpose of Christianity compared to the ancient Egyptian system of Ma'at. An eerie silence has contributed to the prevention of honest biblical discussion, inside and outside religious spaces.

Ma'at, Fruit of the Spirit, and Righteousness

The Bible is continually refuted and charged as being a carbon copy of Kemetic and ancient Egyptian mythical systems. The guiding behavioral source of Kemetic life is Ma'at. The goddess Ma'at is said to be the daughter of the sun god Ra. Through Ma'at multiple life-principles emerged and the Maathian Creed includes living a balanced life of love, truth, wisdom, peace, and justice. After sifting through ancient cultural-historical customs, artifacts, hieroglyphs, literature, and archeological and anthropological discoveries, it drills down to living a righteous and balanced life of love, truth, wisdom, peace, and justice. With this reality, the disdain for Christianity is puzzling. The Maathian Creed speaks of principles designed to ensure a mature and adequate functioning of humanity; and if Christianity seeks a similar end, why the contention? The Bible speaks of a code of life and ontology, not guided by the daughter of Ra, but through the quickening power of the Holy Spirit. One could presume that if a system exists, that is grounded in love, justice, and fairness—groups of people should be able to co-exist and thrive. The goal of this chapter is not to prove ancient extra-biblical systems fraudulent, but to show the precious essence of Christianity and its expectation for righteousness. Each person is free to elect a path that is best for them, but in doing so, do not prematurely cast aside Christianity and a New Testament ethos because of how it has been manipulated and used to oppress and further efforts of coloniality.

Instead of the Maathian Creed, Paul the Apostle instructed the Christians in the Galatian church to not live under carnal habits and appetites, but a life empowered by the fruit of the Spirit. Ancient Egyptians lived by the Maathian Creed and Christians live by the power and manifestations of the Holy Spirit. When this is understood at the basic level of Christian ontology, there is no need for argument. Many people castigate the Christian way because they do not understand its core tenets. In such circumstances they cannot get past the Eurocentric hegemony of a white Jesus hanging on a cross. Paul said, But the fruit of the Spirit is love, joy, peace, longsuffering, gentleness, goodness, faith, [23]Meekness, temperance: against such there is no law" (Galatians 5:22-23 KJV). The *New Living Translation* renders the passage, "But the fruit of the Spirit is love, joy, peace, forbearance, kindness, goodness, faithfulness, [23]gentleness and self-control. Against such things there is no law." The empowered Christian-code of ethics and righteousness is not identical to the

Maathian Creed, but it necessitates the general life themes of love, honesty, patience, and self-accountability. Nothing contained in the manifesting elements of the fruit of the Spirit could justify American chattel slavery, oppression, injustice, racism, white supremacy or any form of genocide, holocaust, or Maafa. Deepening the thrust of radical Christian behavior Paul concluded the chapter saying, "... They that are Christ's have crucified the flesh with the affections and lusts. ²⁵If we live in the Spirit, let us also walk in the Spirit. ²⁶Let us not be desirous of vain glory, provoking one another, envying one another" (Galatians 5:24-26 KJV). Christianity is not a way of life that is negligently passive; it operates out of a profoundly radical agape love that is commanded to offer what is needed over what is wanted. And while the fruit of the Spirit is being executed through faith, Peter said:

> ...Make every effort to add to your faith goodness; and to goodness, knowledge; ⁶and to knowledge, self-control; and to self-control, perseverance; and to perseverance, godliness; ⁷and to godliness, mutual affection; and to mutual affection, love. ⁸For if you possess these qualities in increasing measure, they will keep you from being ineffective and unproductive in your knowledge of our Lord Jesus Christ. (2 Peter 1:5-8 NLT)

Christians are sometimes depicted as negligent, naïve, passive, and unassertive—allowing others to walk over them because they are too timid to defend themselves or actualize opposing opinions. According to the Scriptures, Jesus did not die on a cross because He was passive and could not liberate Himself from the cross; through an unexplainable love, He allowed Himself to become a sacrifice for humanity. About being able to rescue himself from Jewish and Roman persecution He said to Peter, "Do you think I cannot call on my Father, and he will at once put at my disposal more than twelve legions of angels?" (Matthew 26:53 NLT). Christianity is about righteous behavior and its ethos is radical, revolutionary, transformative, and liberating—but many have not patiently explored its tenets, blinded by the stale, sanitized, and colonized version perfected in America. To look at the depths of its radical essence we turn to power, the cross, and bloody mess that resulted in a divine outcome. Historically, blood is an underestimated factor and prefiguring.

The Blood

Eerie silence, white supremacy, and racism have resulted in dulled and distorted biblical pursuits. This section will briefly address the prefiguring of blood and sacrifice and how it has been a cultural staple since the beginning of human existence. Biblical content is shunned, deemed disconnected and silent toward ancient cultural customs and practices. Many societies participated in animal sacrifice, occultism, witchcraft, Vodun, voodoo, and Yorba and the Bible addresses those trajectories in-part, but does not proclaim them as the endorsed path. The Bible does not declare the customs a façade, just not the elected path of the God of the Bible. Since blood and sacrifice connect to the beginning of human existence, it is strange to hear Christianity challenged for its blood linkages and ultimate fulfillment through the cross.

Although the Bible spans dispensational and covenantal epochs, it consistently professed a trust, belief, and faith in God—as opposed to occultism, witchcraft, or mediums. In *Tribal Talk: Black Theology, Hermeneutics, and African/American Ways of "Telling the Story"* (2000), Will Coleman said: "The West African or priestess and early African American conjurer (both male and female) and/or preacher was a mediator of the sacred" (p. 38). He continued, "These religious leaders brought elements of their West African belief system, one that incorporated magic into religion, with them to the Americas" (p. 39). Related to contention between the African enslaved and Christianity versus mediation, Coleman said, "As African American Christianity became more influential within the slave community, there were occasional rivalries between the slave preacher and the conjurers and healers" (p. 40).

The book of First Samuel describes an encounter between fearful King Saul, deceased prophet Samuel, and a woman medium at Endor in the Jezreel Valley. Leading up to the encounter, King Saul disobeyed God twice and the second act of disobedience resulted in the Kingdom being stripped from him. As a result Samuel said to him, "Rebellion is as sinful as witchcraft, and stubbornness as bad as worshiping idols. So because you have rejected the command of the LORD, he has rejected you as king" (1 Samuel 15:23 NLT). Prophet Samuel eventually died and Saul, fearful of not knowing his future and the force of the opposing Philistine army, sought a medium to speak with Samuel from the dead. The Bible records, "Now Samuel was dead, and all Israel had mourned for him and buried him in his own town of Ramah. Saul had expelled the mediums and spiritists from the land" (1 Samuel 28:3 NLT). Despite expelling the mediums, in desperation King Saul wanted one to assist him in consulting with Samuel because God was no longer responding to him. Samuel cried out to God, "...But the LORD DID NOT ANSWER HIM BY DREAMS OR URIM OR PROPHETS. 7Saul then said to his attendants, 'Find me a woman who is a medium, so I may go and inquire of her'" (1 Samuel 28:6-7 NIV).

Saul was told there was a medium at Endor, so he disguised himself, went to her, and inquired. "So Saul disguised himself, putting on other clothes, and at night he and two men went to the woman. 'Consult a spirit for me,' he said, 'and bring up for me the one I name'" (1 Samuel 28:8 NLT). Knowing Saul expelled all mediums from the village, she was fearful and unaware she was talking to King Saul. He assured her she would not be punished for her mediation and she said: "Whom shall I bring up for you?" and he said "Bring up Samuel" (1 Samuel 28:11 NLT). The Bible is not silent in the fact that the medium at Endor conjured Samuel from the dead. The Bible says, "When the woman saw Samuel, she cried out at the top of her voice and said to

Saul, 'Why have you deceived me? You are Saul!'" (1 Samuel 28:11 NLT). The story concluded with 1 Samuel 28:13-19 NLT:

> The king said to her, "Don't be afraid. What do you see?" The woman said, "I see a ghostly figure coming up out of the earth." [14]"What does he look like?" he asked.
>
> "An old man wearing a robe is coming up," she said. Then Saul knew it was Samuel, and he bowed down and prostrated himself with his face to the ground. [15]Samuel said to Saul, "Why have you disturbed me by bringing me up?" "I am in great distress," Saul said. "The Philistines are fighting against me, and God has departed from me. He no longer answers me, either by prophets or by dreams. So I have called on you to tell me what to do." [16]Samuel said, "Why do you consult me, now that the LORD has departed from you and become your enemy? [17]The LORD has done what he predicted through me. The LORD has torn the kingdom out of your hands and given it to one of your neighbors—to David. [18]Because you did not obey the LORD or carry out his fierce wrath against the Amalekites, the LORD has done this to you today. [19]The LORD will deliver both Israel and you into the hands of the Philistines, and tomorrow you and your sons will be with me. The LORD will also give the army of Israel into the hands of the Philistines."

Although not endorsed, the Bible does speak of sorcery, magic, and the occult. The Old and New Testament Scriptures do not ignore the historical realities of the world, they expose and emphasize the theology of God toward them. This is of critical emphasis because some view the Bible as an antiquated and out-of-touch literary source that omits cultures and customs of African, ancient, and ethnic people. This is the result of Eurocentric hegemony and coloniality toward the biblical text. Despite the European hands that touched, transcribed, and translated Scripture, they are not of holistic European origin. We now turn to linkages of the blood.

Historical Linkage and Theological Blood Clarification

As emphasized in chapter 5, God said to Cain after he murdered his sibling, "...Your brother's blood cries out to me from the ground!" (Genesis 4:10). It is critical to note the position of Biblical writ, burrowed within the schematic frame of history. From beginning to end, blood is a prophetic biblical element that must be tracked for comprehensive understanding. It begins with the sacrificial and ceremonial blood of animals and ends with the blood of Christ. Any culture, tribe, or community that has a history of blood usage should find validation and resonance in the Scriptures.

Potentially landing in the realm of lore, some surmise that the first animal sacrifice, according to biblical custom, occurred when Adam and Eve transgressed in the Garden of Eden and discovering their nakedness were ashamed. The Bible records, "Unto Adam also and to his wife did the LORD God make coats of skins, and clothed them" (Genesis 3:21 KJV). Is it possible that the bloodshed in the killing of the animal atoned for their transgression and the skin covered their bodies? Again, this cannot be confirmed, but could also serve as a prophetic shadow of the redemptive cover and blood of Christ. Based on the Genesis account of the Cain and Abel sacrifices offered to God (Genesis 4:3-5), some theologians have postulated that the Abel sacrifice was accepted not just because it was from "the best portions of the firstborn lambs from his flock," but because it included blood. Throughout scripture, blood is symbolically and metaphorically depicted as the primary atoning, cleansing, healing, reconciliatory, and atoning agent.

Earlier in this chapter the prophetic link of biblical circumcision was emphasized. Circumcision was a bloody mess, but the symbolism of its atoning process pointed to the supreme blood of Christ. Although not previously explained, blood is a biblically prominent agent with women and birthing children and their menstruation cycle (1 Timothy 2:15; Leviticus 18:19). Both encounters, like circumcision, point to the perfected and prefigured blood of Christ. Proper Bible interpretation cannot commence without an understanding of the thematic premise of blood. From Old to New Testament atoning blood sacrifices, it shifted from animals to the Christ. The Bible declares the prefigured, symbolic, and sacrificial blood of animals inferior to the blood of Christ. Comparing the blood of the two covenants, the Hebrew writer said:

> Under the old system, the blood of goats and bulls and the ashes of a heifer could cleanse people's bodies from ceremonial impurity. [14]Just think how much more the blood of Christ will purify our consciences from sinful deeds so that we can worship the living God. For by the power of the eternal Spirit, Christ offered himself to God as a perfect sacrifice for our sins. (Hebrews 9:13-14 NLT)

Bloody Mess Foreshadowed and Fulfilled

The God of the Bible elected to use the life-sustaining source of blood as the primary theological stream and theme of atonement. Despite the previously explained encounters of Adam/Eve, Cain/Abel, and Abraham/Isaac, the additional biblical examples are systemic and replete throughout the Bible. In exodus 4:22-26 a story is revealed and it appears that God was upset with Moses and he was close to being killed. Blood was used as a source of atonement and in this case the wife of Moses circumcised their son as a solution. The act of circumcision was depicted as a type of stay and the life of Moses was spared. The Bible says:

> On the way to Egypt, at a place where Moses and his family had stopped for the night, the LORD confronted him and was about to kill him. [25]But Moses' wife, Zipporah, took a flint knife and circumcised her son. She touched his feet with the foreskin and said, "Now you are a bridegroom of blood to me." [26](When she said "a bridegroom of blood," she was referring to the circumcision.) After that, the LORD left him alone. (Exodus 4:22-26 NLT)

The Passover premise is critical to understanding prophetic biblical trajectory and is also controversial because of the Hebrew-Egyptian nexus. Jews of today are phenotypically depicted as European; thus the Passover narrative is falsely intuited as African oppression toward Europe or whiteness. The landscape of white supremacy provokes racial hierarchy into the story, causing some to view the God of the Bible as anti-African. The problem with the premise was previously explained in chapter 5 through the work of J. A. Rogers (1952) when he said about the biblically colorized Hebrew-Egyptian nexus, "Thus the main difference between Hebrew and Egyptian was not racial but religious..." "Miriam's objection to the Ethiopian wife of Moses, Zipporah, was not on color but on religion and more likely on culture" (p. 12). During Old Testament times, Egyptian and Hebrew people were both colorized. Removing the racial element from the story allows for focus on the prophetic pattern of blood within the Passover. Preparing for Hebrew emancipation from Egyptian servitude, God said to Moses:

> On that night I will pass through the land of Egypt and strike down every firstborn son and firstborn male animal in the land of Egypt. I will execute

judgment against all the gods of Egypt, for I am the LORD! ¹³But the blood on your doorposts will serve as a sign, marking the houses where you are staying. When I see the blood, I will pass over you. This plague of death will not touch you when I strike the land of Egypt. (Exodus 12:12-13 NLT)

Blood was the delivering agent through this encounter of emancipation. Moses was told when God "...Sees the blood on the top and sides of the doorframe, the LORD will pass over your home. He will not permit his death angel to enter your house and strike you down" (Exodus 12:23 NLT). Aside from the sovereignty of God, biblical violence cannot be explained but it is frequently used by some to justify atheism and anti-biblical beliefs. Regardless of doctrinal beliefs or a lack thereof, tracking blood across the biblical context is essential. As will be connected later, Passover blood is linked to the blood of Christ on the cross. Instead of being stuck in the mire of biblical race manipulation, understand the purpose of blood and its historic relevance in countless cultures, tribes, and nations. Blood under biblical construction had numerous usages and most of them pointed to the cross. As the Mosaic covenant was being established, sacrificial blood was used to confirm it. According to Mosaic covenant confirmation, the Bible says "And he took the book of the covenant, and read in the audience of the people: and they said, All that the LORD hath said will we do, and be obedient" (Exodus 24:7 KJV). In response to announcing the covenant, the Bible continues stating, "And Moses took the blood, and sprinkled it on the people, and said, Behold the blood of the covenant, which the LORD hath made with you concerning all these words" (Exodus 24:8 KJV).

Today the bible is personally assessed through a racial prism. Race and racism are permanent American fixtures and they influence biblical discernment. Because of racism and white supremacy, the Hebrew people of the Bible are viewed as white, resulting in a destructive form of biblical supremacy and religious confusion. Abram who became

Abraham was selected by God and because he was of Hebrew lineage, by default they became the biblical chosen people of God. Hebrew people were not selected because they were more special, intelligent, or worthy; they were simply descendants of Abraham who responded faithfully to the commandments of God. Because the Bible is written across three covenant systems, the Hebrew people were used as the progenitors and seed through which the Messiah would be born. One of the pivotal annual Hebrew events was the *Great Day of Atonement* or *Yom Kippur*. Even through this critical ceremonial process, blood was central. This annual day served as atonement for the Hebrew people. The High Priest was required to sprinkle the blood of the sin-offering on the altar. Receiving instructions from God, it was said to Moses:

> And Aaron shall make an atonement upon the horns of it once in a year with the blood of the sin offering of atonements: once in the year shall he make atonement upon it throughout your generations: it is most holy unto the LORD. (Exodus 30:10 KJV)

Just like blood is used in many cultures, customs, and tribes, according to the Bible, God first selected blood as a symbolic and literal agent, used in the redemption and salvation plan. Blood is the life-source of humanity; thus it is clear to understand why God elected to use blood as the saving element in the Bible. Any time blood is used or acknowledged ceremonially—it should evoke a person to consider the focus and purpose of blood in the Bible. Although it comes with violent connotation, animal sacrifice is familiar to many cultures, and as a prophetic prefiguration, it also has unavoidable implications in the Scriptures. Blood from animal sacrifices was used to temporarily atone for the transgressions of the Hebrew people and nation. Full atonement and sin remission would not occur until the sacrifice of the Christ. However, until the sacrifice of Jesus, the Hebraic High Priest offered animal sacrifices and sprinkled its blood on the altar for temporary atonement. Moses was provided with Levitical instructions on how to keep the priestly orders organized for the welfare of the Biblical and ancient Nation of Israel. The Bible states:

> And he shall put his hand upon the head of the burnt offering; and it shall be accepted for him to make atonement for him. ⁵And he shall kill the bullock before the LORD: and the priests, Aaron's sons, shall bring the blood, and sprinkle the blood round about upon the altar that is by the door of the tabernacle of the congregation. (Leviticus 1:4-5 KJV)

The Old Testament is replete with examples and prefigured Christly shadows of blood. Sacrifice and blood are two repetitive Old Testament concepts. Their purpose and fulfillment are actualized and expressed in the New Testament. As previously stated, some view the Old Testament as reliable, but the New Testament as purely mythical or fabricated. Because of the prophetic manifestations of the Old Testament structure, coherence is theologically impossible without the linkages to the New Testament. While many people refer to Christianity as the religion of the white man because of how it was manipulated and abused through the institution of American chattel slavery, it is through the New Testament that the universal salvation plan by the blood of Christ is explained. This effort is not designed to convert anyone to Christian principles holistically, but it is an honest attempt at demystifying biblical misrepresentations, helping interested people understand the simplicity within the message and purpose of Christ; especially as it relates to His salvific blood.

One misrepresentation was that first-century Christians were blood drinking cannibals because of a misunderstanding of the gospel message of Jesus, by way of communion or the Eucharist, a spiritual process of drinking His blood and eating of His body, using unleavened bready as the body and grape juice or wine as the blood. S. David Sperling (1998), said in *The Original Torah: The Political Intent of the Bible's Writers*, "Because blood was identified with the life force, biblical legislation allotted the blood to Yahweh alone, who was popularly believed to consume it" (p. 129). Skepticism toward erroneous uses of blood connected to the Bible is conceptually ancient. George Robinson points out a blood fallacy and fixation in *Essential Judaism: A Complete Guide to Beliefs, Customs, and Rituals* (2000) saying, "The accusation that Jews use the blood of Christian children in making *matzot* is an old one, known as the 'blood libel'" (p. 489). The biblical blood of the Messiah is described as emancipatory and about His liberating blood, Jesus proclaimed:

> ...Verily, verily, I say unto you, Except ye eat the flesh of the Son of man, and drink his blood, ye have no life in you. [54]Whoso eateth my flesh, and drinketh my blood, hath eternal life; and I will raise him up at the last day. [55]For my flesh is meat indeed, and my blood is drink indeed. [56]He that eateth my flesh, and drinketh my blood, dwelleth in me, and I in him.
> (John 6:53-56 KJV)

The words of Christ in John 6:53-56 are not a call to cannibalism, blood libel, or a spooky underworld vampire culture; it was a prophetic announcement for the Christian community to maintain the spiritual zeal, stamina, energy, and spirituality displayed by Christ on the cross. While on the cross, the appearance of Jesus was a bloody mess. A crown of thorns were punctured through His skull and before being strapped to the cross He was viciously beaten with a whip with metal fragments at the end, sending chunks of flesh and blood in the air; ripping His back open. The beating alone was severe enough to cause death before His crucified lynching and related to the brutality, the Bible declares that they, "...Scourged him. [2]And the soldiers platted a crown of thorns, and put it on his head, and they put on him a purple robe, [3]And said, Hail, King of the Jews! and they smote him with their hands" (John 19:1-3 KJV).

Based on Roman capital punishment during the epoch of Jesus, either a person was viciously whipped or crucified; Jesus suffered both. Through that bloody scene and sacrifice, spiritual healing is offered. Prophet Isaiah prophetically said about the sacrifice, "…He was wounded for our transgressions, he was bruised for our iniquities: the chastisement of our peace was upon him; and with his stripes we are healed" (Isaiah 53:5 KJV). Pilate did not want to kill Jesus; he knew Christ was innocent. Mockingly, Pilate presented the bloody, battered, and bruised body of Jesus before the Hebrew people, thinking the whipping would be sufficient for His release. It was not, the people screamed for death and blood. About this portion of the bloody encounter the Bible records:

> Pilate went outside again and said to the people, "I am going to bring him out to you now, but understand clearly that I find him not guilty." [5]Then Jesus came out wearing the crown of thorns and the purple robe. And Pilate said, "Look, here is the man!" [6]When they saw him, the leading priests and Temple guards began shouting, "Crucify him! Crucify him!" "Take him yourselves and crucify him," Pilate said. "I find him not guilty." [7]The Jewish leaders replied, "By our law he ought to die because he called himself the Son of God." (John 19:4-7 NLT)

In addition to the blood that poured from the body of Jesus after a Roman soldier pierced Him in the side after His death (John 19:34), all the blood explained through Old Testament animal sacrifices and circumcision was temporary prophetic atonement, pointing to the ultimate blood and sacrifice of the sinless human Messiah. The trauma, pain, and suffering connected to the blood of Christ is what purchased the church. From a biblical perspective the church is referred to as the body of Christ and the institution was paid for by the blood of the Christ. The Apostle Paul had a specific message for the Pastors of the first-century churches that he met with in Ephesus. He exhorted them by saying, "Take heed therefore unto yourselves, and to all the flock, over the which the Holy Ghost hath made you overseers, to feed the church of God, which he hath purchased with his own blood" (Acts 20:28 KJV). As a result to the sacrificial work of Christ on the cross, the church is the fulfillment of the Old Testament redemptive scheme, not ethnically or racially, but spiritually and theologically—founded on the salvific deed of Christ. His work was and remains designed to bring God's most complex and valued earthly creation into harmony and equilibrium with Him.

Under biblical construction and as a result of the sacrificial blood, Christ perpetually reconciles, cleanses, and washes every person who, by faith, repentance, and baptism elects to connect to the body of Christ or church that Jesus paid for with His life and blood. The Apostle Paul said to the Christians of the Colossian church, "And, having made peace through the blood of his cross, by him to reconcile all things unto himself; by him, I say, whether they be things in earth, or things in heaven" (Colossians 1:20 KJV). The blood of Christ serves through the ministry of reconciliation. In addition to reconciliatory blood, it also serves as the spiritual cleansing agent of the New Testament. The Hebrew writer said, "Let us go right into the presence of God with sincere hearts fully trusting him. For our guilty consciences have been sprinkled with Christ's blood to make us clean, and our bodies have been washed with pure water" (Hebrews 10:22 NLT). In addition to the reconciliatory and cleansing blood of Christ, it is critical to note that the cleansing blood operates perpetually in the life of the Christian. John said, "But if we walk in the light, as he is in the light, we have fellowship one with another, and the blood of Jesus Christ his Son cleanseth us from all sin" (1 John 1:7 KJV). As long as the Christian walks in faith, they are cleansed from unrighteousness daily.

The Bible can be difficult to understand without sufficient help, but the overall scheme is simplistic and familiar to surrounding customs found in multiple cultural and tribal settings. During the evangelism of Philip he was instructed to teach the gospel to an Ethiopian eunuch who was also the treasurer of Candace, Queen of Ethiopia. As Philip approached the Ethiopian man he was reading the fifty-third chapter of Isaiah, a narrative that prophesied the crucifixion of the Messiah in gruesome detail. Philip asked him if he understood what he was reading and he responded, "How can I, unless someone instructs me?" (Acts 8:31 NLT). The premise demonstrates that despite the straightforward essence of the Bible, the basic structure of it as a prophetically fulfilled book does initially require a guide. Thus blood and sacrifice are common practices in ancient rituals—thousands of years old, but the blood and sacrifice of Christ was always designed to be preeminent. The Christian religion is based in the blood of Christ and its prophetic shadow began in the Old Testament and was fulfilled in the New Testament.

Conclusion

The first book of the Bible (Genesis) introduces the prophetic blood of Jesus and the last book of the Bible (Revelation) perfects it. As a comprehensive package, the Bible addresses a scheme of redemption for all of humanity. Based on the principles of Christianity, it is never to be forced on a person. The primary thrust of Christianity is love. Jesus told His disciples, "If any household or town refuses to welcome you or listen to your message, shake its dust from your feet as you leave" (Matthew 10:14 NLT). Under a biblical ethos, if a person rejects the message of the Bible it is never to be forced on them. The gospel of Jesus is not designed to be rude, behaviorally offensive, arrogant, conceited, or brash. White supremacy created an un-Christian disposition, forcing Christianity on people across the globe. Eurocentric hegemony compromised the biblically Christian persona (especially in America), distorting it in the minds of those abused and privileged by it.

This chapter creates a context for religious clarification for those misled by a toxic brand of Christianity. Christianity is rooted in love and provides a scheme of redemption for all of humanity. A misnomer is that some racial or ethnic groups cannot or should not be Christian, simply because of their race or ethnicity. Again, that epistemic is the result of white supremacy and the commandeering of Christian principles that created Christian supremacy. Truth is, the gospel of the Bible is not designed to diminish, distort, or reject ethnicity, race, or culture—it serves as a companion that supports interpersonal relationships and human engagement. Christianity is not a white man's religion, and it transcends race, culture, and ethnicity. The book of Revelation provides concluding insight into the blood of Christ for every willing person.

In addition to the biblical reconciliatory and cleansing blood of Jesus, it also spiritually *washes*. John the Apostle said, "And from Jesus Christ, who is the faithful witness, and the first begotten of the dead, and the prince of the kings of the earth. Unto him that loved us, and washed us from our sins in his own blood" (Revelation 1:5 KJV). Many cultural and ethnic groups have rituals and belief systems to help them reach *self-actualized* levels. The principles of scripture create what theologians would consider a divine premise of how to live spiritually and righteously with love, forgiveness, honesty, justice, and repentance as core tenets. The greatest disservice to the Christian faith was its adoption and poisoning by those who used it to further their European agenda of hate and greed. If a person properly understands and can move past the imposter of whiteness, erroneously affixed to the Christian faith, the foundational purpose of the blood of Christ is supremely powerful. Before it is categorically rejected and denied it should first be understood.

Going back to the bloody story of the Passover, every family was spared from death if the blood of the sacrificed lamb was on the three sides of the door post (Exodus 12:7). Each family was authorized to select an unblemished lamb for the sacrifice and blood. Insignificant it may seem, but it was prophetically connected to an unblemished or sinless Savior. Just like the blood of the lamb saved the Hebrew people from oppression and bondage, the blood of Jesus liberates and redeems from spiritual servitude today. According to Scripture Jesus is the unblemished lamb and it was and is His blood that saves today. The problem is that many miss the cohesive story and nexus of the Bible record, unable to decipher its prophetic fulfillment. John the Apostle saw a vision of 144,000 people in heaven, 12,000 from each of the twelve tribes and as he asked for an explanation of who they were he was told, "...These are they which came out of great tribulation, and have washed their robes, and made them white in the blood of the Lamb" (Revelation 7:14 KJV). Thus not only does the Bible provide a blueprint and the cosmic equipment for healthy living, it also redeems through the blood of Jesus the Lamb. In Revelation 13:8 (KJV) Jesus is referred to as "...The Lamb slain from the foundation of the world."

Life is challenging and rarely are things easy. Its survival requires resolve, resilience, patience, help, and support. The Bible does not participate in an eerie silence regarding that reality. Adherence to biblical tenets would be similar to the student applying the concepts learned to manage stress, trauma, and anxiety through the Social-Emotional Learning program at their school. However, for the Christian, embraced biblical principles are supported by the divine power of the Holy Spirit, a subject we do not have time to explore through this project, but undoubtedly a gift for those who elect a life of the Christian faith. Access to the power is received by the blood of Christ. Revelation chapter twelve reveals an apocalyptic story where a war occurred in heaven and the devil and his satanic angelic forces were expelled and cast to earth, causing terrestrial turmoil for humanity (Revelation 12:9). The way the people on earth survived and defeated the evil forces was through the blood of Christ. John the Apostle recorded from his heavenly vision, "And they overcame him by the blood of the Lamb, and by the word of their testimony; and they loved not their lives unto the death" (Revelation 12:11 KJV).

John saw a heavenly image of the Son of God, the Messiah, dipped in blood. Coupled with faith and repentance, baptism is a culminating process where the saving and covering blood of Christ is received. The physical display of bloody animal sacrifices in the Old Testament were concealed messages about the ultimate sacrifice engaged by

Christ. Today faith, repentance, and baptism are the means by which humanity contacts the blood of Christ and the equipping power. The Apostle Paul said to the Christians in the Galatian church, "For ye are all the children of God by faith in Christ Jesus. [27] For as many of you as have been baptized into Christ have put on Christ" (Galatians 3:26-27 KJV). About Jesus Christ, the supreme example of what it means to live under biblically Christian construction, John said:

> His eyes were as a flame of fire, and on his head were many crowns; and he had a name written, that no man knew, but he himself. [13] And he was clothed with a vesture dipped in blood: and his name is called The Word of God. [14] And the armies which were in heaven followed him upon white horses, clothed in fine linen, white and clean. (Revelation 19:12-14 KJV)

Race, racism, racial identity, education, and theology impact the psychology of humanity on monumental levels. Racial hatred and bigotry, coupled with religion, has resulted in distorted education, poor racial identity attitudes, sanitized education, and conceptual whiteness viewed as supreme. Until the eerie silence is broken in these areas, America and the world will continue to promote a dishonest dialogue that results in racial self-hatred, schools that lack wholesome critical pedagogy and paideia, and religious systems, most importantly Christianity, that views theology through a toxic white prism. Until we engage in an intentional interracial-justice dialectic, schools and students will suffer, Eurocentric hegemony will prevail, and religious centers and churches will produce uninspired platforms of ministry that maintain status quo, even in the face of injustice.

It was in 2014 when then-Los Angeles Clippers NBA owner was recorded by his girlfriend making racist remarks about NBA players and Black men in general. In his 2017 *New York Times* interview Jay-Z said, "I thought when Donald Sterling got kicked out the NBA I thought it was a misstep....You also sent everyone else back in

hiding....Getting rid of him just made everyone go back in hiding."
Eerie silence will never be broken through, isolation, inaction, and
avoidance. Wherever you have influence, strategically demand justice
and the breakage of institutional eerie silence.

EPILOGUE
TOWARD EERIE SILENCE
HEALING IN AMERICA

This literary project is a call for American and global repentance toward unjust inaction in the face of systematic mistreatment and marginalization of the *other*. As a collective, America is painfully and critically selective about what causes it to be outraged, often presenting as a double-sided coin, willing to address one societal injustice while remaining silent toward others. After school and mass shootings, analysis of the alarming rates of police killings of unarmed Black people, or racist encounters caught on camera, the same rhetoric follows. As tragic, traumatic, and racist events occur in America, someone casually interjects: "This allows the country to come together for a needed conversation." Someone also declares shock at where the incident occurred or who the victims were. This pattern is not productive. America has an institutionally documented past of racism, denial, and violence. As captured by Kenneth O'Reilly (1989) in *Racial Matters: The FBI's Secret File on Black America, 1960-1972* he shared: "Concluding that second-class citizens would have second-class loyalty, the FBI dismissed every black dissident as subversive, every criticism of American policy as un-American" (p. 12). Speaking against American injustice engenders a price. Follow the pattern of who speaks and what happens to them physically or how their career progress is attacked, marginalized, or thwarted.

The breaking of eerie silence is not just for the moments after a tragedy; the dialogue must be ongoing until we reach a place of local and global healing. Dialectic convening cannot singularly surface as reactive crisis intervention; it needs to serve as proactive and responsive prevention. The narrative needs to change in America. There should be a history in place of courageous dialogue before violent and racist acts occur. The dialogues are difficult, terrifying, emotional, painful, uncomfortable, risky, and radical, but they are of extreme necessity. The embrace and praxis of routine hard dialogue is non-negotiable. The conversations must be normalized, not merely for the sake of a dialectic experience, but for movement into sustained action and healing.

Each person must individually assess whether or not their love is worth the discomfort of breaking the collective eerie silence. Each time we elect to remain silent in the face of injustice, our love and advocacy are being measured. The institution of white supremacy in America has established a fortified platform that supports, promotes, and protects collective silence. The natural American predilection is racial conversation avoidance and denial. Glenn Singleton, in his (2015) book, *Courageous Conversations About Race: A Field Guide for Achieving Equity in Schools*, emphasizes the importance of isolating race dialectically. He said, "It is extremely difficult to keep the conversation focused on race and not drift off into topics that are less emotionally charged and about which people feel more knowledgeable" (p. 100). Singleton acknowledges in *More Courageous Conversations About Race* (2013), the critical importance of focused and well facilitated racial dialogue, especially when conceptions such as "White privilege, White supremacy, and White racial dominance" are introduced. When racial dialogue is not facilitated properly it can "…Quickly escalate into unproductive posturing or deafening silence. Facilitating conversations about race takes courage, but going deeper to unmask issues associated with the racial power dynamic, particularly the impact and role of Whiteness, takes even more. It takes purpose!" (p. 49).

Every aspect of America is challenged to incorporate systems and procedures to normalize racial dialogue that seeks to target, name, identify, and de-link from racist and discriminatory trends that occur overtly or subliminally. Whether spoken or not, race and racism are pervasive elements across every American institution, continually impacting every racial and ethnic group. No one in America escapes the pressure and tension of white supremacy, and that alone illustrates the power of silence. Silence is generated, harnessed, leveraged, and maintained, despite the public visage of glaring injustice, discrimination, or racism. The breakage and healing of eerie silence must transcend race, political affiliation, socio-economic levels, religion, education, or marital status. As an example, political affiliation should not determine the side of the coin a person takes toward injustice. Generally speaking and of course not with absolute accuracy, Republicans are silent in the arena of police violence and Black Lives Matter advocacy, while Democrats are more vocal in those areas. More white people are silent toward racial injustice than Black people and people of color in general. This should not be the case; there should be a collective outrage for any acts of injustice. Historically, the white power structure in America has acted in oblivion and ignorance or arrogance and sadism in the face of unleashed oppression, enslavement, discrimination, and violence.

Intentional participants in the breakage of eerie silence through schools, churches, religious centers, businesses, politics, banking, and community organizations must inspect the racial trends that exist within them and begin the necessary dialogue to create real actions—reversing toxic and adverse racialized outcomes. *American schools* are locations where white supremacy is intentionally and unintentionally reinforced. From elementary through high school, social justice platforms must be developed, instructing students through true paideia, informing them of the real historicity of America, helping them navigate the pitfalls, while preparing them to disrupt and dismantle racist and discriminatory systems. Every American pioneer, *Founding Father,* or President cannot honestly be discussed with angelic and glowing terms. Related to the classroom, diminishment of the institutional scope of American chattel slavery is destructive and the instructional history of Black people must start thousands of years before the Middle-Passage and American enslavement. For healing-actualization, the history of race and racism must be presented candidly in schools.

Discussing race is not racist and dialogue about racism is not beyond the intellectual capabilities of young people. Adult discomfort and struggle through racialized dialogue fail to justify shielding ugly racial truths from children and teenagers. Conceptions of restorative interracial-justice and interracial dialogue must be normalized in school, countering the current system that silently promotes an agenda that extols white superiority ideals. Teachers, principals, instructional leaders, school administrators, counselors, psychologists, Governing Board members, and support staff must invest in the necessary time and education to become social justice advocates, working to not only educate children and young people, but also eradicating practices and policies that hold in place racist outcomes. Any twenty-first century educator, operating outside the realm of an antiracist lens, is not equipped to be a competent and responsible educator of children and teenagers today. Such an individual is guilty of educational malpractice.

Religious centers, but especially *churches* and the Christian community have a huge role in American and international healing. Fred K.C. Price (1999) said in *Race, Religion, & Racism:* "I hold the white Christian church in America responsible for racial and color prejudice in the Church" (p. 134). Just like schools have promoted an eerie silence toward race, racism, and injustice, the same is true for many Christian churches. As already stated in this project, Christianity is the privileged religion in America and has been historically complicit in some of the most violent American institutions. From its first-century inception, Christianity was not designed to be silent toward injustice. Pastors, preachers, ministers, clergy, and church members are required to create platforms within their religious sphere of influence to intentionally break silence and speak words of life, love, and justice into those within and outside the church walls. The church cannot be silent on issues of racism, police brutality, the Prison-industrial complex, and racial disparities in education, but vocal on abortion, same-sex marriage, patriotism, and Make America Great Again allegiance. Through healing, churches must first acknowledge and repent for involvement in the institution of slavery, bigotry, and oppression; not only must churches be prepared to respond to national crisis and disaster, but there must also be a readiness to respond to racial crisis.

A silent gospel message toward injustice, discrimination, and racial superiority is antithetical to the core teaching and missional premise of Christ. Pockets of the church are ready for the radical breaking of eerie silence, but far too many are comfortable with the current postmodern scheme of American silence. It has created an uneasy tension and church-level identity crisis. Many segments of young people today are thirsty for radical change and want to see their collective Christian communities engaged in a transformative fight of love that does not ignore injustice, racial inequality, and marginalization. Dottie Schulz (2018) stated in the Christian Chronicle:

> I know there are those among us who express they wish things would get back to normal. My reply is, 'This is the new normal.' The younger generations do not care what the name is on the church building. They want to be with a church that is making a difference in their neighborhoods, and in the world, who will mentor them and hold them personally accountable. (p. 15)

While most churches in America are in the midst of a spiritual identity crisis, some people are in a *racial identity* crisis. The weight of white supremacy cajoled many Europeans in America to meld into an identity of whiteness, which has subliminally influenced many colorized people into adopting an internalized racial psychology, philosophy, and sociology that declares whiteness superior. This is not done intentionally, but because eerie silence works without oration, many people are unaware of this adopted custom and racial manifestation. This dynamic requires healing because its unconscious behaviors result in Black and other colorized groups of people being first deemed guilty or blamed for the outcome, without the institution of white supremacy every being analyzed for situational and generational contributory impact. For example, this is where the Black person is coached in proper conduct when approached by police, without police being coached in issues of implicit bias and cultural responsiveness. When racial identity attitudes are poor, misguided, and unanalyzed—the default is whiteness; and whiteness is inherently problematic because it is established on the premise of non-white inferiority.

Justice aspects related to gender, sexism, classism, patriarchy, economics, gentrification, and housing/homelessness are additional aspects that require dedicated attention and solution, yet this project briefly focused on the maladies and intersections of race, racism, religion, and education. As a systematic continuance within the current struggles of racial equality across all spectrums, joining countless social justice warriors across the globe, let us radically ensure that advocacy is established and eerie silence broken throughout educational, religious, racist, and positive racial identity development frameworks. Regardless of race, class, political affiliation, social-economic-status, or education level, it is never too late to join the most honorable and courageous work in America as a bold antiracist leader and advocate. It was Cornell West who once said, "Tenderness is what love feels like in private. Justice is what love looks like in public." Check your love and break the *Eerie Silence* toward injustice.

REFERENCES

Adair, A. V. (1984). *Desegregation: The illusion of Black progress.* London, England: University Press of America.

Akbar, N. (1979). Mental Disorder Among African Americans. Paper presented at the 13th Annual Convention of the Association of Black Psychologists, Atlanta, GA, August.

Alexander, M. (2011). *The New Jim Crow: Mass Incarceration in the Age of Colorblindness.* New York: The New Press.

Allen, J., Als, H., Lewis, J., & Litwack L. F. (2000). *Without Sanctuary: Lynching Photography in America.* Santa Fe, NM: Twin Palms.

Anderson, C. (2016). *White Rage: The Unspoken Truth of Our Racial Divide.* New York: Bloomsbury.

Ani, M. (1994). *Yurugu: An African-Centered Critique of European Cultural Thought and Behavior.* Baltimore: Afrikan World Books.

Ani, M. (1980). *Let the Circle Be Unbroken: The Implications of African Spirituality in the Diaspora.* Baltimore: Afrikan World Books.

Bailey, K. E. (2011). *Paul Through Mediterranean Eyes. Cultural Studies in 1 Corinthians.* Downers Grove, ILL: Inter-Varsity Press.

Baquet, D. (November, 2017). On Therapy, Politics, the State of Rap and Being a Black Man in Trump's America. *New York Times* Retrieved from https://www.nytimes.com/interactive/2017/11/29/t-magazine/jay-z-dean-baquet-interview.html

Barashango, I. (2001). *Afrikan People and European Holidays: A Mental Genocide (Book I).* Baltimore, MD: Afrikan World Books.

Barth, R. S. (2007). *Culture in Question*. In *The Jossey-Bass Reader on Educational Leadership* (pp. 159-168). San Francisco: Jossey-Bass.

Battalora, J. (2013). *Birth of a White Nation: The Invention of White People and Its Relevance Today*. Houston: Strategic Book and Rights.

Bayless, P. D. (1991). Teachers' Critical Reflections on Cross-cultural Understanding Through Participatory Research. *Dissertation Abstracts International*. (UMI No. 9322380).

Bell, D. (1992). *Faces at the Bottom of the Well: The Permanence of Racism*. New York: Basic Books.

Blomberg, C. L. (2016). *The Historical Reliability of the New Testament: Countering the Challenges to Evangelical Christian Beliefs*. Nashville: B&H Academic.

Blomberg, C. L. (2007). *The Historical Reliability of the Gospels*. Downers Grove, ILL: Inter-Varsity Press Academic.

Brodkin, K. (2004). *How Did Jews Become White Folks?* In Burns, A., Fine, M., Powell, L., Weis, L. (Ed), *Off White: Readings on Power, Privilege, and Resistance* (pp. 17-36). New York: Routledge.

Brown II, R. J. (2012). *Walking the Equity Talk: A Guide for Culturally Courageous Leadership in School Communities*. Thousand Oaks, CA: Corwin.

Browder, A. (2006). *Egypt on the Potomac: A Guide to Decoding Egyptian Architecture and Symbolism in Washington, D.C.* Washington, D.C.: IKG.

Browder, A. T. (1996). *Survival Strategies for Africans in America: 13 Steps to Freedom*. Washington D.C.: The Institute of Karmic Guidance.

Browder, A. T. (1992). *Nile Valley Contributions to Civilization: Exploding the Myths Vol 1*. Washington D.C.: The Institute of Karmic Guidance.

Bruce, F. F. (1981). *The New Testament Documents: Are They Reliable?* Grand Rapids: William B. Eerdmans Publishing Company.

Butler, H. (2009). *When Rocks Cry Out*. Fort Worth: Stone River Publishing.

Castro-Klaren, S. (2008). *A Companion to Latin American Literature and Culture*. Malden, MA: Blackwell Publishing.

Coe, M. D., & Koontz, R. (2013). *Mexico: From the Olmecs to the Aztecs*. New York: Thames & Hudson.

Coleman, W. (2000). *Tribal Talk: Black Theology, Hermeneutics, and African/American Ways of "Telling the Story"*. University Park, PA: The Pennsylvania State University Press.

Coates, T. (2017). *We Were Eight Years in Power: An American Tragedy*. New York: One World.

Comer, J. P. (1972). *Beyond Black and White*. New York: Quadrangle Books, Inc.

Cone, J. H. (2016). *The Cross and the Lynching Tree*. Maryknoll, NY: Orbis Books.

Cone, J. H. (1997). *The God of the Oppressed*. Maryknoll, NY: Orbis Books.

Copan, P. & Craig, W. L. (2012). *Come Let Us Reason: New Essays in Christian Apologetics*. Nashville: B&H Publishing Group.

Crenshaw Williams, K., Ocen, P., & Nanda, J. (2015). *Black Girls Matter: Pushed Out, Overpoliced, and Underprotected*. Center for Intersectionality and Social Policy Studies and African American Policy Forum.

Crenshaw Williams, K. (1993). *Beyond Racism and Misogyny: Black Feminism and 2 Live Crew*. In K. Matsuda, M. J., Lawrence III, L. R., & Delgado, R., *Words That Wound: Critical Race Theory, Assaultive Speech, and the First Amendment (pp. 111-136)*. Boulder, CO: Westview Press.

Cress Welsing, F. (1991). *The Isis Papers: The Keys to the Colors*. Washington, D.C.: C.W. Publishing.

Dalton, H. L. (1995). *Racial Healing: Confronting the Fear Between Blacks & Whites*. New York: Anchor Books.

DeGruy, J. (2005). *Post Traumatic Slave Syndrome: America's Legacy of Enduring Injury and Healing.* Portland: Uptone Press.

Delgado, R., & Stefancic, J. (2001). *Critical Race Theory: An Introduction.* New York: New York University Press.

Delgado, R. (1993). *Words that Wound: A Tort Action for Racial Insults, and Name Calling.* In K. Matsuda, M. J., Lawrence III, L. R., & Crenshaw Williams, K., *Words That Wound: Critical Race Theory, Assaultive Speech, and the First Amendment (pp. 89-110).* Boulder, CO: Westview Press.

DiAngelo, R. (2018). *White Fragility: Why It's So Hard for White People to Talk About Racism.* Boston: Beacon Press.

DiAngelo, R. (2011). White Fragility. *International Journal of Critical Pedagogy,* Vol 3 (3), pp. 54-70.

Diop, C. A. (1991). *Civilization or Barbarism: An Authentic Anthropology.* Brooklyn: Lawrence Hill Books.

Du Bois, W. E. B. (1999). *Darkwater: Voices from Within the Veil.* Mineola, New York: Dover Publications, Inc.

Dudley, D. (2001). *History of the First Council of Nice: A World's Christian Convention A.D. 325 With a Life of Constantine.* Buffalo, NY: Eworld Inc.

Durant, W. (1957). *The Reformation: The Story of Civilization, Part VI.* New York: Simon and Schuster.

Dyson, M. E. (2017). *Tears We Cannot Stop: A Sermon to White America.* New York: St. Martin's Press.

Elias, J. L. (1994). *Paulo Freire: Pedagogue of Liberation.* Melbourne, FL: Krieger Publishing Company.

Epperson, R. (1995). *The Unseen Hand: An Introduction to the Conspiratorial View of History.* Tucson, AZ: Publius Press.

Fanon, F. (1963). *The Wretched of the Earth.* New York: Grove Press.

Fine, M., Weis, L., Powell-Pruitt, L., & Burns, A. (2004). *Off White: Readings on Power, Privilege, and Resistance.* New York & London: Routledge.

Finegan, J. (1989). *Myth & Mystery: An Introduction of the Pagan Religions of the Biblical World*. Grand Rapids: Baker Book House.

Finley, T. (2015, December). Jesus Wasn't White and Here's Why that Matters. *HuffPost*. Retrieved from https://www.huffingtonpost.com/entry/jesus-wasnt-white-and-heres-why-that-matters_us_567968c9e4b014efe0d6bea5

Foreman, M. W. (2012). Challenging the Zeitgeist Movie: Paralellomania on Steroids. In Copan, P. & Craig, W. L. (Ed.), *Come Let Us Reason: New Essays in Christian Apologetics* (pp. 169-185). Nashville: B&H Publishing Group.

Foster, D. (2018, March, Vol. 75, No. 3). What is a Church of Christ? *The Christian Chronicle*, pp. 17-19.

Freedman, D. N. (1992). *The Anchor Yale Bible Dictionary*, Volume 1, A-C. New Haven: Yale University Press.

Freire, P. (2017). *Pedagogy of the Oppressed*. New York: Bloomsbury.

Freire, P. (1973). *Education for Critical Consciousness*. New York: The Continuum Publishing Company.

Fridman, R. E. (1987). *Who Wrote the Bible?* New York: Summit Books.

Fuller Jr., N. (2016). *The United-Independent Compensatory Code/System/Concept: A Compensatory Counter-Racist Code*. Produce Justice.

Gajanan, M. (2018, May). It's Crippling to See What's Happened. Why TMZ Producer Confronted Kanye West Over Slavery Claims. *Time*. Retrieved from http://time.com/5263677/van-lathan-kanye-west-tmz-slavery/

Gay, G. (2010). *Culturally Responsive Teaching: Theory Research, and Practice*. New York: Teachers College Press.

Gerbner, K. (2018). *Christian Slavery: Conversion and Race in the Protestant Atlantic World*. Philadelphia: University of Pennsylvania Press.

Ginzburg, R. (1988). *100 Years of Lynchings*. Baltimore: Black Classic Press.

Goodspeed, E. J. (1981). *How Came the Bible: The Turbulent and Fascinating History of the World's Greatest Book*. Nashville: Abingdon Press.

Green, E. (2016, December). Are Jews White? *The Atlantic*. Retrieved from https://www.theatlantic.com/politics/archive/2016/12/are-jews-white/509453/

Harpaz, B. J. (2018, May). Lynching Memorial May be Game-changer for Montgomery Tourism. *The Washington Post*. Retrieved from https://www.washingtonpost.com/lifestyle/travel/lynching-memorial-may-be-game-changer-for-montgomery-tourism/2018/05/16/f0061a5c-5913-11e8-9889-07bcc1327f4b_story.html?utm_term=.95d584ae8f49

Hays, J. D. (2016). *The Temple and the Tabernacle: A Study of God's Dwelling Places from Genesis to Revelation*. Grand Rapids: Baker Books.

Heyward, O. J. (2017). *Baptism: Dead, Dipped, Delivered. A Grammatical and Contextual Analysis of Baptism Passages*. Pennsauken, NJ: Book Baby.

Hilliard, A. (1995). *The Maroon Within Us*. Baltimore: Black Press.

Hollie, S. (2013). *Culturally and Linguistically Responsive Teaching and Learning: Classroom Practices for Student Success*. Huntington Beach, CA: Shell Education.

Hooks, B. (1993). *Teaching to Transgress: Education as the Practice of Freedom*. New York: Routledge.

Howard, T. C. (2010). *Why Race & Culture Matter in Schools: Closing the Achievement Gap in America's Classrooms*. New York: Teachers College Press.

Hughes, R. T. & Allen C. L. (1988). *Illusions of Innocence: Protestant Primitivism in America, 1630-1875*. Chicago: University of Chicago Press.

Ilona, R. (2014). *The Igbos and Israel: An Inter-Cultural Study of the Largest Jewish Diaspora*. Washington, DC: Street to Street EpicCenter Stories.

Imhotep, D. (2012). *The First Americans Were Africans Revisited*. Bloomington, IN: Author House.

Jacques-Garvey, A. (2014). *Philosophy and Opinions of Marcus Garvey*. Mansfield-Centre, CT: Martino Publishing.

Kambon, K. K. (1998) *African/Black Psychology in the American Context: An African Centered Approach*. Tallahassee, FL: Nubian Nations Publications.

Kieffer, C. II. (1981, April). *Doing Dialogical Retrospection: Approaching Empowerment Through Participatory Research*. Paper presented at the International Meeting of the Society of Applied Anthropology, University of Edinburg. Edinburg, Scotland.

Kindi, I. X. (2016). *Stamped from the Beginning: The Definitive History of Racist Ideas in America*. New York: Nation Books.

Kivel, P. (1996). *Uprooting Racism: How White People can Work for Racial Justice*. Gabriola Island, BC: New Society Publishers.

Kolbert, E. (2018, April). Skin Deep. *National Geographic*, 233(4), pp. 30-41.

Kuhn, A. B. (2007). *Shadow of the Third Century: A Revaluation of Christianity*. Minneapolis, MN: Filiquarian Publishing.

Ladson-Billings, G. (2009). *The Dream Keepers: Successful Teachers of African American Children*. San Francisco: Jossey-Bass.

Lebron, C. (2018, February). Black Panther is Not the Movie We Deserve. *Boston Review*. Retrieved from http://bostonreview.net/race/christopher-lebron-black-panther

Lee, B. (2016). *Best Practices in Community Consciousness Policing: A Reflection on Law Enforcement Community Building Workshops*. Indianapolis: Dog Ear Publishing.

Makesi-Tehuti, K. (2006). *How to Make a Negro Christian: A Reprinting of the Religious Instruction of the Negroes and Other Works by Dr. Reverend Charles Colcock Jones.* Raleigh, NC: Lulu Press.

Manigault Newman, O. (2018). *Unhinged: An Insider's Account of the Trump White House.* New York: Gallery Books.

Marble, M. (2016). *Beyond Black and White: From Civil Rights to Barack Obama.* Brooklyn: Verso.

Marble, M. (2007). *Race, Reform, and Rebellion: The Second Reconstruction and Beyond in Black America, 1945-2006, Third Edition.* Jackson: University Press of Mississippi.

Marble, M. (1999). *Introduction.* In Du Bois, W. E. B, *Darkwater: Voices from Within the Veil* (pp. v-viii). Mineola, NY: Dover.

Martin, S. J., Goldstein, N. J. & Cialdini R. (2014). *The Small BIG: Small Changes that Spark Big Influence.* New York: Grand Ventral Publishing.

Martin, T. (1993). *The Jewish Onslaught: Dispatches from thee Wellesley Battlefront.* Dover, MASS: The Majority Press.

Matsuda, M. J., Lawrence III, L. R., Delgado. R., & Crenshaw Williams, K. (1993). *Words That Wound: Critical Race Theory, Assaultive Speech, and the First Amendment.* Boulder, CO: Westview Press.

Menakem, R. (2017). *My Grandmother's Hands: Racialized Trauma and the Pathway to Mending Our Hearts and Bodies.* Las Vegas: Central Recovery Press.

Mignolo, W. D. (2011). *The Darker Side of Western Modernity: Global Futures, Decolonial Options.* Durham: Duke University Press.

Mignolo, W. D. (2008). Preamble: The Historical Foundation of Modernity/Coloniality and the Emergence of Decolonial Thinking. In Castro-Klaren, S. (Ed.), *A Companion to Latin American Literature and Culture* (pp. 12-32). Malden, MA: Blackwell.

Moraña, M., Dussel, E., Jáuregui, C. A. (2008). *Coloniality At Large: Latin America and the Postcolonial Debate.* Durham: Duke University Press.

Moulton, J. H., & Milligan, G. (1930). *Vocabulary of the Greek Testament.* Peabody, MA: Hendrickson Publishers.

Murakawa, N. (2014). *The First Civil Right: How Liberals Built Prison America.* New York: Oxford University Press.

Oden, T. C. (2014, June). How Africa Shaped the Christian Mind (an InterVaristy Press interview). Retrieved from https://www.youtube.com/watch?v=biEWUed41pM

Oden, T. C. (2007). *How Africa Shaped the Christian Mind: Rediscovering the African Seedbed of Western Christianity.* Downer Grove, ILL: InterVarsity Press.

O'Reilly, K. (1989). *Racial Matters: The FBI's Secret File on Black America, 1960-1972.* New York; The Free Press.

Painter, I. P. (2010). *The History of White People.* New York: W.W. Norton & Company.

Payne, A. A. & Welch, K. (2015). Restorative Justice in Schools: The Influence of Race on Restorative Discipline. *Youth & Society.* Vol 47(4), pp. 539-564.

Perry, T., Steele, C., & Hilliard, A. (2003). *Young Gifted and Black: Promoting Achievement Among African American Students.* Boston: Beacon Press.

Price, F. K. C. (1999). *Race, Religion & Racism, Volume I: A Bold Encounter With Division in the Church.* Los Angeles: Faith One Publishing.

Randall, L. B., Graham, S. M., Westphal Jr., C. R., & Jew, C. L. (2008). *Culturally Proficient Inquiry: A Lens for Identifying and Examining Educational Gaps.* Thousand Oaks, CA: Corwin Press.

Reece, R. L. (2018, Spring). Debunking the Mobility Myth. *Teaching Tolerance,* (Issue 58), pp. 23-26.

Revilla, A. T., Stuart Well, A., & Jellison Holme, J. (2004). We Didn't see Color: The Salience of Color Blindness in Desegregated Schools: In Fine, M., Weis, L., Powell-Pruitt, L., & Burns, A. (Ed.), *Off White: Readings on Power, Privilege, and Resistance* (pp. 284-301). New York & London: Routledge.

Rieder, J. (2013). *Gospel of Freedom: Martin Luther King, Jr.'s Letter from Birmingham Jail and the Struggle that Changed a Nation.* New York: Bloomsbury Press.

Robertson, C. (April, 2018). A Lynching Memorial Is Opening; The Country Has Never Seen Anything Like It. *The New York Times.* Retrieved from https://www.nytimes.com/2018/04/25/us/lynching-memorial-alabama.html

Roberts, J. D. (2005). *Liberation and Reconciliation: A Black Theology.* Louisville: Westminster John Knox Press.

Robinson, G. (2000). *Essential Judaism: A Complete Guide to Beliefs, Customs, and Rituals.* New York: Pocket Books.

Rogers, J. A. (1952). *Nature Knows No Color-Line: Research into the Negro Ancestry in the White Race.* Middletown, CT: Wesleyan University Press.

Ross Jr. B. & Harris, H. R. (2018, July). Fifty Years After Historic Meeting, Race Still Divides Churches of Christ. *The Christian Chronicle.* Retrieved from https://christianchronicle.org/we-still-have-two-brotherhoods/

Rouff, R. A. (2010). *Ida B. Wells: A Woman of Courage.* Berlin, NJ: The Townsend Library.

Rozenberg, H. (June, 2017). Black People Are the 12 Tribes of Israel. Retrieved from https://www.youtube.com/watch?v=KbYZozeIWV8

Saheli, A. (2003). *From Nigger to African American: Education and Critical Consciousness as Crucial Components to Positive Black Racial Label Development* (Doctoral dissertation). Ann Arbor, MI: ProQuest. (UMI number: 3113330).

Saheli, T. (2013). *The Memoirs of a Young Millennium Preacher's Wife: A Story of Life, Love and the Testing of Faith.* Maitland, FL: Xulon Press.

Saldivar, J. D. (2012). *Trans-Americanity: Subaltern Modernities, Global Coloniality, and the Cultures of Greater Mexico.* Durham & London: Duke University Press.

Sharp, M. J. (2012). Does the Story of Jesus Mimic Pagan Mystery Stories? In Copan, P. & Craig, W. L. (Ed.), *Come Let Us Reason: New Essays in Christian Apologetics* (pp. 151-168). Nashville: B&H Publishing Group.

Schrum, B. (2018, March, Vol. 75, No. 3). The Words We Use to Define or Faith. *The Christian Chronicle,* pp. 17-19.

Schulz, Dottie. (2018, March, Vol. 75, No. 3). What is a Church of Christ? *The Christian Chronicle,* pp. 15-17.

Singleton, G. E. (2015). *Courageous Conversations About Race: A Field Guide for Achieving Equity in Schools.* Thousand Oaks, CA: Corwin.

Singleton, G. E. (2013). *More Courageous Conversations About Race.* Thousand Oaks, CA: Corwin.

Smiley, T. (2014). *Death of a King: The Real Story of Dr. Martin Luther King Jr's Final Year.* New York: Little, Brown and Company.

Sperling, D. S. (1998). *The Original Torah: The Political Intent of the Bible's Writers.* New York: New York University Press.

Stannard, D. E (1992). *The Conquest of the New World: American Holocaust.* New York: Oxford University Press.

Sussman, W. S. (2017). *The Myth of Race: The Troubling Persistence of an Unscientific Idea.* Cambridge, MASS: Harvard University Press.

Tatum, B. D. (1997). *Why Are All the Black Kids Sitting Together in the Cafeteria? And Other Conversations About Race.* New York: Basic Books.

Taylor, J. L. (2015). *Black Nationalism in the United States: From Malcom X to Barack Obama*. Boulder, CO: Lynne Rienner.

Thompson II, M. (2017). *Golden: The Miraculous Rise of Steph Curry*. New York: Touchstone.

Tryggestad, E. (2018, March, Vol. 75, No. 3). The Words We Use to Define or Faith. *The Christian Chronicle*, pp. 17-20.

Tryggestad, E. (2018, March, Vol. 75, No. 3). What is a Church of Christ? *The Christian Chronicle*, pp. 1, 14-15.

Tyson, T. B. (2017). *The Blood of Emmett Till*. New York: Simon & Schuster.

Van Sertima, I. (2003). *They Came Before Columbus: The African Presence in Ancient America*. New York: Random House.

Van Der Valk, A. (2018, Spring). Teaching Hard History: Educators Talk about How to Teach American Slavery. *Teaching Tolerance*, (Issue 58), pp. 50-54.

Walker, D. (1829). *David Walker's Appeal in Four Articles*. Mansfield Centre, CT: Martino Publishing.

Walker R. (December, 2016). Quick Overview of Religion in African History. Retrieved from https://www.youtube.com/watch?v=7FtE7AWww9Q

Walker, R. (2014). *Blacks and Religion: Volume One*. London: Reklaw Education Limited.

Walls, A. F. (2012). Two Thousand Years in African Christian History. Video retrieved from https://www.youtube.com/watch?v=IAJeo6kybMk

Warnock, R. G. (2014). *The Divided Mind of the Black Church: Theology, Piety & Witness*. New York: New York University Press.

Weiner, M. F. (2010). *Power, Protest and the Public Schools: Jewish and African American Struggles in New York City*. New Jersey: Rutgers University Press.

Wells, I. B. (2010). *Southern Horrors: Lynch Law in All Its Phases*. Venice, CA: SWB Books.

West, C. (2015). *Struggle for Honesty, Decency and Integrity in Modern America*. Video retrieved from https://www.youtube.com/watch?v=CXw37Pr5CDw.

West, C. (2014). *Black Prophetic Fire*. Boston: Beacon Press.

West, C. (2002). *Prophesy Delivered: An Afro American Revolutionary Christianity*. Louisville: Westminster John Knox Press.

West, C. (1999). *The Cornel West Reader*. New York: Basic Civitas Books.

West, C. (1988). *Prophetic Fragments: Illuminations of the Crisis in American Religion & Culture*. Grand Rapids: William B. Erdmans Publishing Company.

Williams, C. (1987). *The Destruction of Black Civilization: Great Issues of Race from 4500 B.C. to 2000 A.D.* Chicago: Third World Press.

Williams, Jr., R. A. (2012). *Savage Anxieties: The Invention of Western Civilization*. New York: Palgrave Macmillan.

Williams, W. (2011). *The Historical Origins of Christianity*. Chicago, Ill: Maathian Press.

Wood, J. L., Harris III, F., & Howard, T. C. (2018). *Get Out! Black Male Suspensions in California Public Schools*. San Diego, CA: Community College Equity Assessment Lab and the UCLA Black Male Institute.

Woodson, C. G. (1933). *The Mis-Education of the Negro*. Trenton, NJ: First Africa World Press.